Practical Systems Design

By the same authors
Basic Systems Analysis

Practical Systems Design

Edited by

Alan Daniels

Director
Institute for Industrial Training,
Brunel University

Don Yeates

General Manager
Datasolve Education

PITMAN

PITMAN PUBLISHING LIMITED
128 Long Acre, London WC2E 9AN

PITMAN PUBLISHING INC
1020 Plain Street, Marshfield, Massachusetts 02050

Associated Companies
Pitman Publishing Pty Ltd, Melbourne
Pitman Publishing New Zealand Ltd, Wellington
Copp Clark Pitman, Toronto

© Alan Daniels and Don Yeates 1984

First published in Great Britain 1984

British Library Cataloguing in Publication Data
Practical systems design.
  1. System analysis
  I. Daniels, Alan   II. Yeates, Don
  003   QA402

  ISBN 0–273–01939–2

Library of Congress Cataloging in Publication Data

Main entry under title:

Practical systems design.
  Bibliography: p.
  Includes index.
  1. System design.   2. System analysis.   I. Daniels,
Alan.   II. Yeates, Donald.
QA76.9.S88P73 1984   003   84-1877
ISBN 0–273–01939–2

Printed in Great Britain at The Pitman Press, Bath

Contents

Foreword

The need for more information on systems analysis at a time when the use of technology in business and industry is growing rapidly and causing great change has brought about this second book. Systems analysis is an area of growing professionalism. Systems analysts are the individuals with primary responsibilities for implementing change. They are the staff professionals. The 'system' has developed as an activity encompassing people, procedures, materials, and equipment coordinated to provide a service and produce an end-product.

At the beginning of the 1960s, computers were considered technological marvels which awed many, especially management personnel. Today, technology has been recognized as an asset in the work-a-day environment and as a management tool, though it does have its own problems and solutions. It is essential for individuals who assist management to be well informed on the technological advances and on better ways to solve problems.

The changes which are occurring at a very rapid rate in our society are treated in this text. Each chapter moves from the philosophical to the practical, concentrating on the 'doing' aspects of the subjects discussed. The text presents philosophies, approaches, and proven techniques by which successful implementation can occur. Emphasis is placed upon the end-product. However, flexibility, intelligent caution, and considered decision-making are encouraged. The wide range of topics covered in this text provides an over-view of the increasing number of tools available to systems analysts and practical suggestions for their utilization.

I appreciate the opportunity for my continued involvement in this important endeavour.

S. Charp
President
American Federation
of Information Processing Societies

Preface

This book is intended for students and practitioners in systems analysis and design who have gone beyond the basic concepts of systems work and now find themselves concerned with a wider range of systems problems and solutions. It therefore assumes an understanding of systems work as described in *Basic Systems Analysis*.

The book begins with a review of the scope of systems analysis and design, with emphasis on the role of the analyst as an agent of change.

Chapter 2 reviews the types of system with which analysts are now involved and categorizes systems according to their goals of processing transactions and providing operational and management control or information for strategic planning.

Chapter 3 deals with the management of systems development activities and is followed, in Chapter 4, by a more detailed treatment of structured design methodologies.

Chapters 5, 6 and 7 consider some typical systems design solutions and include a discussion of database, distributed and realtime systems. Data communications is dealt with separately in Chapter 8.

The role of the analyst in the design of office automation systems is considered in Chapter 9 and the 'people' side of systems work is brought together in Chapter 10.

The book is thus an introduction—and in some areas more than that—to a range of new or more advanced systems problems which a senior student or practitioner is likely to face. Inevitably, there is much more that could be written, but we think that this book is a digestible further bite into the world of systems analysis and design.

Alan Daniels
Don Yeates

Acknowledgements

It is not possible to produce a book which covers such a wide range of topics as this without being able to draw on the help, advice and contributions of many friends and colleagues who are expert in their chosen fields. We are very fortunate that so many people have been willing to help. In particular, we would like to acknowledge the contributions of

Neville Boxer of
Software Sciences

Brian Davis,
Computer Consultant

Alan Peck of
Datasolve Education

Dr Pete Thomas of the
Open University

Derrick Croisdale, formerly
with the UK Civil Service

Professor Frank Land of the
London School of Economics

Stuart Rostron, a specialist
consultant in office systems
and technology

Martin Ould of Logica

Jim Wood of
Brunel University

We are also grateful to Simpact Systems Ltd of Shedfield, Southampton, England, for allowing us to use PROMPT to illustrate methodologies for the management of systems development.

Finally, thanks to Sue Baker and Margaret Lailey for word processing it all.

1 The scope of systems analysis

In this introductory chapter there is one idea that is more important than any other; it is *change*. Typically, systems analysts are taught about the impact of change on people, how people cope with change and how changed systems and working practices can be implemented. Indeed, in our earlier book—*Basic Systems Analysis*—we talk about the systems analyst as an implementer of change or as a change agent. In this book we are concerned with the impact of change on the systems analyst. How is our analyst prepared to take his—or her—own medicine?

In principle, of course, we are all prepared to take our own medicine—so long as we think that we need it! The difficulty lies in the fact that we generally assume that we are fit and healthy and in no need of medication. Before reading on, therefore, we must ask you to recognize that, however things are now, they could be better; however your systems work is going, it could go more effectively. With this thought in mind, let us examine three fruitful areas for improvement: our own performance as analysts and the way we do our job; the way our systems projects are managed; and the intractable 'people' problem.

The way we were
In *Basic Systems Analysis* we represent the activities of the systems analyst as being neat and tidy, with a simple methodology to follow. Our analyst is described as '. . . able to discover the fundamental logic of a system, produce sound plans and appreciate the effects of new facts in planning. The analyst must be perceptive, but must not jump to quick conclusions, be persistent to overcome difficulties and obstacles, and maintain a planned course of action in spite of setbacks'. We also talk of a 'need for stamina, strength of character and a sense of purpose; a broad, flexible outlook, an orderly mind, a disciplined approach and logical neatness'.

While no apology is made for describing such a paragon, we must take for granted that, wherever a systems analyst finds himself, he is what he is—paragon or not. It seems most unlikely that there will be sufficient systems analysts to meet the increasing need for their skills and although some people are more readily suited to systems work than others, we do all need to stop and take stock of the way we do our work to see if we can do it better and to see if we can identify those essential characteristics of the systems analyst.

One model, proposed by Parkin, puts systems analysis under the microscope and examines it in the light of the skills and knowledge

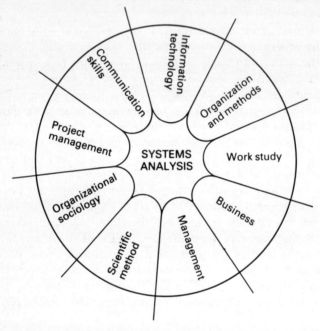

Fig. 1.1 Under the microscope

borrowed from other business or academic activities. This is shown in Figure 1.1. We can see from this model that skills and methods have been borrowed:

● from *other changemakers*: traditionally the pursuits of O & M and work study were the precursors of systems analysis and indeed provided an active pool from which analysts were recruited in the 1960s;
● from *business and management*: analysts solve business problems for managers—or such is a common view. It seems then only sensible to understand the problem areas and the client;

- from *science*—a twofold contribution: firstly, the approach to problem solving in a scientific way to imply the disinterested and completely objective method so necessary to systems work; secondly, the study of organizations and their social make-up which provides the backcloth against which the analyst works;
- from *project management*—included since all of our activities are carried out in a project structure;
- from *communications skills*—clearly important since a substantial part of the analyst's job is to listen, discuss and persuade.

Last of all is information technology: the thing which sets the systems analyst apart from other change-makers and which puts him in the driving seat of the new industrial revolution.

There remains, however, the as yet undefined 'something in the middle' which characterizes the mind or the attitude of an analyst. There are three words which fit this remaining gap:

- *Eclecticism*—our systems analyst has a greedy mind and collects ideas and experiences from all walks of life to apply to his work. The very thought of rejecting something because it is 'not invented here' is anathema.
- *Syncretism*—the nature of systems analysis is to reconcile technology and people in order to solve problems in a changing world. The ability to reconcile differing attitudes and to present solutions that are capable of wide acceptance is therefore clearly of importance.
- *Congruence*—the solution of problems is much easier when resources are unlimited and the time available is infinite. The analyst, however, is expected to deliver a system which is not only effective but also efficient. In other words, a congruent solution is required. Using a sledgehammer to crack a nut—the opposite of a congruent solution—is not appropriate.

This gets us started in knowing about our 'profession'—for such is it called these days. Indeed the very use of the word 'professional' when describing our activities implies a great deal: a 'computer professional' is not merely someone who is paid to do a specific job—a professional footballer as opposed to an amateur—but someone who applies himself to his job in a thoughtful, ethical, comprehensive and thorough way. There are no halfway houses on the road to professional systems analysis.

Innovating force

The systems analyst as the innovating force finds himself at the centre of a network of attitudes and practices which set the climate for the work he does (see Figure 1.2). Innovation in an organization will not

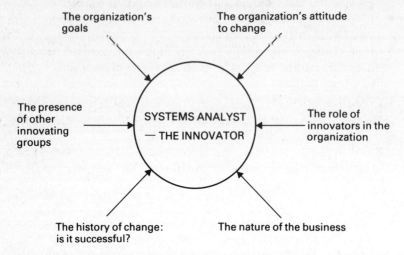

Fig. 1.2 The innovator

take place without the recognition and belief that a specific problem exists and that there is a mechanism, process or means to solve it. Management's appreciation of these factors—problem and solution—is, however, unlikely to be sufficient on its own to change the situation. An essential ingredient is the presence of innovating or change agent groups who have a vested interest in the implementation of change. Innovative activities typically occur through the efforts of groups who are outside the programmed activities of production deadlines and who have a specific responsibility for planning and improvement. Some researchers point to the need for social scientists to provide the drive needed by organizations pursuing a program of innovation in systems design and management control and, while many of their aims are far outside the scope of systems analysis, there is in one important area a role for systems analysts to play. This is concerned with the recognition of the importance of human factors in the design of new systems. We believe this to be of such importance to the success of systems analysis and design in the 1980s that Chapter 10 of this book deals with it in detail.

Such recognition cannot, however, be made without a change in the way systems work is done. Typically analysts are concerned with reconciling:

(1) organizational needs and objectives,
(2) the tasks to be done,
(3) technology,
(4) the individual's objectives and needs,

and usually in that order. If, however, we establish a design group drawn from both the client department and the systems development group, the system that is eventually designed represents the concentrated efforts of both groups and should be highly acceptable to users and to computer people.

Such a design is seen by the users as very much their own solution and highly acceptable as a future way of working. For the systems analyst, however, it requires a change of role from technical expert to that of an adviser able to offer a variety of solutions from which a choice can be made, rather than presenting the one unique solution. In addition, it requires that the human and technical parts of the design proceed together instead of the human parts being forced to fit a rigid technical solution. Also, we must accept the validity of participation by users and their right to develop the skills to enable them to design their own systems. Last of all we must recognize that a system which optimizes technical efficiency but which does not contribute to job satisfaction is unlikely to be adopted by the user group.

The driving force that will initiate this change will come either from systems users via revolution or from us by evolution; we can either plan for it or have it forced upon us. The reason is simple: our clients—and let us call them that since it begins to give them a wholly new role—have higher expectations of us than hitherto and a much lower tolerance threshold of incompetence. Attitudes towards information technology generally are often either hostile, as a result of bad experience, or expectant of a greater level of satisfaction than has previously been delivered. In short, the game's up; either we deliver or we are ignored.

Delivering new systems
A substantial part of the problem of delivering new systems to clients lies in the way we plan, control and manage the activities of ourselves and our systems teams. Chapter 4 draws a stark contrast between the traditional staged approach to conventional systems project development and the more rigorous and responsive approach being proposed in

some of the newer methodologies. Let us consider here just two additional points.

(1) *Getting started*

The beginnings of a systems project are entirely creative. This does not come about through the earth moving or in a sudden flash of lightning, but is the result of discussion, consultation and contemplation. Problems unresolved here can never be satisfactorily eliminated later. It is therefore a slow process and, while it may prove tedious, frustrating or even obstructionist to insist on a clear and widely accepted view of what is to be achieved, a slow start is a good start. Taking drastic action at the end of a project to tighten up and to control more and more of less and less of the work remaining is not the solution—it is putting all the effort in the wrong place.

(2) *Projects are people*

Projects and systems are run by people, and the interrelationships between the members of the development team and the client staff are complex. The effects of bargaining between groups and the use of informal systems complicates the analyst's tasks. Recognizing this, accepting it and using it where one can speeds the project, and although the participative approach and newer methodologies aim to avoid the need for such methods, for the time being we must accept that they have a place now.

In this chapter we have been able to do no more than touch on some of the issues which will tax the mind and heart of the systems analyst over the next few years. A recently published *A-Z of Information Technology* uses the term 'forgiving systems' to describe systems which allow a novice to make mistakes without chaotic or disastrous consequences and which enable confused users to call for help and to be led out of trouble. There seems no doubt that we shall need such systems ourselves.

2 Systems application studies

2.1 Introduction

Organizations of any size whatsoever are constantly involved in the collection, processing and transmission of data and information about their various activities. These data processing systems range from informal verbal discussions between individuals to sophisticated management information systems utilizing the very latest communications technology. All such systems, however, whatever their nature, have in common the fact that they reflect the procedures of the organizations within which they operate. It is the organization that provides the environment within which each information system is contained and therefore it is the characteristics of the organization that determine the characteristics of the information system and not vice versa. Members of the organizations are the users and the customers of the information system and in most cases it is a subset of these groups—management—that also allocates resources for the development and operation of these information systems. Therefore, in designing computer-based data processing and information systems, the analyst has to consider carefully the particular role of the manager concerned with using the information provided, the kinds of decision to be supported and the general nature of the problem involved.

When computers were first introduced into business organizations on any considerable scale few people on either side of the development divide had any clear idea of the situation that faced them. General management had little or no knowledge of how computers worked or what they were capable of achieving. Devoid of such technical know-how, managers substituted their understanding of what they saw as a similar area, production engineering. The computer was viewed as another machine whose performance was measured in terms of the amount of 'work' it was performing. Data processing departments were pressurized into ensuring that the computer was actually performing tangible tasks for a large proportion of the working day. When this was achieved, firms moved to shift systems in order to increase the amount of time that the computer was actually in operation, thus allowing management to spread the very large fixed costs over a larger workload even at the price of increasing variable costs, since at this time these were significantly smaller.

The result of this policy, coupled with the generally held view that computers were best used to deal with repetitive, routine tasks such as calculations, sorting and printing, was the era of application development characterized by the use of the computer as a 'super-clerk'. In other words, the main application areas that were computerized were concerned with transaction processing and the production of routine, regular paperwork such as wages, sales orders and invoices. It was felt that these areas represented the kinds of application that were both the most suitable for replacement by programmed procedures and also offered scope for the kinds of cost-saving that would justify the large expenditure involved in acquiring computer resources. These projected savings, particularly in the reduced staffing levels expected, seldom seem to have materialized in practice and many organizations were left with uneasy feelings about the merits of the new systems that had been introduced. It is now widely recognized that many mistakes were made, quite understandably, in those pioneering days and that the filling of machines with low-level operational systems was misguided.

The reason for this relative failure, which is still with us to a certain extent today, is not that such systems are not suitable for computerization—since clearly they are—but rather that the benefits which can be obtained from electronic data processing are not to be found in such applications, or are at best somewhat limited. The computerization of low-level transaction processing systems needs to be seen in the light of their interaction with the other information systems of the organization of which they form only a part, albeit an initially crucial one. The benefits to be obtained, therefore, will come from improvements brought about in the higher-level information systems and not from the operational level *per se*, although increases in efficiency and effectiveness at any level will always bring with them cost-savings and hence increased profitability.

The hierarchy displayed in Figure 2.1 may be seen as forming layers of a pyramid structure, each level providing information to the higher levels. Associated with each level is the notion of information as the means by which an organization may control its activities, thus ensuring that the company does not deviate from its plans. It can be seen, therefore, that any modern organization requires information systems which support its managerial and decision-making functions. Computer-based information systems can encompass many different types of requirements such as the provision of:

- information on the routine processing of transactions;
- information for the day-to-day planning of operations and associated decision making;
- information to support tactical planning and associated decision-making;
- information to support strategic planning and associated decision-making.

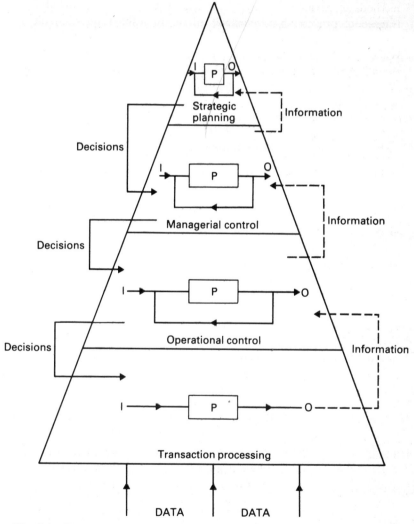

Fig. 2.1 The information hierarchy

Table 2.1 sets out the kinds of decisions that have to be made at each information level within two different types of organization. It can be seen that these differing classes of decisions will be the main determinant of the kind of information system developed in each case.

Given the extent of computerization over the last decade there are now potentially far fewer new transaction systems to develop and therefore the concentration in the future will be on the design and implementation of decision-oriented applications. Whether the methods of development that have been used in the past to produce transaction processing systems will still be applicable is questionable; it is possible that new methods and approaches will arise over the next few years to deal specifically with the production of information systems at the tactical and strategic planning levels. We shall now consider

Table 2.1 Typical decisions at various information levels

	Type of decision/function	
Level	*Manufacturing firm*	*Local authority*
Transaction processing	Wages payments Preparation of invoices Calculating the level of raw material stocks	Wages payments Processing of rate payments Maintaining rent accounts
Operational control	Determining the need for overtime working Credit control Determining reorder levels	Ensuring cover for illness/absenteeism Calculating changes in rateable value Dealing with rent arrears
Managerial control	Training and recruitment of staff Determining the pricing structure Deciding on a change supplier	Implementing cutbacks in staffing levels Determining a change in the rating structure Determining a suitable method of collection
Planning	Manpower planning Forecasting market changes Predicting long-term availability of raw materials	Manpower planning Estimating population changes Evaluating a change to home ownership

operational, control and planning systems in turn, identify their own particular features and discuss the analyst's approach to the development of each kind of application. We shall also summarize some of the essential design features of these kinds of system.

2.2 Operational systems

Any organization carries out a multitude of activities such as selling products, producing goods and services, storing items in stock and paying wages, all of which need to be described and recorded at varying intervals of time. Wages are paid weekly, salaries monthly, bills may be settled every three months and published sets of accounts are prepared annually. Such basic activities are regular, relatively unchanging and routine; all features that inevitably make them attractive for computerization. The ability to store and process large amounts of data very rapidly indeed meant that the mainframe computer soon found itself carrying out these clerical tasks in most medium-to-large organizations. Firms had little hesitation in converting their manual procedures into computer-based ones, believing that this would bring realizable benefits in terms of faster processing, the more efficient use of resources and a consequent reduction in the numbers of clerical staff required. These were the objectives pursued by systems analysts as they designed and implemented computer-based transaction processing systems.

2.2.1 Defining the system

Operational systems are generally characterized by their use of clearly specified routine operations which lend themselves fairly readily to being automated. The listing of items on an invoice and the calculation of the total amount payable by the customer are, in most cases, straightforward procedures and any problems are likely to be concerned with variations from standard conditions. For example, difficulties may be caused by a customer who insists on having the items described in a particular way or by uncertainty over whether or not a specific discount applies to an individual case. As long as the analyst can ascertain all the possible variations, however, the description of the system should be relatively straightforward.

The production of paperwork still figures strongly at the transaction processing level even with the advent of computers. The idea of the 'paper-less' office—which we discuss later—still seems to be far in the future as activities continue to be recorded on forms or documents which may then be used internally within the company, or provide external communication with other organizations. A wage slip or a despatch note may well be the tangible output from a computer system and is often seen as being the objective of the system as well. Documents, however, often perform a multitude of functions ranging from simply being an internal record of a particular transaction to representing the organization in its dealings with the outside world. In some cases it may be necessary for the same document to perform both functions. For example, a requisition note from the production department to the stores may be used by the latter as an order form to the supplier. Even at this level, therefore, there may be conflicting design requirements which the analyst has to reconcile and which almost certainly will involve some kind of trade-off between differing views of the system.

Increasingly, in transaction processing systems, forms and documents are being replaced by screen layouts for visual display units. The design considerations, however, are often similar, the major concern being the reactions of users to particular formats. James Martin in his book *Design of Man–Computer Dialogues* describes twenty-three different types of on-line computer interaction, with the type of dialogue chosen depending primarily on the application. The major design consideration is which format will be convenient for the user and will make it as simple as possible to enter the data correctly.

2.2.2 Operational system outputs

It is common to define a system in terms of its production of some tangible, physical output, e.g. 'A payroll system is a system for producing wage slips', or 'A sales order processing system is a system for producing invoices'. This gives a flavour of manufacturing to the process rather than stressing the informational nature of the outputs produced by the system. In other words, it does not say what the system is for. Perhaps with the advent of screen-based reports and a decline in the reliance on hardcopy output this view will alter and greater attention will be paid to the information content of the material produced rather than its physical characteristics.

Output represents the primary area of contact between a system and its users. The quality and perceived usefulness of the output determine whether or not such a system will be a 'success'. With operational systems, measuring performance in this way may not be considered necessary, since the system must of necessity exist. Unlike other types of information system which we shall consider later, transaction processing systems are not, in the main, able to be ignored or bypassed. Simply because such a system exists, however, does not mean that it is successful, since users may vent their displeasure on other applications which are voluntary in nature (e.g. inquiry systems or forecasting systems). Dissatisfaction with lower-level operational systems may also lead managers to distrust figures produced by higher-level planning systems: they feel that if the computer cannot perform simple clerical functions efficiently, it cannot be relied upon at the more rarefied atmosphere of managerial decision-making.

Outputs from computer-based application systems are used primarily to communicate the results of processing to the users concerned. They also often provide a permanent copy of the results of such processing which can then be used at some later stage for reference purposes. There are a number of different types of output, the main distinction being between internal and external outputs. Internal outputs are used only within the organization itself and represent the major interface with the user. External outputs, on the other hand, are destined for use with other organizations and therefore are subject to different or additional design considerations. These outputs represent the company's dealings with its environment and therefore must project and uphold its image in the outside world. The analyst may also have to take account of pressures from the recipients of external outputs, as well as giving consideration to the usual factors associated with designing output.

The first area of concern is to identify the type of output being dealt with in a particular system. Some output requirements offer little scope for change or flexibility, as for example with pre-printed stationery or statutory documents. As we have seen, however, it is important for the analyst to distinguish between internal and external outputs, and to identify outputs which may be operational or interactive in character or which may be used as turnround documents. Each of these types of output will have its own particular requirements, but the overall objective of producing any form of output is to communicate its contents to some individual or group. It is likely that these individuals or groups will be very different in nature (e.g. programmers, clerks, managers) and the effect of such differences needs to be taken into account.

Perhaps the area which is given most consideration during the specification of output requirements is that of the actual content of the material. Lengthy discussions may well take place on precisely what the user would like to see contained on a form or document. The exact titles for headings will be specified, together with the nature of the data contained within such headings, and the need for totals, subtotals and so on. If the output fulfills a number of different functions these may well place conflicting demands on the content and layout. If, for example, an output document is used for turnround purposes and re-enters the system at some later stage as a source document, the features required for its use as output may well differ from those required for punching purposes. Clarity of format and the choice of meaningful headings are important if users are to react favourably to the design. The analyst should avoid the use of obscure codes or acronyms and should provide an explanation of any unclear or difficult features of the output. If sequences of items are used (e.g. customer number within sales area) they should, as far as possible, relate to well-understood methods that the company has used previously or in other areas of their business.

The final area to be explored is that of the frequency with which the output is required together with the speed of response necessary in a particular application area. Most transaction processing systems have a fixed, regular processing cycle which may be measured by the hour, day, week, month or even year, depending upon the nature of the company's business. Such applications clearly lend themselves to batch processing since this approach is characterized by the periodic processing of batches of accumulated transactions. Generally these transactions need to be sorted into some required order before the transactions are processed against a master file. For this approach to be economically feasible, however, it is necessary to accumulate a sufficient number of transactions before processing takes place.

Batch processing may take place with both sequential files and direct files. In the former case the whole master file is read and written every time transactions are processed and therefore it is necessary for this method to be justified by the level of the activity of the file. If the degree of activity is sufficiently high, it generally costs less per transaction to process batches than to process each transaction on an on-line basis. As mentioned previously, however, it is necessary to sort the input data into the same sequence as the master file and this requirement may slow down the provision of information for decision-making purposes to an unacceptable degree. The approach described in Figure 2.2 is, therefore, generally limited to straightforward operational systems such as payroll and accounts payable.

Batch processing is not limited to sequential access files since the method can also be used with direct access storage devices such as magnetic disks. If the hit rate is sufficiently low, the direct access

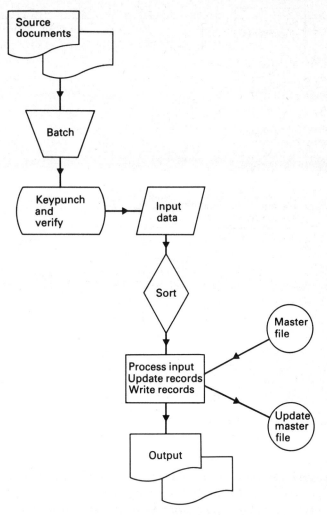

Fig. 2.2 Batch processing with a sequential access file

approach is relatively efficient. With such an approach, illustrated in Figure 2.3, it is not necessary to sort the input data into some predetermined sequence. This can be advantageous where input transactions enter the system in a completely random manner but at fairly regular intervals as, for example, with customer orders that are received by post once in the morning and once in the afternoon. Finally, since the master file data is held on a direct access storage device, it may be possible to offer the provision of an on-line

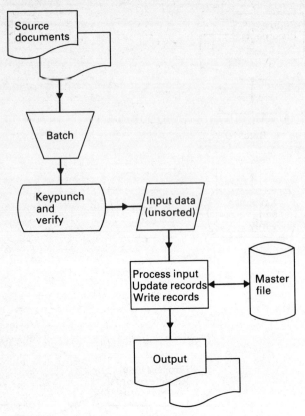

Fig. 2.3 Batch processing with a direct access file

information service to management as well as the more routine batch data processing service. Thus it is necessary to decide whether a particular application lends itself better to sequential access batch processing or to direct access batch processing.

Batch processing can also be carried out either on a local basis or utilizing remote job entry methods. In the case of local batch processing the input data is accumulated in batches on the premises of the organization and then sent directly to the computer department for processing, after which the outputs from the system are returned to the user department. With remote job entry, however, the input data is communicated over a data transmission system, then processed by the central computer department. The outputs from the system are returned to the user department by the same data transmission system.

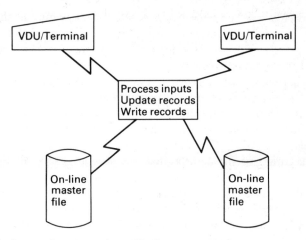

Fig. 2.4 Interactive processing with direct access storage device

Remote job entry thus combines batch data processing with the facilities of data transmission. Data is transferred over the communications channel according to some previously established timetable in either an off-line or an on-line fashion, depending upon whether or not there is a need for an immediate response. With an off-line approach the data is written on to magnetic tape or disk for processing at some future time, whereas with the on-line method the data is fed into the computer itself for immediate processing. The output which is produced is subject to the same stages as the input in each case, but is sent in the opposite direction, that is, back to the dispersed user centres.

In conclusion, it should be noted that the trend in operational systems is toward more interactive processing, that is, dealing with transactions and inquiries as and when they occur, as illustrated in Figure 2.4. This enables operational systems to contribute much more toward the effectiveness of the organization's information systems in total, as was outlined in the introduction to this chapter.

2.2.3 Operational system inputs

The trend in recent years has been towards collecting data as close to its source as possible in order to eliminate costly transcription processes which increase both the number of errors in the data and the time taken to get data into the computer. Techniques for source data collection include on-line terminals located in the workplace, turnround documents and a variety of optical character and mark-reading equipment.

The particular method chosen will depend on the nature of the data, the working environment (e.g. an engineering factory shopfloor or a company with salesmen 'on the road') and the number of people involved in the input process.

It is normally advantageous if system designers stick closely to existing form layouts for new documents and screen-based systems. This helps users to assimilate the new forms far more quickly, thus causing them to make fewer mistakes and to accept the new methods more readily.

The accuracy of the data produced at this level is vital since, for example, wages must be calculated correctly, invoices must be submitted for the right amounts and delivery quantities must tally with the amount of goods received if the firm is to maintain its reputation and efficiency, not to mention its profit level. Most problems with accuracy occur at the data input stage of any transaction processing system so it is important that the analyst takes all steps necessary to ensure the accuracy and validity of the data entering the system. Such steps range from instituting clerical checks on source documents to detailed programming procedures which validate incoming data. Well-designed systems deal with errors either by correcting them or by informing someone about the error while continuing to produce valid and correct output.

Where input is batched together and entered all at the same time, some process of key-verification is usually employed in order to check for recording errors. By having two separate operators key-punch the same data, discrepancies can be identified and corrected. However, this process assumes that the data is recorded accurately at the outset, therefore nothing can be done about items which are provided in an incorrect state. Instead of a lengthy verification process, we may rely on the computer to identify transcription errors through the use of check digits. Batch totals and hash totals may be used after transcription in order to ensure that all the data has been entered correctly into the computer. Individual fields are examined at the editing stage to check that they contain the correct format of either numeric or alphabetic characters, as appropriate. Finally, 'reasonableness' checks can be applied to the data during processing in order to verify that a data item falls between acceptable limits.

If data is rejected under a batch system it may be necessary for a designated individual to discover the reason for the error, correct it and then resubmit the offending item. This may lead in some cases to a serious increase in the overall processing time and to the compounding of errors if subsequent processing depends in some way on the incorrect item. In moving to on-line input, one aim is to allow the terminal operator to correct errors immediately by reference to the appropriate source document. On-line systems make use of many of the previously mentioned input checks such as check digits, field checking, upper and lower bounds for values and comparing for numeric and alphabetic characters. They should also use consistency checks which ensure that the same conditions are fulfilled each time an input entry is made. In general, important data should be echoed back to the operator for eye checking and final confirmation. Finally, it may be possible to incorporate into an on-line input operation a batch element, allowing the designer to utilize batch and hash totals as well as all the other mechanisms available.

2.3 Characteristics of control systems

The word 'control' normally carries implications of regulation, as in 'to restrain', 'to check', 'to command' or 'to order'. A control system can be viewed as some arrangement of entities interrelated in such a way that they achieve the regulation or direction of another system of which they may or may not form a part (i.e. control may be internally or externally induced). Such control systems are usually described as either open-loop or closed-loop in nature (Figure 2.5) although in practice it can sometimes be difficult to categorize exactly a given control system application.

Open-loop control systems operate effectively if the relationships between the inputs and outputs in a particular process are known. This may occur where human beings have learnt these relationships through experience and can anticipate changes in the input conditions. If, however, the relationships are not clearly understood or if environmental change is unpredictable, closed-loop control is generally far more effective. This is because open-loop systems simply transform inputs into outputs in some invariant manner. Such systems are designed to act in a prescribed way and therefore they are unable to adjust their responses. They will continue to produce the desired output for so long as the inputs do not alter, but if any change occurs an open-loop system will not be able to respond to it.

Certain systems, however, have the property that a portion of their outputs or behaviour is fed back to the input in order to affect or influence succeeding outputs. Control, then, can be seen to be any process or procedure designed to influence the behaviour of the system to be controlled, by affecting in some way the system's inputs, outputs

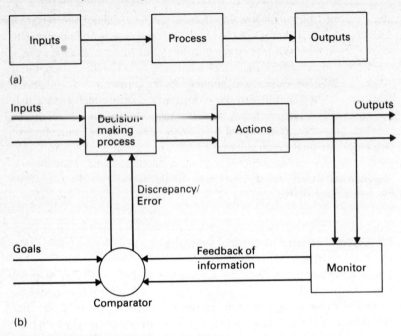

Fig. 2.5   (a) Open-loop control system
             (b) Closed-loop control system

or states. Control action is taken after a comparison has been made
between the goals of the system and its actual performance, based on
some quantitative measure of such performance. If this comparison
shows that there is a significant discrepancy between actual and desired
output, the necessary control action is initiated in order to bring the
behaviour of the system back into line.

All such adjusting systems have a basic feature, the closed loop,
which enables them to behave in some required fashion. If an
operational system is to be able to achieve the goals set for it, it has to
have some way of comparing its present position with some desired
state of affairs. This means that the system must also have some way of
sensing what its current state is, together with some way of using the
knowledge about the discrepancy between actual and desired states in
order to correct the imbalance. In most cases which we consider,
the feedback loop acts to reduce this discrepancy, hence the term
'negative feedback' is applied to this type of control mechanism.
Negative feedback systems generally act to move the present output of
the system towards some desired value and then keep it stable around
that level. Such a system will respond appropriately to any disturbance

that may arise and the desired output is maintained by a process of self-regulation, since the input is adjusted by the output itself and both settle down to steady operation. One point of great importance here is that a feedback system of this kind is effective not only against one given kind of disturbance: it should be able to deal with all kinds of disturbance, even those whose causes are unknown.

Figure 2.6 gives the basic structure of a feedback loop. This is a closed path connecting, in sequence, a decision that controls action, and information about the system which then returns to the decision-making point. The decision activity may be human or mechanical. The action results from the decision and the information feedback reports on the action. The process of control is therefore continuous, and the available information that exists at any given moment is the basis for the current decision that controls the action stream. This action, in turn, alters the state of the system. The true state of the system is the generator of information about that system, but the information can be late or incorrect. Thus the information gives the apparent state of the system and this may well differ from the true state because of such delays and inaccuracies. It is the apparent state of the system, therefore, and not the true state which is often the basis of the decision process. The single-loop structure is the simplest form of feedback system and there may well be additional delays and distortions appearing sequentially in the loop, as well as many loop interconnections.

In our case we are dealing with a control system in which the input is information about the desired level of some variable, and the output is information about its current level. Such a system, therefore, is dealing with *information* and not with goods, expenditure or some other physical or material flow. A control system is thus an information processing system that operates on some external operational system in order to maintain a particular variable at some desired level. This illustrates an important point: the distinction is between a general system that does something and a control system that uses information to exercise control over another system (see Figure 2.7).

2.3.1 Control system outputs

The format and content of the output from a control system depend first of all on whether the system is concerned with operational control or managerial control. Generally operational control systems function in the short run and deal with those things which affect day-to-day activities (e.g. 'What should we produce today?', or 'How much stock

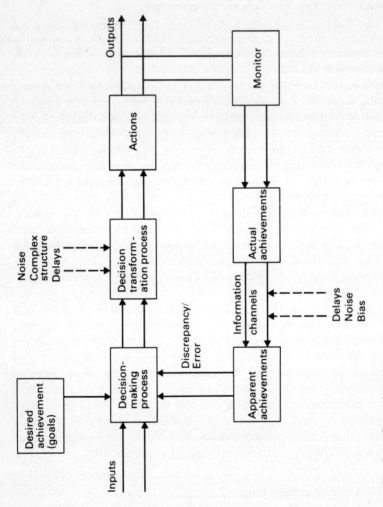

Fig. 2.6 Control system structure

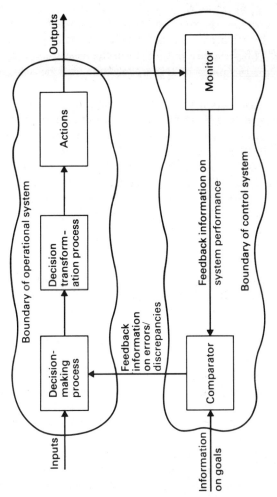

Fig. 2.7   The different functions of an operational system and a control system

should we re-order?'). Managerial control, on the other hand, has a longer time-span and deals in the main with the use of resources within the organization. Operational control often involves materials and other physical factors, whereas managerial control focuses more on financial and personnel considerations.

Outputs from operational systems are normally specific in nature such as, for example, production schedules showing which items to produce on which machines, using which raw materials and by what finishing date. These factual outputs form the basis for control. If they are adhered to, the plans of the organization will be achieved and, assuming that the plans have been correctly formulated, the goals laid down by the organization will also be achieved. However, there also need to be mechanisms by which the plans can be altered in the face of changing conditions such as delayed deliveries, price increases or absenteeism. It may be necessary, therefore, to allow space on output documents for such changes to be included, or to offer a set of alternatives with guidelines on how to select the appropriate action in a given set of circumstances. The output may be produced as a screen layout or as hardcopy, depending on the degree of interaction required in the system.

Output for managerial control systems, on the other hand, should be far more selective in nature and should be based on the principle of exception reporting. In exception reports only the unusual or critical items are highlighted for management attention, so that it is not necessary to search through large amounts of data for the important areas for consideration. This requires a set of rules that allow the system to determine what is and what is not 'unusual' or 'critical'. Most managerial control systems, therefore, are based on the approach of variance analysis, whereby the difference between some actual figure and its budgeted or target level is assessed. If the discrepancy lies within an acceptable range of variation from the budget, no corrective action is yet necessary; a discrepancy greater than is acceptable should be highlighted so that the necessary corrective action can be taken to bring the variable back within the given limits. Although couched in standard accountancy terms, this approach is clearly based on the same principles as the negative feedback view of control described earlier in this section.

2.3.2 Control system inputs

As we have seen, the input to any control system is information about the current state of some variable or variables. This information may be obtained as the byproduct of some already established transaction processing system or it may have to be collected by some newly designed procedures. Also, in order to control operational processes it is necessary to specify their goals and these need to be available to the control system in some way so that the comparison with actual performance can be computed and any discrepancy between the two dealt with. These goals vary in nature from application to application with, for example, cost minimization as a typical goal for production systems, whereas the sales operation may be more concerned with the maximization of revenue.

It is often difficult to specify an overall goal for a group or organization and it is important that individuals or subgroups should be able to quantify their goals in terms of cost, quantity, quality and so on, in order that they can understand their role in the wider operational system which is related to the control system. In a production department, for example, if the basic goal is 'to minimize costs' then it must be clear which costs (i.e. fixed, variable or total) are referred to. Moreover, it is likely that the department has been set goals for the quantity to be produced, the quality to be achieved and the time to be taken, as well as the cost at which all this is to be done. It can be seen that there are several goals to be achieved here which may well be mutually contradictory in nature; their relative importance within the control system therefore needs to be clear (e.g. 'Do we keep to the times laid down at the expense of the quality of the product?').

If the goal for the sales department is to maximize revenue, this may bring it into conflict with the production department, in that its insistence on being able to meet customers' orders as and when they arise increases the variable costs of production. Such a conflict can only be resolved satisfactorily by some higher-order control system of which these two operational systems are simply parts (see Figure 2.8). It can be seen that any organization contains a hierarchy of such interlocking negative feedback control systems. Computer-based information systems should be designed accordingly.

As the main input to the control system is information about the current state of the output of some operational system, this information has to be collected in some way. There must be some process by which operational outputs are monitored and the required information is collected and fed back to the decision-making process. The main problem area here is the time delay while these processes are being carried out, followed by the distortion of feedback information caused by such delays. As we have seen, the result of this distortion is that a comparison is made between the goals of the system and its apparent

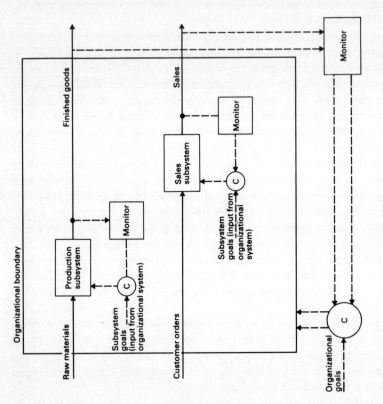

Fig. 2.8 Hierarchy of feedback control loops

achievements and not, as required, between the goals and the real achievements. The net result of all this, of course, is that management may well decide on the wrong course of corrective action. In theory, the monitoring and feedback of control information should be a continuous process so that the action taken is always based upon the most up-to-date information possible.

It may be necessary to use workstations on the shop floor to provide the data collection function which will generate the feedback of information to update the master files. There are currently several ways of collecting data from such workstations. These include automatic counters of some description which record each event completed at a workstation, without the intervention of the operator. Alternatively, the operator can input data through a simple terminal which is designed to accept only certain kinds of data and which cannot record any special events or output data. Finally there are multi-purpose data collection centres which are designed to process a large variety of data to be received as well as transmitted.

Clearly the implementation of computer-generated schedules and plans is a complicated process and is generally more difficult than actually developing the schedules in the first place, although the system has to be capable of handling uncertainty, breakdown and emergencies whatever their causes.

Data inputs take the form of items such as sales forecasts, new orders and the current status of the production schedule showing orders already in process. Incoming data is integrated with stored data such as production capacity, inventory status and machine set-up and run times in order to produce the required outputs (which were described in the previous section). Overall organizational policy acts as a constraint on the production of outputs as, for example, with customer-priority rules, overtime budgets and holiday arrangements.

Control systems of this kind are each a subsystem of the total organization and therefore must be designed to interact with other subsystems on a continuous basis, particularly at the tactical and strategic planning levels.

2.4 Characteristics of planning systems

All management activity begins with planning and the success of other organizational functions depends on how well the process of planning is carried out. Planning is concerned with deciding how an organization gets from where it is now to where it wants to be at some future date, by deciding in advance what has to be done, how, when and by whom. Management must develop objectives and then allocate resources appropriately in order to attain these objectives.

Strategic planning decisions are taken over long periods of time, although the exact time-span involved may well vary from organization to organization. Such decisions often involve a substantial effort and investment on the part of the company involved as, for example, in the case of a plan to develop and introduce a new product. The problems to be faced at the strategic planning level are clearly of an unstructured kind which may well deal with novel situations as far as the particular organization is concerned. There will be no easily described procedure for the solution of such a problem and in many cases managers resort to the notions of intuition and 'feel' when faced with the degree of uncertainty involved. This is probably why the development of computer-based information systems to support decision-making at the strategic level has been so slow. It is often difficult to convince management that computers have a major contribution to make at a level so intimately concerned with uncertainty and lack of precision.

The planning function can be viewed in two ways. In 'top-down' planning, general objectives are set at the top of the organizational hierarchy and then filter down the structure to be translated into the divisional targets, departmental goals and production schedules which are appropriate. The structure of the plans parallels the work structure in the organization, different plans being set for the control and operational levels which were considered earlier in this chapter. With 'bottom-up' planning, on the other hand, individual plans are formulated by the subsystems within the organization, having regard for their own circumstances and problems. When these subsystems, goals and targets have been set they are then passed up the organization to be combined and integrated into a coherent strategic plan for the whole organization.

Business survival is concerned with the ability of an organization to adapt to a rapidly changing environment. A firm requires information in order to evaluate its own performance and that of the environment within which it exists, as well as to attempt to specify the alternative futures that may be available to it. The planning and change decisions that affect any organization are often to do with the goods or services which the firm produces, for instance:

- what business to be in;
- what new products or services to offer in order to stay in that business;

- the product strategy necessary to produce profits and growth;
- what prices to charge for such products;
- the level of market share needed by the company to sustain itself.

The strategic planning process consists first of all of developing a strategy and, secondly, of formulating the steps necessary to achieve this strategy. The strategy will be described as a set of goals and objectives which the organization as a whole is to pursue. The steps in implementing the strategy will be defined as the courses of action to be taken, the allocation of resources selected and the tasks to be carried out by the relevant subsystems in order to achieve the organization's goals and objectives.

Strategic planning, therefore, is an important activity for any organization, since management is constantly confronted by many candidates for the allocation of the company's scarce resources. The planning system should thus increase the effectiveness of management in this area by allowing it to focus its attention on the key variables, providing it with rapid feedback information and allowing decision-makers to analyze and evaluate a large number of alternative scenarios for resource allocation. A planning system, therefore, will not simply be a single model but rather a collection of models coordinated by a computer system, which may include:

- simulation models to consider the detailed implications of various alternatives;
- econometric models to supply external data and projections about the national economy or specific markets;
- optimizing models to generate optimal overall performance;
- financial models to evaluate the investment implications of the various strategic alternatives put forward.

Such a system would look something like that illustrated in Figure 2.9: the aim would be to support the strategic planning function rather than to supplant it.

In developing a strategy, an organization has to take a series of separate but related steps.

(1) It is necessary to analyze the environment within which it operates and identify those conditions which have some influence on the company's behaviour. In particular, the organization should look for possible changes occurring within the environment and try to anticipate their effects.

(2) The company should identify its own strengths and weaknesses,

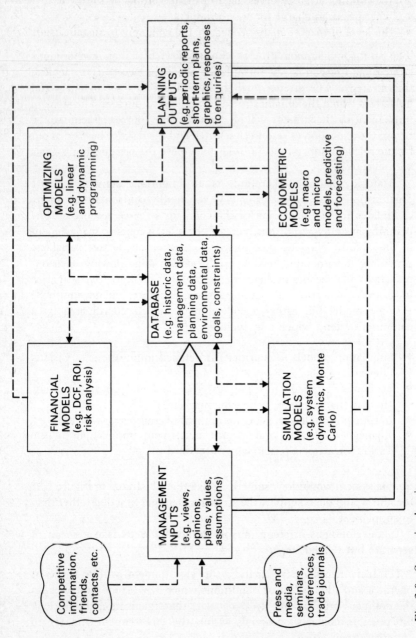

Fig. 2.9 Strategic planning system

particularly in relation to its competitors and to the market. The organization should establish the level of risk which it is prepared to accept in respect of taking decisions, at the same time clarifying the value systems of its own management so that the two areas are compatible.

(3) The next stage is to match the company's strengths with the future trends that have been identified, so pinpointing the environmental opportunities to be exploited. Having done this, management should be able to specify the range of products to be offered, the markets to be in and the general scope of the company's activities. At the same time the organization should formulate its ideas on quality, price, service and the other factors which will differentiate its products from those of its competitors.

(4) Finally, it will be necessary to set quantitative objectives and measures of performance in order to assess the contribution made to the achievement of the overall goals and objectives by each subsystem, and to decide on the optimum allocation of resources between these various subsystems.

Computer-based information systems can play an important part in the development of such planning systems as they can provide a formalized, organized and continuous means of gathering internal and external information (see Figure 2.9).

A number of problems are associated with the development of computer-based planning systems, some of which are common to other types of computer application but which tend to be more serious in the planning area. Inflexibility, lack of cost-effectiveness and expensive development are all criticisms which have been levelled at computer systems at one time or another. Also it is often assumed that managers are short of information and that there is therefore a need to provide far more of it. However, the lack is usually of information that is up-to-date and relevant, whereas the total amount provided is often excessive. This may well be because managers do not know what information they need in order to make a particular decision and therefore play safe by asking for everything they can get their hands on.

Even when relevant information is provided, it may not be used correctly if insufficient care has been taken in designing its format or specifying the bases upon which it may be employed by a manager in his decision-making. Typically there is a general lack of management skill in the areas of quantitative analysis and scientific modelling. As has already been mentioned, strategic planning decisions are often taken on the basis of experience and intuition and it may well be that management will choose to ignore the output from a sophisticated computer-based planning system because the analyses provided are not understood and consequently not trusted.

Finally, it is often difficult in practice to demonstrate the tangible benefits of a system inherently concerned with long-term effects, compared with the day-to-day operational problems being faced by functional management. However, the argument all through this chapter has been that all the information systems within an organization are conceptually intertwined and therefore cannot be practically isolated.

2.4.1 Planning system outputs

The determining of what information is needed as output from a strategic planning system is even more difficult than it is under normal circumstances, that is, for other kinds of application systems. When determining such output requirements the analyst must work closely with those people who will be using the information output. Managers and system designers must work together to decide the form and content of the output if the new system is to be successful in involving the users to the degree required for effective planning.

It is likely that past examples of output, if they exist at all, will be inappropriate at this level and therefore the need to consider them is less important than is usual with transaction processing or control systems. The analyst, however, needs to be aware, as always, of the extent to which existing planning documents or reports need to be incorporated into the new system. It is more important, however, to be able to offer the user a variety of different forms of output for his consideration and then guide him in his selection of the most appropriate layout. The use of sample outputs and prototype reports is particularly valuable at the level of strategic planning since much of the design will be based on the individual's 'feel' for what is appropriate to his requirements; there is less call for standardized routines than in other types of information systems.

Although planning systems demand a much greater degree of interaction than other systems there will still be a requirement for printed outputs produced in a batch mode. However, reports produced in this way are likely to incorporate either the principle of 'management by exception' or that of 'management by perception', or both. As we have already seen with control systems, it is important for management to be able to compare what is happening with what should be happening.

Exception reports highlight the significant deviations from established plans that have occurred either in sections of the organization or at the level of the organization as a whole, depending on the status of the manager receiving the output. Such exception items may be the only content of an output report or they may be indicated in some way within a complete list of the items concerned with some particular area. In planning systems the former method is likely to be the more appropriate, since the aim should be to minimize the amount of detail presented to the decision-maker. Some managers, however, prefer to keep track of the non-varying items as well as those that are deviating in some way from the plan. Such an approach also caters for the problem of deciding whether or not to furnish an exception report that contains no items!

The principle of 'management by perception' suggests that output reports should have the ability to display important trends and should attempt to show the impact of these on the future performance of the organization. In other words, management reports at this level should be forward-looking rather than backward-looking. The planning system should also produce regular summary reports of important information. As one moves from the lowest to the highest management levels, information becomes more and more summarized and at the planning level may well be little more than an overview of a department or even of the whole organization.

Although there is the need for any planning system to produce regular printed management reports in order to help the planning process it is the requirement for interactive output that particularly distinguishes this level of information system. In an interactive processing mode, exception and summary reports may be produced as with batch processing, but the emphasis is on the visual presentation of such material rather than on producing hardcopy. The interactive mode should be oriented toward obtaining inquiry information from the system in order to answer questions of interest to management.

Of particular importance is the ability of the planning system to handle the 'what if?' questions of particular users. The director of marketing, for instance, may want to know the likely effect on the general sales level of a product if its price is increased by 10 per cent relative to that being charged by the competition, if such an increase is backed up by a major promotional campaign on television and in the press. What if the price increase is only five per cent? What if the advertising is based only on television?

The ability to explore alternative strategies in this way by utilizing the ability of the computer to handle numerous complex interactive variables represents the major challenge faced by system designers at the present time.

2.4.2 Planning system inputs

An information system designed to support strategic planning utilizes a wide variety of inputs, ranging from organized contributions from individual managers to wide-ranging environmental data culled from many different sources. The strategic planning system also makes use of information obtained from the manipulation of control, operational and transactional data. Thus it is necessary to integrate the planning system with the lower-level information systems already discussed, as well as to provide the individual features required by the higher-level system.

The most obvious difference between the planning system and the others is its need for external information in order that the company can decide what kind of business it wants to be in, what products to develop and what markets to be in. External information can be classified as either general environmental information or competitive information. General environmental information comprises such areas as general economic trends, technological, social and political change as well as details of factors of production such as cost and availability. Competitive information, on the other hand, obviously covers details of the marketing and financial policies of major competitors as well as estimation of future demand and markets for the company's products.

This kind of input information is clearly difficult and expensive to obtain and is often of a qualitative and judgemental nature. Formal information systems, particularly computer-based ones, traditionally have not dealt with such areas because of their inherently subjective nature. In practice, planning decisions are often based on knowledge and information which is obtained informally through personal contacts, friendships or an undirected scanning of the environment using such sources as the press, trade journals and conferences. It may be possible to organize such activities on a rather more formal basis, but judgement and experience will still play an important part in selecting the relevant input data to the planning system.

An analyst should not allow his interest in formal procedures to blind him to the importance of such individual, informal information-gathering networks. Rather he should harness such sources and integrate them with the formal procedures of the computer through which environmental data can be analyzed and made sense of. The analyst will therefore have to pay even greater concern than usual to the human factors involved in designing input. The level of the management involved in strategic planning systems is likely to require input methods to be easy and convenient for the user. The more time-consuming and complex the methods, the less likely it is that they will facilitate the gathering of such difficult, often intuitive, input data. Managers will need a lot of encouragement and education to help to feed their opinions, feelings and judgements into a computer-based planning system.

In contrast, it might be assumed that the collection and input of internal information into the planning system is a relatively straightforward process. Although it is true that the internal information should already be available through the existing transaction processing and operational and managerial control information systems, a number of difficulties are still associated with the use of such information at the planning level. Firstly, much of the established data on, for instance, costs and prices will be historical in nature, whereas the requirement of a planning system obviously concerns the future. Although historical data may be useful as a guide to the future if events remain fairly constant in nature, it is of little help in periods of rapid change or where the organization is deliberately attempting to plan a new future for itself. Secondly, internal data may have been collected for a purpose that has nothing to do with planning and is therefore in an unhelpful or unsuitable format. Even if the planning function is recognized from the outset, the system designer may not be able to take account of its needs because the requirements of planning may be very difficult to specify in advance and may ultimately differ from the requirements of transaction processing or operational control. The analyst may therefore have to interface the planning system with the other information systems within the organization, taking the structure and format of the data as it is presented and adapting it to the particular needs of the planning system as and when required. This obviously makes the specification stage of such a system even more crucial than it is with more conventional computer-based applications.

2.5 Summary

In this chapter we have drawn the contrast between traditional transaction processing systems and the present need for decision support systems to enable users to improve the quality of the work they do rather than just complete it in a shorter time. This does not imply that new operational systems will not be developed but it emphasizes that analysts have at their disposal the most powerful set of methods and techniques yet assembled for developing computer-based information systems. The benefits of using computers at all levels in an enterprise are still to be fully realized in many cases because the full advantages will come only from their effective involvement in all types of system, from transaction processing to decision support systems.

3 Managing systems development

3.1 Introduction

Far too many computer-based systems fail to realize their expected potential: either they are not as efficient as expected—more time and money than were estimated are needed to produce a given output; or they are not as effective—they do not do what the user wants. Yet in many such cases project management may have been exemplary and all systems work done to perfection. Clearly this paradox has to be investigated and resolved.

In computer work, project management is intimately connected with systems development and its purpose is to ensure that all the phases of the systems life-cycle are correctly executed. Traditional project management is linked with a particular variety of systems analysis which emerged in the 1950s and early 1960s from the RAND Corporation and Bell Telephone Laboratories in the USA. In these versions of systems analysis the end-product (the 'what is to be delivered') was assumed to be known and capable of reasonably precise definition. The methodology concentrated on the 'how to produce it', and in essence consisted of a critical appraisal of alternative approaches to the solution of the 'how' problem. The main techniques embedded in the methodology enabled solution models to be specified, compared, evaluated and costed. In today's terminology this kind of systems analysis is known as 'hard systems engineering' and is typified by, for example, the specification, design and construction of a new hospital.

In the 1960s and 1970s hardly anyone questioned the appropriateness of this methodology to the specification, design and implementation of computer systems for business uses. It was taken as axiomatic that business systems were the same as 'hard' engineered systems. In fact many systems are not 'hard' at all, but 'soft'; they are difficult to define precisely and indeed the actual problem under investigation may not be at all obvious. They are more analogous to saying 'We want to improve the treatment of sick people'—and it is only with the passage of time and expenditure of much effort that it emerges that a hospital may be the best way of tackling the problem. In these circumstances one should be wary of using only the 'hard' systems engineering approach. It may not be self-sufficient because it lacks the methodologies, the techniques and the tools for a searching analysis of the problem.

However inappropriate it may therefore appear in theory, there is no denying that systems analysis has been used on practically all computer projects. It has been 'forced' to do the job; it has been modified, fixed, adapted, squeezed in parts, expanded in others in order to achieve results. But its inherent imperfection for the job manifests itself during system tests, trials, changeover and live operations when operational imperfections come to light. As a generalization one could say that small, highly technological systems with stable requirements are most suitable for the use of the 'hard' systems engineering approach, whereas large systems involving a considerable element of human activity coupled with unstable requirements will encounter most difficulty if a traditional approach is used.

The basic methodology of 'hard' systems engineering is the system life-cycle which, as adapted to computer systems development, may be considered as a list of stages (see Table 3.1). To monitor and control

Table 3.1 Typical stages of system development

Project initiation
Feasibility study
Detailed study
Outline system design
(Hardware evaluation and procurement if necessary)
Detailed system design
Programming
Conversion and changeover
Operational running
System evaluation

these stages of work, project management was imported in the early 1960s from industry and civil engineering where it had proved to be effective for such requirements as new product development and major capital works, but where the objectives were relatively 'hard' and capable of reasonably precise definition. A project manager was then appointed to plan, monitor and control all the activities which needed to be completed in order to produce the end-product.

The main technique that was developed to help the project manager was project network analysis—a valuable technique in its own right and certainly deserving consideration for the planning and control of the development of large computer systems. This kind of project management tends to require a powerful, dictatorial style of management—capable of driving a project through the successive stages of the system's life-cycle. A typical feature is that stages, or activities within stages, must be completed to allow later ones to begin. If this style of management is unthinkingly transplanted to computer systems work, the result is excessive attention to detail early in a project in order to specify all the requirements; orders to 'freeze' specifications at various stages to allow other stages to proceed and a race against time irrespective of the quality of the product. Here is the cause of the paradox. This style of project management almost guarantees that the operational system will be inflexible and out-of-date and will fail to satisfy the users' needs—even though it may be implemented on time.

Project management as applied to computer work tends to encourage the completion of an activity or a stage without sufficient reference to the ultimate acceptability of the final product. Even where it is acknowledged that a stage product needs to be revised, the techniques and tools available to the project manager have, in the past, often been inadequate to control the consequences of such a revision. A defective end-product results.

3.2 Traditional project management

Traditional project management is a style of management which aims to ensure that a system is produced to specification within the permitted limits laid down for money, time, manpower and materials. Virtually without exception, project managers adopt the staged approach to systems development based upon the system life-cycle. In many cases this is not a conscious decision by the project manager—indeed, he may not be appointed until after some of the early stages of the system development process have been completed and management has given the go-ahead for detailed design work to begin.

3.2.1 The project manager

Where the project manager sits in the organization will vary according to the relative size and influence of the data processing department and its relationship with other functional departments, but the project manager's immediate organizational environment is likely to be as shown in Figure 3.1.

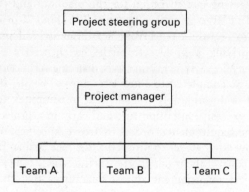

Fig. 3.1 The project manager's organizational environment

The project manager's scope, authority, objectives and constraints stem from a steering group, board or committee. This is usually a pluralist body because it has to represent the many interests of the user, the data processing department and the organization's financial and general business interests. Depending on the size of the project, the project manager may have one or several teams to direct.

In a small organization a project team may be constituted to work together more or less for the duration of the system development process and may include users, analysts and programmers. In many organizations one person is responsible for both analysis and programming (the analyst/programmer). With such a team the project manager may be able to generate a good team spirit with high motivation, job satisfaction and pride in the product. The team may respond readily to *ad hoc* demands upon their time and effort. A deep understanding of the existing system and its new requirements may be developed in the team and communication is easy between team members. A word of caution, however: such teams may operate so informally that formal procedures and documentation are neglected—a project manager may be pleased with the apparently rapid progress of a project team, only to find during systems changeover and live operations that errors are troublesome to rectify because of inadequate documentation. Later in the system's life, changes to the user requirements may be difficult and expensive to accommodate—again because of inadequate documentation. One of the project manager's most important tasks, therefore, when directing a project-oriented team, is to ensure that standard procedures and documentation are fully observed or produced.

By contrast, in a bigger organization one might find specialist groups organized on a functional basis, resulting in some form of matrix organization for project purposes (see Figure 3.2); this is not uncommon in software houses. In this kind of organization the project

	Manager	Manager	Manager	Manager
	Business analysts	System designers	Programmers	Other specialists
Project manager A				
B				
C				
D				

Fig. 3.2   Matrix organization for project work

manager acquires resources from a functional manager to perform the work of a particular stage of project. The advantages are that the specialist skills can be exercised, developed and rewarded within each speciality—helped by professional, functional management; formal procedures and documentation are essential for communication between the specialist groups, and this encourages good overall documentation for the project; staff are employed on the project only for the duration of their task; accounting for work done is easier than with a general-purpose project team; each specialist can keep abreast of the latest professional developments and therefore methodologies, techniques and tools used for the project work are likely to be up-to-date. Staff turnover is less of a problem than with the team-based organization.

Possible disadvantages are that team spirit is difficult to create and sustain because of the changing composition of the project team, and *ad hoc* work may be difficult to organize, especially at short notice. Commitment to the user may also be weak, as the specialist's commitment may be to his specialist group, although experience of this kind of team indicates that a good project manager quickly motivates his team to accomplish the team's goals.

Products to be delivered by the project manager
However the team is organized, project management is a means to an end and is a necessary production overhead. In this sense it is similar to a production control function. The project manager's performance is

Table 3.2 Major products

PRODUCT
Feasibility study report
Functional specification of the user requirement
System proposal
Invitations to tender
Evaluation report
Contracts
Detailed system specifications
Programs
Procedures, forms and user manuals
Staff training plans
Test criteria and plans
Conversion and changeover plans
The operational system
Operational review

judged by his ability to deliver the goods on time, within budget and to specification. It would be undesirable to confine the products of project management to one only, namely the operational system. This is because most computer projects are, relatively speaking, risky and costly exercises and in most cases outcomes cannot, at the outset of a system study, be predicted with absolute certainty. It is prudent therefore for the project manager to produce a stream of intermediate products to enable judgements to be made about the quality of the work being done, whether the project should continue, the accuracy of past estimates of future resources, the validity of cost–benefit assumptions, etc.

Table 3.2. lists the major products associated with a typical medium-sized project which requires the procurement of extra computer facilities.

Techniques for project management
A project manager is a special kind of manager. He is responsible for managing change—a formidable task. He is required to have good management qualities of a general nature such as the ability to communicate, motivate, plan, control and hold down cost. In addition he must be able to manage multi-discipline teams, cope with a changing environment and understand the relative significance of the technical products he will be handling.

In three areas he has tools and techniques to help him: in planning and control, investment appraisal and estimating application software effort. These are discussed in turn below.

3.2.2 Planning and control aids

There are two common aids to planning and control. These are charts and networks. Charts and networks are familiar and are covered in *Basic Systems Analysis*; Figure 3.3 shows a typical bar chart. The

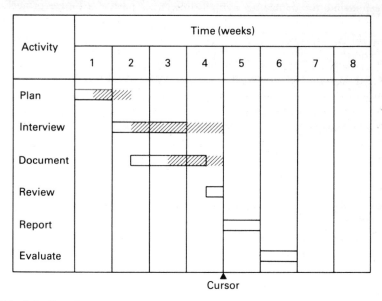

Fig. 3.3 Bar chart

hollow rectangles indicate a planned activity, its estimated elapsed time and when it is due to begin and end. The shaded rectangles indicate actual performance. A moving cursor can be constructed from pins and string to show the current date at a glance. A chart does little more than give a pictorial representation of estimates of activities and subsequent performance. It does not allow any numerical analysis to be made and the overall effect of variations in performance against estimates is not readily revealed by such charts. However they are useful for high-level presentations—they are strikingly simple! At the other end of the spectrum, bar charts are useful for small teams. They may be displayed on a wall and are a visible reminder of how the team is progressing.

Where a large number of time-critical interrelated activities have to be planned and controlled, a project manager may well find that network analysis is a useful tool. There are a number of related products such as PERT (Programme Evaluation and Review Technique) and CPA (Critical Path Analysis) and these can be studied separately. Suffice it to say, however, that project network diagrams and analyses may be used on projects of all sizes. Obviously the larger and more complex the project, the greater the resources needed to produce and maintain the network. If a systems analyst were made responsible for managing a small project, or part of a bigger project, and he used networking diagrams to assist in planning and control, he would be required:

- to draft networks and check their validity
- to negotiate estimates of activity durations and resources
- to produce analyses of project time and float
- to produce bar charts and resource histograms
- to renegotiate as necessary and produce revised diagrams, etc.
- to secure user–management agreement
- to monitor progress
- to revise networks and analyses
- to act as progress-chaser
- to report to user–management at progress meetings

Project network techniques are useful when a project has the following chacteristics:

- Many interrelated activities
- A need for careful coordination of the work of several separate departments
- A critical completion date
- Limited resources
- A need to educate many managers about the project as a whole and the part their department plays in the whole scheme
- A need to react quickly to changing circumstances

3.2.3 Investment appraisal

In spite of the falling cost of raw computing power through the evolution of microelectronic technology, a computer system for a business application is still a relatively expensive purchase and the outcome in terms of benefit to the organization it serves is by no means certain. Hence the procurement of computer facilities should be treated with appropriate business caution—indeed, some would say it should be treated as a high-risk, high-cost investment.

Investment appraisal requires someone to ascertain the total costs associated with, say, a system proposal—and this amounts to a great deal more than the mere cost of the computer hardware and system software—and to compare them with the expected benefits. Management then has to decide whether the organization is getting 'value for money' in authorizing the project.

There are two problems to be mentioned at the outset. Firstly, in recent years hardware costs have been decreasing while manpower-related costs have been increasing. During the period 1955–1970 one could estimate that for every pound spent on hardware another pound would be spent on analysis, programming, operating, data entry and control. Today the ratio of hardware costs to manpower costs is about 1 : 3. The problem this creates is that manpower-related costs tend to be more difficult to predict than hardware costs. Secondly, there has been a convergence of computers and telecommunications coupled with a proliferation in the variety of on-line peripheral devices of all shapes, sizes and prices. Thus the development of systems has become more pervasive in an organizational sense, and the introduction of many more variables has made it much more difficult to predict costs and benefits.

At the outset of this section some terms need clarification. *Evaluation*, as required to be performed by a systems analyst during the course of a project or system development, is the process of forecasting the likely impact and value of a new system or system change. *Cost-justification or cost–benefit* analysis is the process of justifying expenditure on a new system or of making a change to an existing system. A comparison is made between the expected costs and forecast benefits.

Benefits may be tangible or intangible. *Tangible benefits* fall into two categories. First, *hard* tangible benefits: these are benefits to which monetary value can readily be assigned, for example, manpower, plant machinery, buildings, etc. Such benefits are treated as *realizable*. Second, *soft* tangible benefits: those to which it may be difficult or impossible to assign a monetary value, such as improvements in labour–turnover, or savings in time. Such benefits are best treated as *unrealizable*. An element of pessimism in estimating savings is justifiable and prudent. *Intangible* benefits are those that are wholly unquantifiable, such as improved decision-making, increased job satisfaction, better business image, etc. No savings whatsoever should be claimed for intangible benefits.

Cost-effectiveness is the state of affairs where the cost, in quantifiable monetary terms, of providing a service is less than the cost of providing it by any other practicable means. Cost-effectiveness, rather than cost-justification, may more often be the objective of an investment appraisal of a computer system proposal, since in many circumstances it has already been decided by management that a service, or a particular level or standard of service, should be provided. That service has been properly defined, justified and agreed, and the only question that remains is how the defined level of service can be provided most economically—that is, the question of cost-effectiveness.

Although 'value for money' is undoubtedly a key aspect of investment appraisal for senior management, there are other aspects which perhaps bear more directly upon the systems analyst involved in project management. Investment appraisal, properly executed, enables a project manager to demonstrate that he has planned and costed the development and the operation of the new or revised system, and compared the costs with those of the existing system (if there is one—or of an alternative if there is not), and is satisfied that the user's objectives can be attained economically.

The appraisal also provides a basis for monitoring the project's progress and final outcome—and in this sense the analyst's professional competence is exposed to scrutiny. Investment appraisals also help user–management to decide priorities between projects. Investment appraisal, essential though it is, is not a guarantee of project success. The realization of the project objectives depends entirely on the skilful management of the whole process of system development and on the harmonious working relationships of users and computer specialist.

Before considering two typical techniques for investment appraisal there are three matters for consideration which are common to all such techniques:

(1) *The system boundary must be defined.* If the boundary is drawn too tightly, relevant costs or benefits may be excluded from the appraisal; if it is drawn too loosely, the result may be an excessive amount of work in collecting costing data and making estimates. Generally, the boundary must be defined to encompass all significant changes to the existing system; this is especially true for cost–benefit purposes. However, if it is only a question of comparing competing configurations of hardware—all of which provide the facilities required—then the boundary needs to encompass only the computer system itself.

(2) *The system life must be determined.* The system life is not the same as the physical life-expectancy of the equipment to be used. One must consider the economic life-expectancy of the equipment. Is it

likely to become obsolete and therefore expensive or impossible to maintain? On the other hand, the system life-expectancy may be shorter than the economic life of the equipment, and in this case the question of residual value of the equipment arises.

(3) *All appraisal elements must be identified.* The most common elements are the following:

Manpower
    Project management
    Systems
    Programming
    Operations (including data entry)
    User management and operational manpower

Decisions must be taken about the basis of manpower costing, such as whether current actual earnings are used, what assumptions are made about new jobs, likely future wage increases, etc. If redundancies are likely, what will they cost? If staff are to be redeployed and retrained, what will be the cost?

Equipment
    Computer and peripheral devices
    Terminals and communications
    Off-line devices
    Installation and commissioning
    Bureau facilities
    Maintenance
    Unbundled software
    Consultancy services for procurement

Accommodation
    Project and system development staff
    User staff and facilities
    Computer facilities
    Computer operations staff
    Air conditioning, if necessary

Other
    Training
    Consumables
    External services (transport, post, telecommunications)
    Power

Discounted cash flow
The most widely used appraisal technique is probably that known as

discounted cash flow; this will be described in some detail and contrasted with another technique known as the payback method.

Discounted cash flow (DCF) provides a method of putting costs on a comparable basis and of taking account of the time-value of money. To use this technique the analyst estimates the sums of money needed year by year to cover the annual outgoings. All expenditure is recorded in the year in which it arises and current and capital expenditure are treated alike.

There are several ways in which DCF comparisons can be made. The most straightforward is to draw up the life-time annual cash flows for the proposed system and for the existing system. The cash flows for the proposed system are deducted from the cash flows for the existing system, to arrive at a net cash flow, and then discounted by a given 'test discount rate' (TDR). The annual discounted cash flows are ' then summed to give a single value called the net present value (NPV). For the proposal to be cost-effective, the NPV should be greater than zero. Another way of using DCF, say for cost-justification, would be first to estimate the annual cash flows for the proposed system, then to estimate the monetary value of the tangible benefits year by year and record these. Subtract the cash of the proposed system from the benefits for each year and apply the TDR to the annual net results, compounded as before. Sum the discounted net results to give a single NPV. If this is positive then, on the given assumptions, the system has passed its cost-justification or cost–benefit test. Once practised, these techniques give a useful way of assessing cost-benefit. Some help from an accounting colleague may prove useful.

Standard forms may be produced for using DCF and examples are shown. Figure 3.4 shows a general-purpose form for summarizing the annual cash flows associated with a proposed system, an existing system or an alternative system. Figure 3.5 shows a form for summarizing the benefits, and the form in Figure 3.6 takes the totals from the previous forms and shows the NPV. This should be a positive amount; if it is not, the project may be relying heavily upon benefits which are other than tangible and realizable.

Figure 3.7 shows a form for comparing proposed costs with either existing or alternative system costs (the form depicted in Figure 3.4 may be used for arriving at these costs—one for each system being compared) and, like the Figure 3.6 form, arrives at the NPV.

A danger in using techniques like DCF is that the results assume an unjustified significance. Typing the costing data into the costing forms immediately enhances their credibility! One should never forget that many of the costing elements are subject to a considerable degree of

Units: £

Type of expenditure	Supporting documentation reference	Year										
		0	1	2	3	4	5	6	7	8	9	10
MANPOWER Management Systems Programming Operations User management User staff													
TOTAL													
EQUIPMENT Computer Terminals+comm. Offline Installation Bureau Maintenance Software Services													
TOTAL													
ACCOMMODATION Project Users Computer Air-conditioning													
TOTAL													
OTHER Training Consumables Services Power													
TOTAL													
GRAND TOTAL													

Fig. 3.4 Cash flows of proposed project and system life or existing/alternative system

Units: £

Type of benefit	Supporting documentation reference	Year										
		0	1	2	3	4	5	6	7	8	9	10
TANGIBLE (realizable) Manpower Buildings Plant Machinery Consumables Services													
TOTAL													
TANGIBLE (but realization uncertain) To be specified:													

INTANGIBLE Brief description	

Fig. 3.5 Estimates of benefits

Units: £

	Year										
	0	1	2	3	4	5	6	7	8	9	10
(A) COSTS OF PROPOSED PROJECT AND SYSTEM Grand total											
(B) TANGIBLE BENEFITS Total realizable											
NET CASH FLOW (B) – (A)											
DISCOUNT FACTOR @ 7%	1.0	0.935	0.873	0.816	0.763	0.713	0.666	0.623	0.582	0.544	0.508
ANNUAL NPV											
TOTAL NPV											

Fig. 3.6 Summary of costs and benefits

Units: £

	Year										
	0	1	2	3	4	5	6	7	8	9	10
(A) CASH FLOW: PROPOSED Grand total											
(B) CASH FLOW: EXISTING/ALTERNATIVE Grand total											
(C) OTHER TANGIBLE BENEFITS (realizable) Specify:											
NET CASH FLOW (C) + (B) − (A)											
DISCOUNT FACTOR @ 7%	1.0	0.935	0.873	0.816	0.763	0.713	0.666	0.623	0.582	0.544	0.508
ANNUAL NPV											
TOTAL NPV											

Fig. 3.7 Comparison of costs of proposed and existing/alternative systems

Managing systems development **53**

uncertainty—especially if the system life is more than, say, 5 years. A technique known as sensitivity analysis tests the sensitivity of the DCF results to changes in the assumptions, and this helps to identify key assumptions which have a range of uncertainty associated with them. With computer projects these are usually obvious, for example, labour cost and market assumptions. The sensitivity analysis in essence takes a range of assumptions and reworks the NPV.

The best advice, then, is to ensure that the basic assumptions and costing elements are as accurate as possible and seasoned with a sprinkling of pessimism.

Payback period
This approach to investment appraisal is based upon a simple concept—how long will it take to recoup the money invested in a new system? It is generally used in cases where the payback period is unlikely to exceed 5 years. It is rough and ready but it gives management a simple no-nonsense indicator of 'value for money'. It is best confined to small rather than large systems proposals and short time-scales rather than long (Figure 3.8).

Of course, the work of estimating all the costing elements is, in theory, just the same as for DCF. But in practice the payback calculation tends to encourage 'back-of-an-envelope' estimates. The simplicity of the calculation results partly from ignoring all of the time aspects of the costs and benefits—this is similar to using a zero TDR for a DCF analysis. But 'payback period' tends to be used for quick payoffs—and this would imply a high rate of return consistent with high interest rates!

Investment appraisal—conclusion
Whatever method of appraisal is used by the analyst it must be remembered that it depends absolutely upon the estimates of cost and benefits. These should be fully documented so that assumptions may be referred to or updated easily. Treat with special care the one or two key elements which probably determine the outcome of the appraisal. Remember that small adjustments in TDR for DCF purposes can easily turn an unprofitable investment into a profitable one—and vice versa. Be consistent in the use of an appraisal method throughout the life of the project and update the appraisal at all key stages.

3.2.4 Estimating application software effort

Experience suggests that software development must still be regarded

```
┌─────────────────────────────────────────────────────────────────┐
│                                                                   │
│    1. NON-RECURRING PROJECT COSTS                         £       │
│         Feasibility study                                         │
│         Detailed design                                           │
│         Equipment                                                 │
│         Programming                                               │
│         Testing                                                   │
│         Conversion                                                │
│         Other                                                     │
│                                                    _____       │
│                                         TOTAL (A) _____        │
│                                                                   │
│                                                                   │
│    2. ANNUAL OPERATIONAL COSTS        Existing        Proposed    │
│         Manpower                          £               £       │
│         Accommodation                                             │
│         Equipment                                                 │
│         Maintenance                                               │
│         Consumables                                               │
│         Other                                                     │
│                                    _____       _____        │
│                            (B) _____      (C) _____         │
│                                                                   │
│                                                                   │
│    3. ANNUAL BENEFIT                                              │
│                                                                   │
│                            (B)  less  (C)  =  (D) _____        │
│                                                                   │
│                                                                   │
│    4. PAYBACK PERIOD                                             │
│                                                                   │
│                            (A) ÷ (D) = _____ YEARS            │
│                                                                   │
└───────────────────────────────────────────────────────────────────┘
```

Fig. 3.8 Payback period calculation

as a high risk activity. Many projects succumb to one or more of the
following:

- Failure to meet operational requirements
- Late delivery
- Inadequate reliability
- Excessive development cost
- Excessive maintenance cost

Estimates of application software development costs have been wide
of the mark in far too many cases. Similarly, the cost of maintaining
programs seems to have been consistently and often seriously underesti-
mated, and it is not uncommon to find that the maintenance cost is

several times the development cost—and rarely is this foreseen at the time of the investment appraisal of the system proposal! However great may be the direct cost of delay and poor estimating, the indirect costs should not be overlooked—obsolete equipment may have to be retained, new equipment may be under-utilized, trained personnel may have little or no work to do, system benefits may be delayed, customers may lose confidence in a company which fails to meet the deadline date for introduction of a new service, etc. While it is true that for some years there has been recognition of the need to improve the estimation, planning and control of programming projects, what is recognized is not easily achieved!

Let us say first of all that there is no method or technique available to the project or programming manager that will eliminate all of the areas of uncertainty. The best that can be done is to use methods and techniques to minimize the risks associated with the major areas of uncertainty. The main resources involved in this aspect of the project are:

- Time
- Personnel
- Money
- Computer facilities
- Consumables

In addition, cutting across all estimating and planning of production and maintenance costs is the quality of the product to be delivered. What are the targets for reliability, maintainability, adherence to standards, readability, execution speed, memory utilization and documentation? Often these are compromised in an attempt to keep within resource estimates and this is something the project manager must guard against. A programming manager may claim to have kept within budget, while what started as a high-quality product has ended as a low-grade product deficient in many of the above requirements. In other words, the promised product has not been delivered and an inferior one is being foisted upon the customer. Later in this chapter we shall examine a methodology for systems development which makes a conscious effort to overcome problems of this kind.

The approach to estimating
Estimates are required for different purposes at different stages of a project. The early estimates are required for cost-justification of the project and tend to be 'broad-brush'. Later estimates are required to determine the number of programmers and support staff needed, to

determine the project duration time, to cost the project, to determine the computer resources required and to specify performance characteristics; these are normally made during the detailed design stage of the project.

A factor which further complicates estimating is the need to deal with changes to the operational requirements. The specification may have to be 'frozen' at some stage, but it should be as late as possible; it was pointed out at the very beginning of this chapter that early freezing only ensures that the user is provided with something he does not want! The project manager must ensure that the cost of coping with changes is fully accounted for. Changes involve:

- defining the tasks needed to implement the change
- estimating the resources needed
- scheduling the resources
- determining the overall impact on the project
- estimating the cost

The project manager should bear in mind that any estimate can only be as good as the factors which influence it, such as the accuracy of the data on which estimates are founded, the experience and ability of the estimator, the time allowed for making estimates and the organization's experience of comparing estimates with actual performance.

One estimating method which is applied widely is to call for three estimates: (a) an optimistic, (b) a pessimistic and (c) a most likely estimate. These are then combined to provide a realistic estimate by averaging them according to weights assigned on the basis of experience. For example:

$$\text{Realistic estimate} = \frac{\text{optimistic} + (3 \times \text{most likely}) + (2 \times \text{pessimistic})}{6}$$

Clearly the values used will be arrived at subjectively, but at least they provide a starting-point.

Estimating by comparison
This method is usually confined to estimating man-days of effort and is based upon the experience of the estimator and his skill in applying past experience to future work. The method can be used at all stages of a project. Even in the earliest stages it is possible to take the outline of a new system and subdivide it. Subdivision will undoubtedly reveal elements which are recognizably similar to programming tasks performed in the past. The estimate will be improved if there are accurate records of past work and resources used. Some elements may be unlike

anything within the estimator's experience—but at least this can be recognized to be the case and enquiries may be made elsewhere for guidance on resources needed. A contingency factor can be incorporated.

This is a simple method which is adequate in many circumstances. For example, in a database environment with good adherence to installation standards, many requirements may result in similar kinds of programs. The method may be improved by averaging two or three estimates by experienced managers or team leaders.

The method, however, may suffer from some or all of the following:

- The new requirements may not be as similar to past work as the estimator thinks
- The programming environment may have changed considerably
- The programming objectives may not be the same
- The recording or recall of past work may be defective

A record of previous estimates is essential.

Estimating by formula
This method is mostly confined to estimating man-days of effort required. A formula is employed which takes into account the most significant factors that influence the completion of the programming task. Estimates are made of the values of the factors and, as with comparative estimating, subjectivity plays a part. However, use of a formula forces the estimator to think consciously about the factors, their significance and their value. Moreover, if information about tasks and resource utilization is collected on a regular basis the formula method can be refined and improved with the passage of time.

A typical formula-based method requires an estimate of program size measured in units which can also be used to express a programmer's output. The program size can then be divided by the average programmer's output to give the average number of programmer-days needed to complete the task. Two commonly used units are (a) number of memory locations occupied by the program when consolidated and loaded and (b) number of source statements. The latter is preferable because it more directly relates to a programmer's work—the former is influenced by compiler and consolidation software. The source statements used as units of measure are those which are fully tested, debugged and documented—in other words, they are part of a product delivered to specification, are quality-assured and include data definitions as well as procedural instructions. The average number of such source lines per programmer is surprisingly low at many installations and it often falls within 10–20 per programmer-day.

To arrive at the total cost of programming effort several other costs must be included, such as those relating to clerical support, data entry, computer facilities and consumables. However, the above method is too crude to be widely acceptable—it assumes that all programs and programmers conform to the average. In fact there are four major factors which should be taken into account:

(1) Degree of complexity (e.g. data types and file structures)
(2) Working environment (e.g. quality of specifications and technical supervision; working conditions)
(3) Tools and techniques (e.g. design methodology, languages, software aids, workstations)
(4) Personnel (e.g. programmer's experience, ability, etc.)

Not all relevant factors can be taken into account, however, as some are impossible to measure, being too subjective or lacking significance. Those which can be taken into account include, for instance:

- The complexity of the program logic
- Input–output complexity
- Size
- Language
- Testing facilities
- Programmer experience
- Size of programming team
- Degree of program novelty
- Time available for completion
- Programming objectives
- Management and organization of the team

One of the most significant factors influencing the time required to complete a major software project is its novelty. The degree and extent of innovation is often not appreciated. Not only may a system be new but there may be a high degree of innovation in hardware, system software, design methodologies, languages, management style etc. Another significant factor is size. Large programming teams seem to be less productive than small ones; productivity of programmers working on large programs seems to be much less than that of those working on small ones. The reasons for this are not clearly understood.

An individual formula must be devised for an installation or project, based upon trial and error and using factors which have been found from experience to be relevant. The final formula may be like this:

$$\text{Man-days} = \frac{\text{Estimated size of program}}{\text{Average daily programmer output}} \times F_1 \times F_2 \times F_3 \times F_4$$

where $F_1 - F_4$ are factors deemed to be relevant, such as

$$F_1 = \text{programmer experience} = \text{trainee} = 1.5$$
$$6\text{--}12 \text{ mths} = 1.2$$
$$12\text{--}24 \text{ mths} = 1.1$$
$$\text{over } 24 \text{ mths} = 1.0$$

$$F_2 = \text{coding complexity} = \text{simple} = 0.8$$
$$\text{normal} = 1.0$$
$$\text{difficult} = 1.3$$
$$\text{very complex} = 1.5$$

and so on. A formula is no more than a formal statement of the data and factors to be taken into account and the values attached to the factors are quantifications of the assumptions made. Nevertheless this is better than snatching a figure out of thin air and it is capable of improvement with use.

3.2.5 Traditional project management—conclusions

A project is a means of implementing a new system or a change to an existing one. The manager is responsible for ensuring that this happens within constraints laid down by senior management. Planning, estimating and control feature large in the project manager's tasks; he must also be able to direct and motivate a variety of people; he is responsible for the entire conduct of the project and its products. His appointment commonly starts early in the project and he stays at his post until the plans have been fully implemented.

In most projects the staged development of systems analysis is used as the methodology for systems development (see Table 3.3). By applying this methodology a logical stream of products is produced—both by the project manager himself as a means of determining progress and by those over whom he is exercising control. These streams can be related to the project stages.

Obviously, project management can be scaled in size and importance, depending on the circumstances, from a two-man team of analyst–programmers working together for six months to a very large mixed team of users, computer specialists, management services

Table 3.3 Staged development of systems analysis

Stage	Project manager's product	Technical products
Project initiation	1. Evaluation and recommendations 2. Plan for feasibility study 3. Outline plan of further stages	Terms of reference
Feasibility study	1. Stage report 2. Plan for detailed study 3. Outline plan of further stages	1. Review of current system 2. System objectives 3. Strategies for change 4. Cost–benefit appraisals
Detailed study	1. Stage report 2. Plan for outline system design 3. Outline plan of further stages	1. Job specification 2. Detailed description of existing system
Outline system design	1. Stage report 2. Procurement plans and documentation 3. Detailed plans	1. Proposed system specification (incorporating user requirement and system design) 2. Cost-effectiveness analyses
Hardware procurement	1. Evaluation report 2. Detailed plans	1. Technical evaluations 2. Cost-effectiveness analyses
Detailed system design	1. Stage report 2. Detailed plans	1. Detailed specification 2. Program designs

Stage	Project manager's product	Technical products
		3. Clerical procedure specifications 4. Training plans 5. Testing, file conversion and changeover strategies
Programming	1. Stage report 2. Detailed plans	1. Programs 2. Test results 3. Trained operatives, etc. 4. User manuals
Conversion and changeover	1. Stage report 2. Proposal for operations review	1. Converted files 2. Converted system
Operations	1. Report 2. Close project	System performance measurements

practitioners, communication specialist, trainers etc., working together for two or three years and perhaps requiring one or two people to assist the project manager.

Traditional project management will be around for a long time to come. Applied intelligently and flexibly it is a good method of securing change. Its dependence upon one person—the project manager—is perhaps its weakness. Any deficiency on his part may affect the whole project team.

3.3 Improving project management

3.3.1 Introduction

Traditional project management has not had such a good track record that no improvements need be sought. On the contrary, the weight of evidence, anecdotal though much of it may be, has led to a search for improvements. The search has been directed towards solving some of the problems that seem to arise in spite of project management:

- Systems delivered late
- Costs exceeded
- Benefits below expectations
- Dissatisfied users
- Poor documentation
- Managers and users feeling ignored
- Unreliable system performance

It is likely that some of these problems arise because computer people take upon themselves, or are forced to accept, responsibilities for which they may not be adequately equipped, such as specification of user requirements, design of clerical systems, costing, planning (in an organizational dimension) and project management itself. It is not difficult, in the light of the above findings, to make some proposals for improving the system development process. These in turn help to formulate the kind of methodology needed to implement them.

(1) *More management involvement*, especially at senior levels: this is needed for such tasks as strategy approval, priority ordering, planning and resource authorization and progress monitoring. These are all tasks appropriate to senior management's normal role. They do not need extensive detailed knowledge of data processing.

(2) *More user involvement* at all levels: when all is said and done, the user should regard the system as his, not something that has been developed for him and 'sold' to him. User managers should not have to acquire extensive new knowledge—the tasks they may be required to do should be within their normal management skills. However, some users may be required to devote a substantial amount of their time for several weeks or months to such tasks as business analysis, data analysis, clerical procedure design, etc., for which training is desirable.

(3) *The system development methodology* should be visible to all concerned and be seen to be sensible and supportive. The methodology should encourage team work and discourage conflict. The 'charismatic' project manager, introducing a new system by force of personality, should become a phenomenon of the past. There are not enough of such people and, in any case, their performance is unpredictable.

(4) *Changes requested during the system development stages* should not be treated as hindrances to progress and nuisances to be rejected if at all possible. Changes are simply manifestations of flexible, responsive systems and are a fact of business life; it is unrealistic to freeze a user specification and expect it to hold good for months or years. This is not

to say that all changes should be accepted uncritically, but that the system development methodology must have an effective and realistic mechanism for dealing with them.

(5) *Budgeting and progress monitoring* should be strengthened so that the system development process becomes more predictable. They should be based upon defined deliverable products which can be seen, examined, tested and approved.

(6) *The system development process* should be a 'corporate' process and not something managed exclusively by the data processing department. Indeed, computer people should concentrate on doing computer work and not assume responsibility for work for which they have neither the qualifications nor the experience. They should be partners, not overlords.

3.3.2 Desirable features of a methodology

The first step in the crystallization of methodology is to identify some of the major characteristics of a desirable system development process. These may be summarized as:

- An organizational framework appropriate to the work needing to be done
- A variety of resources able to perform particular tasks
- A finite life-span, subdivided into stages
- Tangible products produced at defined points in time—at the very least at the end of each stage of the life-span
- Plans produced and progress monitored

Analysis of the work to be done and products to be delivered reveals that, broadly speaking, they fall into two categories: management and technical. These categories provide the main dimensions of the organizational structure needed to accommodate the system development process. Analysis of the technical products reveals that there are three groups of people interested in reviewing the product quality. They represent the technical aspects (computer programs) the systems aspects (user procedures) and the business aspects (budgets), and this should be reflected in the way products are produced, reviewed for quality and accepted.

On the whole, team structures seem to be the preferred way to organize people for system development work. The composition of teams should reflect the technical skills needed for the job to be done and the personalities of the people with such skills.

Planning is an activity which permeates all system development work. Plans need to be produced at different levels of detail depending on their purpose. Some plans will be technical in nature, such as those for system testing; others will relate to the management process, for example resource scheduling and budgeting.

Controls are an essential feature of any management process and the monitoring of plans helps to control time, costs and quality. Corrective actions must be integral and natural activities of the process

Activities are the tasks that must be accomplished to ensure that planned objectives are achieved. They result in specified, tangible products which can be reviewed, accepted, rejected or amended. There are two main groups of activities—management activities, which result in the products needed to plan, organize and control the system development process, and technical activities, which result in the products needed to construct or operate the system.

Systems development is concerned with the delivery of products. These are tangible things which may be specified, costed, timed and examined for acceptability. The vast majority are in documentary form—not surprising when one recognizes that the system development process, whether it be large or small, is a process of turning ideas into reality. In so doing, the intermediate work is aimed at creating models of the ultimate reality, most of which are theoretical models described by means of symbols and text, such as system and program specifications, data definitions, program listings, flow diagrams, testing strategies, user procedures and training plans. When a system becomes operational, reality becomes apparent—but there should be in existence a complete documentary model of the system which is accurate and readable. This model is by no means redundant—it is vital for dealing with operational trouble-shooting and changing user requirements. The concept of a flexible, responsive operational system can become a reality only if the system documentation is complete, accurate and properly managed.

Quality assurance is rarely a central or dominating feature of traditional project management. If practised at all, it is on an *ad hoc* basis, or perhaps confined to a small technical area such as programming walkthroughs. Even that may have come about only through the initiative or enthusiasm of a single team leader—it may not be a mandatory or universal installation practice. Too often the quality of products arising from traditional project management is taken for granted; testing, trials, conversion and changeover are assumed to be the safety nets which will prevent system failures arising as a result of defective components. What management should grasp, however, is that the cost of repairing defective system components increases with

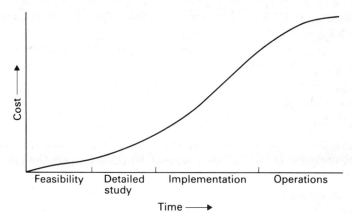

Fig. 3.9 Relative cost of correcting errors

the passage of time (see Figure 3.9). Furthermore, defective documentation is a permanent system overhead. It makes system changes and error corrections, which are labour-intensive tasks, more expensive than they need be. It is believed that 'maintenance' work may account for about 80% of the total data-processing costs over the life of a typical business system.

To create an efficient and effective system it is necessary to elevate quality assurance to a much more prominent position. It must become the focal point of all activities and it must be applied universally to all products, whether they be technical (e.g. a design specification) or business (e.g. a costing statement).

3.3.3 A methodology for managing systems development

A number of products are marketed to help with project management and systems development. To differentiate between traditional project management and the more modern approaches, the term 'management of systems development' is sometimes used. Both terms are based on the system life-cycle and both are claimed to be systems analysis in practice! A modern methodology, however, is a non-charismatic, ego-less approach which lays great stress on defined products, quality assurance and corporate responsibility. One example of this approach is PROMPT (Project Resource Organization and Management Planning Techniques), developed and marketed by Simpact Systems of the UK. It typifies the modern approach to project management by incorporating most of the desirable features previously mentioned, and is used here to illustrate the trend in methodologies for management of systems development. Liberties have inevitably been taken in the interest of brevity.

PROMPT is a methodology for systems development and operation and is in three parts:

PROMPT I   Strategic systems planning
PROMPT II   Systems development and procurement
PROMPT III   Systems operation

This brief description does not include PROMPT III, but concentrates on PROMPT II, including a little of PROMPT I for the sake of completeness of presentation.

It is no surprise that PROMPT is based upon the stages of the systems life-cycle:

- Feasibility investigation
- Initiation
- Specification
- Design
- Development
- Installation
- Operation

The first three, which are preceded by a feasibility study, are mainly planning stages and the last three are mainly implementation stages; design is the fulcrum. Within each stage five components are defined and the system development process cannot continue unless all are satisfactorily completed:

(1) Organization
(2) Plans
(3) Controls
(4) End-products
(5) Activities

(1) *Organization*

The organization component of each stage requires the appropriate management structure to be created. The outline standard organizational structure is shown in Figure 3.10.

The composition of the *project board* reflects the three main interests in the systems developments process, namely, a senior business manager who chairs the board, a senior user manager representing the end-users of the system, and a senior data-processing manager representing the technological system interests.

Each stage in the development process has a *stage manager*. He is

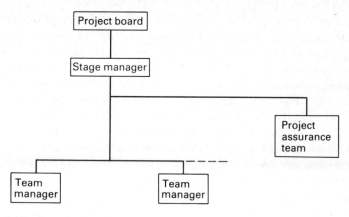

Fig. 3.10   Organizational structure for systems development

appointed by the board and may manage more than one stage. A stage manager's task is to ensure that the stage end-products are produced on time, within budget and to specification.

Supporting the stage manager is a *project assurance team* which functions throughout the project's life to provide continuity of control. The team provides staff support to the stage manager for the preparation of plans, monitoring of progress, estimation of budgets, calculation of expenditure and the monitoring of quality assurance of the end-products. The team's composition reflects three interests: business, end-user and technical.

A stage manager will require one or more teams under *team managers* to do the work needed to produce end-products. The team size and composition are variable.

(2) *Plans*

Three standard plans are defined in the methodology:

- Resource plans
- Technical plans
- Exception plans

The resource plans are produced at three levels. Firstly there is a *project resource plan* produced for the project board in the early part of the system development process—probably during the initiation stage. It will cover the remaining stages of the project.

A *stage resource plan* contains all the resources needed for a particular stage. It is submitted to the board for approval before the commencement of a stage and will be compared with actual utilization at the end of a stage. A *detailed resource plan* is a further breakdown of stage resources if an activity or group of activities is sufficiently large or important as, for example, when there are several teams reporting to a stage manager. The technical plans are subdivided by level, like the resource plans, with the addition of an individual work plan for team members. The technical plans show the sequence and timetable of activities needed to produce end-products. The *exception plans* are required whenever tolerances are exceeded or are likely to be exceeded; such tolerances are set by the project board at the outset of a stage. The stage manager uses an exception plan to report the deviation, its consequences and what remedial action he is proposing, for the board's approval.

(3) *Controls*
There are three main groups of controls: *end-stage* and *mid-stage assessments*, which are controls exercised by the project board; *quality assurance reviews* of tangible products, which are controls within a stage—exercised by either the stage manager or a team leader; finally, *checkpoint reviews* are held at regular time intervals and are conducted by the project team.

(4) *End-products and* (5) *activities*
The methodology defines standard products for the effective conduct of the system development process.

These are summarized in Table 3.4.

3.3.4 What the methodology aims to achieve

What this and other similar methodologies do is to take all the best features from traditional project management and put them together in a coherent management framework. Lessons have been learned from past failures and weaknesses, and efforts made to avoid or overcome them through the correct use of good management principles.

Some of the outstanding features of such a methodology are the following:

(1) The roles of senior business management, user management and data processing people are clearly defined and appropriate for them to perform within their normal bounds of knowledge and skills. The methodology virtually compels top managers and users to participate. The data processing people are put firmly, but quite properly, in their

Table 3.4 Standard products and activities in the system development process

Stage	End-product	Activity
Investigation	Investigation study report	Define the problem Investigate user requirements Evaluate alternative solutions Recommend course of action

Initiation	Project business case
	Project technical plan
	Project resource plan
	Technical and resource plans
	  for next stage
	Approval to proceed
		Prepare business case and
		  all plans

Specification	User specification
	Acceptance criteria
	Installation strategy
	Education and training
	  strategy
	Technical and resource
	  plans for next stage
	Approval to proceed
		Analyse detailed user
		  requirements and determine
		  acceptance criteria
		Devise strategies
		Prepare all plans

Design	System design System construction strategy Testing strategy Technical and resource plans for the next stage Approval to proceed	Produce system design Devise strategies Prepare all plans

Development	Programs
	Procedures
	Systems documentation
	Education and training
	  material
	Technical and resource
	  plans for next stage
	Approval to proceed
		Design, write and test
		  programs
		Devise procedures and forms
		Complete documentation
		Conduct systems tests
		Prepare all plans

Installation	User-accepted system
	Technical and resource
	  plans for next stage
	Approval to proceed
		Prepare systems environment
		  for conversion
		Convert
		Conduct acceptance tests
		Prepare all plans

Operation	Operational and maintainable system Final report to project board	Post-implementation review

correct place—which is to concern themselves with the design and construction of the computer system itself.

(2) End-products are defined for every stage of the system development process; these are tangible deliverables which have to be specified, planned, designed, built, tested and approved.

(3) Quality assurance is built into the management process and operates at all levels.

(4) Control is exercised at all levels in an appropriate way; monitoring and reporting are standardized throughout the life of the process.

Traditionally, projects head out to sea with only vague ideas about speed, direction, fuel consumption and state of the weather. They proceed like a ship without instruments on the bridge and with a crew who seem to want to do everybody else's job but their own. By contrast a modern methodology at least provides charts and instrumentation and defines who should do what.

Figure 3.11 portrays the relationships between the three resource levels—project board, stage manager and team manager. The team manager's role is to produce a steady stream of end-products which are quality assured by appropriate groups of reviewers and approved by the project assurance team. The stage manager's role is to see that all the end-products of his stage are produced to time and within cost. At the start of a stage he will receive the technical and resource plans. During the stage he may be required to submit periodic checkpoint reports highlighting current activities and progress, and may also be required to submit a mid-stage assessment of progress to date, resources used and estimates for the second half-stage. If during the stage any of the tolerances laid down by the project board are exceeded, or likely to be, an exception report will be put before the board with recommendations for action and their clearance. Finally at the end of the stage comes the end-stage assessment and compilation of plans for the next stage.

By these simple means, knowledge of the state of the project is always relatively up-to-date. Methodologies such as the one briefly outlined specify the documentary filing system to be used to ensure that project documentation is accumulated in an orderly fashion. The control procedures make sure that correct documenation of the right quality is produced.

3.3.5 Quality assurance

The control of quality assurance rests with the stage manager, assisted by his project assurance team; quality assurance is achieved through an appropriate agreed method of reviewing a product. The most common method is a form of 'structured walk-through' and the objective of such a review is to detect errors in the product. The quality is evaluated by reference to the product specification and any standards that govern it. Quality assurance encourages the acceptance of the concept of public property; helps to eradicate bad practices and to promote good practices; helps to train new personnel; monitors standards; and

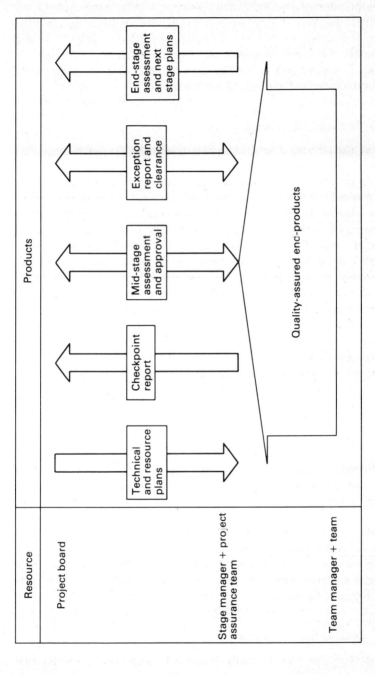

Fig. 3.11 Flow of end-products and reports

provides information on product status. If only minor actions are required, the product may be conditionally accepted; for major actions, the reviewing body will be reconvened for a further review. At the end of the day it is the project assurance team who satisfy themselves that quality is assured and advise the stage manager that the end-product has been completed and can be accepted.

3.3.6 Coping with change

One of the criticisms levelled against traditional project management is that it encourages a 'freezing' of specifications all along the line. This is good from the project manager's point of view, because it allows the project to roll forward without troublesome interruptions and he knows that his performance will be judged on completing the project on time: whether the system he has created satisfies the user is im-material—or so it may seem. With modern methodologies the emphasis is rather more on creating a system which the user wants—but still within time and cost budgets. This explains why control procedures are so well developed and formalized; they have to be so, if they are to absorb changes as the project proceeds. Without them, the choice is either to say 'No' to changes—once frozen, no thaw allowed—or to allow changes, and struggle to live with the muddle and anarchy that will certainly ensue.

Typically, changes result from one of three types of occurrence:

(1) change in requirements (from the user or data processing department);
(2) discovery of an error;
(3) variance from a specification.

All changes should be systematically logged by the project assurance team and an evaluation made of their impact. If implementation can be achieved within the resource tolerances laid down by the project board, the stage manager can approve the change; otherwise, an exception report will have to be submitted to the project board with amended technical and resource plans.

Any change that results in a new end-product will automatically generate the appropriate documentation, which will find its way into the project filing system.

3.3.7 Scaling the methodology

The description of such a methodology may create the impression that it is suitable only for medium to large-scale projects. This is not true. The methodology can be scaled down to make it perfectly appropriate for small projects occupying two or three people for a few months. On a large project the project assurance team may comprise full-time members representing the senior business management, user management and data processing management. On a small project they may operate as a team only on a part-time basis and the same person may represent the first two interests. What is important, even for a small project, is that the standard planning, control and quality assurance procedures should be observed, using the standard documentation provided. The number of stages may be reduced to as few as two—for example, planning and implementation. At the other extreme, a project board may well be dealing with many different projects simultaneously—and they do not necessarily have to be computer-based. The methodology is applicable whatever the system technology may be.

3.3.8 Techniques within the methodology

Standard techniques for planning, costing and estimating may be used with the methodology. Planning may be aided by the use of bar charts or networks; costing should be based on whatever is required by the host organization; the estimation of resource requirements nearly always comes down to experience, whether recalled from memory or recorded on documentation. A methodology such as PROMPT encourages the creation of a database of resource utilization which will help improve future estimating. All of these aids are likely to be available on microcomputers in the near future, which will help to speed and standardize their use.

3.4 Summary

Unquestionably project management, in any form, is an overhead. As yet, however, no other management style is appearing on the horizon which seems likely to displace project management (in all its manifestations) to ensure that systems analysis, design and implementation are performed efficiently. Money cannot be saved by dispensing with project management. Indeed, in most cases not enough money is spent on project management, with the result that over the life of a typical business system much more may be spent than has been 'saved'—this being the result of poor documentation, faulty system components, user dissatisfaction and delays.

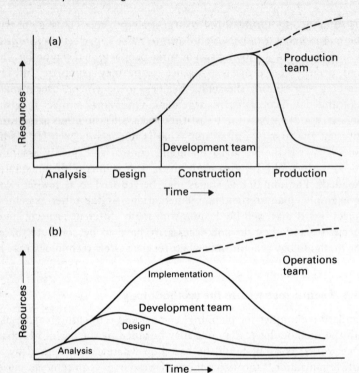

Fig. 3.12 (a) The consecutive stages of traditional project management and
(b) the concurrent processes of project management in business
systems

The actual cost of analysis, design, construction and changeover may typically be about 20% of the total system life costs. This is the cost of the project. The cost of the delivered system will account for 80% of total costs. Hence what is done during the project life is crucial to the longer-term system life. The trouble with too many projects is that they are not managed adequately, in that saving costs during the project period has the effect of loading costs on to the operational system, which thus may well start its life in an unsatisfactory state of acceptability. Management should preferably aim to spend proportionately rather more on the project phase, so as to reduce costs during the operational system phase—say 30% and 70% respectively. By so doing, total absolute costs may well be reduced through the improved efficiency, resilience and flexibility of the new system.

This is not to say that savings cannot be achieved within the project phase. The traditional distribution of costs for development of a computer system is along the following lines:

Analysis and design	35%
Programming	15%
Testing	50%

This suggests that testing is the activity to attack in seeking to reduce these development costs. However, the effort required to achieve a reduction of these costs needs to be expended in the earlier phases and on such things as quality assurance, better documentation and a better control of changes. In other words, a better methodology is needed for managing the development. Only this is likely to lead to lasting improvements and overall reduction of costs.

Traditional project management works well when 'hard' objectives can be specified, as in an engineering product. In these circumstances it may well be appropriate to represent the stages of the project as in Figure 3.12(a). What seems to have been overlooked, in transplanting project management into business systems, is that the 'soft' nature of business systems is inappropriate for the 'freezing' of specifications. The processes of analysis, design and implementation are concurrent for extensive periods of time—and it is this factor more than any other which gives rise to problems in project management (Figure 3.12(b)). The modern methodologies recognize these problems and offer effective organizational and management solutions.

4 Structured methodologies

4.1 Introduction

Many people have argued that programming and systems design lean more towards art than towards science. One celebrated university examination question—surely apocryphal!—asked 'Is computing science?' In this chapter we try to set out a scientific approach to the creative process of systems design and have used the title 'structured methodologies' to encompass this. Since inevitably the word 'structured' tends to be associated more with programming than with design, and since it is easier to begin by addressing programming aspects, that is where we start.

If a hundred engineers were set the same design task, their responses could probably be grouped into a relatively small number of broadly similar solutions. By contrast, if ten programmers were given the same specification, they would more than likely come up with twelve solutions, two of which might meet the requirements that the author of the specification meant to define. Whether this view is unduly cynical or just realistic may depend on personal experience, but it is undeniable that, given a quite unambiguous yet complete specification, all programming languages provide the means of implementation in an almost infinite variety of ways. While this may present a diverting intellectual challenge, it offers little to support the maintenance and robustness of a product which has to last for five years—the typical life of a commercial program. The days when ingenuity was a praiseworthy program characteristic are long gone.

This does not mean, however, that programming is reduced to a mechanical process requiring negligible thought; it is just that a disciplined, consistent approach is needed. When core storage was expensive in relation to programmer time, compact code was highly desirable. Nowadays, considerations are completely different.

Program design and system design
Irrespective of whether design is structured or not, the first distinction to

be drawn is between program design and system design. In crude terms, program design is concerned with how individual programs are made to perform their specified functions. System design deals with splitting the overall requirements down into those programs in the first place. While program design has attracted the attention of many first-class brains over the years, it is nevertheless a much narrower field than system design. Having said that, however, developments on the system design front owe much to the earlier work on program design.

4.2 Structured program design

4.2.1 Origins of structured design

As programs became larger and as the amount of available memory increased, there was a marked increase in time spent on testing and maintenance and consequently a decrease in programming productivity. A number of attempts were made to reverse this trend, including the adoption of a modular approach to programming. Success, though, was at best marginal since the lack of consistent guidelines for the breakdown of programs into modules generated a haphazard approach.

The breakthrough came in 1965, when Professor Dijkstra of Eindhoven University presented a paper at the IFIP Congress in New York suggesting that the GOTO statement should be eliminated from programming languages altogether, since programmer quality was inversely proportional to the number of GOTO statements per program. This idea was developed and repeated in a now renowned letter to the *Communications of the ACM* in March 1968. Böhm and Jacopini subsequently showed also that any program with single entry and exit points could be expressed in terms of just three basic constructs:

- Sequence
- Selection
- Iteration

From these beginnings structured methodologies can be said to have sprung.

4.2.2 Basic constructs

The three basic constructs of sequence, selection and iteration are illustrated in familiar flowchart terms in Figure 4.1. It is important to note that a sequence may logically comprise not just individual programming statements but any combination of statements (e.g. a subroutine) provided always that there is just one entry and one exit point.

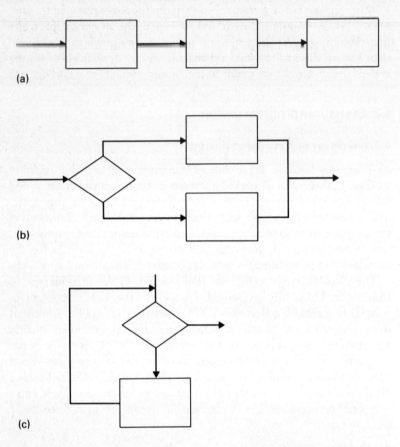

Fig. 4.1 Basic constructs: (a) sequence; (b) selection; (c) iteration

The most obvious way of implementing selection is by using the IF–THEN–ELSE type of programming statement. Iteration is implemented in various ways in different programming languages, e.g. DO–WHILE in ALGOL, PL/1 or CORAL 66, and PERFORM–UNTIL in COBOL. The representation in Figure 4.1(c) deliberately implies that the process within the loop may be performed zero times, which, as we shall see later, is extremely useful.

4.2.3 Objectives of the structured approach

The reason for adopting a more disciplined approach to programming was the need to improve productivity, not just by increasing the average number of statements written in a given period of time, but also by increasing the likelihood that those statements perform the intended task correctly without having to be modified at a later stage. The fact that the usual interface between analyst and programmer is provided by systems and program specifications means, therefore, that the analyst should at least be aware of the essential considerations of program design.

In recent years, investigation has revealed that the maintenance workload—defined as modification of existing systems as well as 'bug-fixing'—can absorb up to 80% of an organization's programming and analytical resources. Since, however, one of the main factors determining the useful life of a system is its ability to accept modification, there is then a vicious circle; increased modification means a shorter useful life with fewer staff available to implement new systems. Moreover, the degree of control that can be exercised over requests for modification is also limited, if demand is not to be stifled altogether.

One way, therefore, to break out of this vicious circle is to ensure that the initial design improves the 'maintainability' of the original program. Arguably the best way of achieving this is to ensure that the program is constructed in a consistent fashion and one that is well documented, so that someone other than the original author can see how to implement the required modification and recognize the likely implications of the change. Apart from making the maintenance programmer's life less tedious, this releases more staff for more creative work. Taken further, a really significant improvement in productivity must reduce overhead costs and expand data processing into areas not previously considered cost justifiable. Improvements in hardware price–performance have always moved in this direction, but hardware costs now account, on average, for much less than 50% of total installation costs and this proportion is ever reducing. So, far from reducing the demand for computer staff at all levels, higher productivity may actually increase demand.

Of course, program modification may be necessary even before a system becomes operational, in which case it can hardly be classed as maintenance. Testing is generally carried out at several levels in the software development life-cycle. The original author carries out some kind of testing at the individual module level and this is further extended when separate modules are combined progressively into the ultimate system. This kind of integration testing can easily take longer than the elapsed time required to write the individual modules, since there is less opportunity for parallel working. In extreme circumstances, implementation of an entire system may be frozen while a single module is rewritten. Thus anything that can be done to reduce the likelihood of such an occurrence or, at least, to identify the problem as early as possible, must be worthwhile.

In brief, then, the objectives of structured programming extend far beyond the negative task of eliminating GOTO statements and reach out to the positive goal of raising productivity:

- by improving understandability to simplify maintenance;
- by minimizing the time required for testing by ensuring that the original design is sound.

4.3 Alternative approaches to program design

Program design can be described as the process whereby the requirements defined in the specification are converted into code. Since the

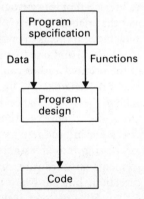

Fig. 4.2　The role of program specification

essential role of the program specification is to show how input is transformed into output, the process may be represented schematically as in Figure 4.2. From this, it is quite easy to see how the two alternative basic approaches to structured program design arose, by taking as the starting-point either the functions or the data. The former route gave rise to techniques such as composite design and functional decomposition, propounded by the likes of Myers, Constantine and Yourdon in the USA, which to some extent preceded the data-oriented approach as developed, *inter alia*, by Jackson and Warnier in the UK and France respectively.

4.3.1 Functional decomposition

As a very simple illustration, consider the task of implementing a payroll system. Ideally, we would like a compiler that could interpret directly the instruction 'Produce payroll'. Since this is not possible, we must decompose the requirement into smaller functions such as 'Calculate gross pay', 'Calculate deductions' and 'Print output'. These cannot yet be interpreted directly, however, so we must continue the process until we reach the level of our chosen programming language, using approved means of implementing the basic constructs of sequence, selection and iteration.

Now this does not really tell us whether we have an inherently good or bad design, as the decomposition process is largely intuitive. What is neded is some means of assessing the quality of the design, for which Yourdon and Constantine offer the concepts of coupling and cohesion. Coupling is a measure of the interdependence between modules, while cohesion is a function of how closely the elements within a single module are related to one another. An ideal design minimizes coupling and maximizes cohesion. Clearly the two are interrelated in that the greater the cohesion within the individual modules, the lower the coupling between the modules is likely to be. Although the correlation is not perfect, it is sufficiently strong to support the practical recommendation to concentrate on cohesion.

4.3.2 Data-oriented design

The basic premise of data-oriented program design is that the structure of the data processes dictates the structure of the program itself. This in turn tends towards a more quantitative approach, of which probably the best known and almost certainly the best documented is the structured program design methodology developed by Michael Jackson in the early to mid-1970s. MJSPD was subsequently chosen as a standard for all UK government installations as Structured Design Methodology (SDM); although special documentation standards have been applied, the basis is still pure Jackson.

Notation
Since structured programming permits just three basic constructs, the first requirement is for a notation to represent sequence, selection and

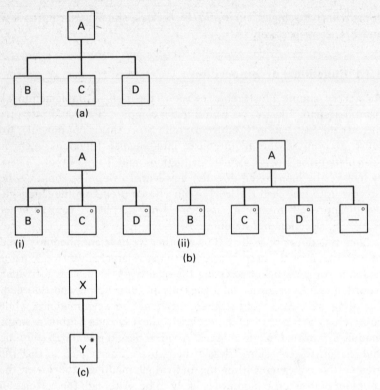

Fig. 4.3 (a) Sequence; (b) selection; (c) iteration

iteration. The Jackson notation is shown in Figure 4.3. This notation is absolutely specific. In (a), A is a sequence of operation B, followed by operation C, followed by operation D, all of which are always performed, and in that order. In (b), A is a selection under which one out of B, C and D must be performed as in (i) or, if it is a logical possibility that none of the three possibilities may be performed under the execution of A, then a fourth (null) choice must be shown, as in (ii). In (c), X is an iteration under which the iterated part, Y, may be performed any number of times, including zero.

The three constructs may be combined hierarchically in any way to represent complex structures, taking care to preserve the integrity of the notation by ensuring that:

- all boxes with a common parent are of the same type;
- an iteration has only one iterated part.

For example, if a file comprises a header record followed by any

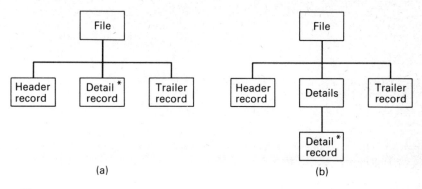

Fig. 4.4 (a) Invalid structure; (b) valid structure

number of detail records and terminated by a trailer then, of the alternatives in Figure 4.4, only (b) is valid. The reason that structure (a) is invalid is because it shows 'FILE' as a mixture of two sequence elements and one iterated part; in (b), 'FILE' is a straightforward sequence of three, one of which ('DETAILS') is an iteration in its own right. If the detail records, in turn, could be defined as any number of 'A' records followed by any number of 'B' records, the structure could be shown as in Figure 4.5(a) or (b), but not (c).

Design stages
MJSPD/SDM comprises five quite distinct design stages, always performed in the same sequence. These are:

(a) Draw a separate data structure for each input and each output.
(b) Identify correspondences between the data structures.
(c) Use the correspondences to combine the separate data structures into a single program structure.
(d) List the executable operations and allocate them to appropriate places within the program structure.
(e) Write schematic logic (sometimes referred to as 'structured text').

These steps are described in more detail in the following sections and are illustrated by reference to an extremely simple specification of requirements, namely: 'A program is required to process a file containing transactions in account number sequence to produce a printed summary report. In addition to account number, each input record contains a sterling amount and an indicator to show whether the amount is a credit or a debit. The report, headed 'Account summary', is to have one line per account showing the net value for the whole file'.

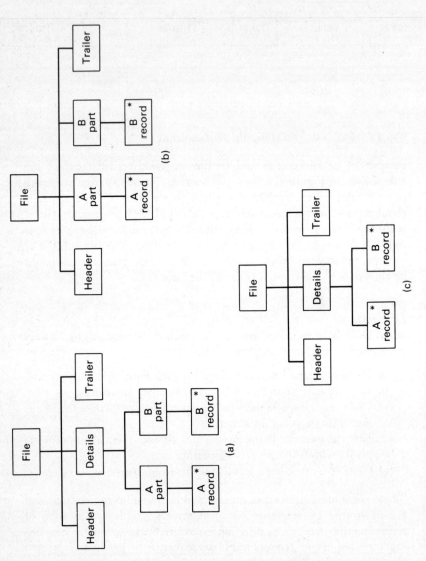

Fig. 4.5 (a, b) Valid structures; (c) invalid structure

(a) *Draw data structures.* For each input and output defined in the specification, a separate data structure must be drawn using the notation described above. In this case there is just one of each with the data structures as shown in Figure 4.6.

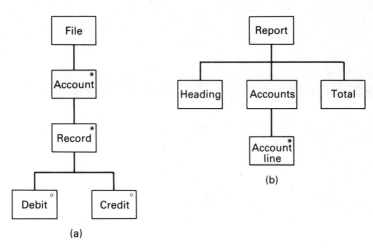

Fig. 4.6 (a) Input data structure; (b) output data structure

(b) *Identify correspondences.* If entities from different data structures are required to be processed together, they must correspond with one another. For correspondence to exist, the following conditions must be satisfied:

- each item must occur the same number of times; and
- the items must be in the same sequence.

The number of correspondences required depends on the type of task but, in general terms, the more the better. The number may well be affected by the way in which the data is viewed; with nontrivial problems the logical structure is usually more significant than the physical structure. In our example, 'FILE' corresponds with 'REPORT', since there is only one of each for each program execution so they must be in the same sequence. The system can always be represented so that there is correspondence at the highest level. The other, more useful correspondence is between 'ACCOUNT' and 'ACCOUNT LINE'.

(c) *Form the program structure.* The essential concept is that each correspondence in the component data structures is combined into a single box in the program structure and then the remaining, noncorresponding boxes from each data structure are added in turn, preserving the original hierarchy. The simplest way of doing this in practice is to draw the data structure with the greatest number of boxes and then progressively add the others. The program structure for our example is shown in Figure 4.7.

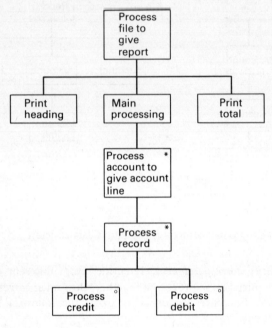

Fig. 4.7 The program structure

(d) *List and allocate executable operations.* Listing the operations seems at first sight to be a somewhat intuitive process. While the sequence of listing is quite immaterial, the following simple check-list may be found useful:

- (i) Terminate (normally 'STOP' for a main program, 'RETURN' for a subroutine).
- (ii) Open and close all files.
- (iii) Produce output (e.g. 'PRINT', 'WRITE', 'PUT').
- (iv) Perform calculations to produce output.
- (v) Acquire input (e.g. 'READ', 'GET').
- (vi) Manage internal variables (notably initialization).

The form in which the operations are expressed may be narrative or, as in our example, in programming notation, which is more compact.

(i)   (1) STOP

_ _ _ _ _ _ _ _ _ _ _ _ _ _ _ _ _

(ii)   (2) Open FILE, REPORT
        (3) Close FILE, REPORT

_ _ _ _ _ _ _ _ _ _ _ _ _ _ _ _ _

(iii)   (4) Print title
        (5) Print account line
        (6) Print total

_ _ _ _ _ _ _ _ _ _ _ _ _ _ _ _ _

(iv)   (7) ACCOUNT : = ACCOUNT + CREDIT
        (8) ACCOUNT : = ACCOUNT − DEBIT
        (9) TOTAL   : = TOTAL + ACCOUNT

_ _ _ _ _ _ _ _ _ _ _ _ _ _ _ _ _

(v) (10) Read FILE record

_ _ _ _ _ _ _ _ _ _ _ _ _ _ _ _ _

(vi) (11) ACCOUNT : = 0
        (12) TOTAL : = 0
        (13) Store account number

Having listed the operations, the next step is to allocate them to the appropriate point or points in the program structure. Strictly speaking, operations can only be allocated to sequence components, and this may entail the addition of 'dummy' boxes to the program structure. Two questions have to be answered for each operation in turn:

- With which component box (or boxes) is the operation associated?
- Whereabouts in sequence does it belong (beginning, end or elsewhere)?

The only exceptions to this are 'read' operations where the 'read ahead' rule is applied. This postulates that the first record is read immediately after opening the file and subsequently whenever a record is consumed. The program structure with operations allocated and dummy boxes added for the example is shown in Figure 4.8.

The allocation of the operations provides a valuable check as to the correctness of the program structure and hence the component data structures. If it is not simple, it is wrong.

(e) *Write schematic logic.* Schematic logic, or structured text, is a language-independent pseudocode which simply puts the program structure with allocated operations into narrative form. Its main purpose is to specify the conditions for selection and iteration. With SDM documentation this is done by means of a condition list. The

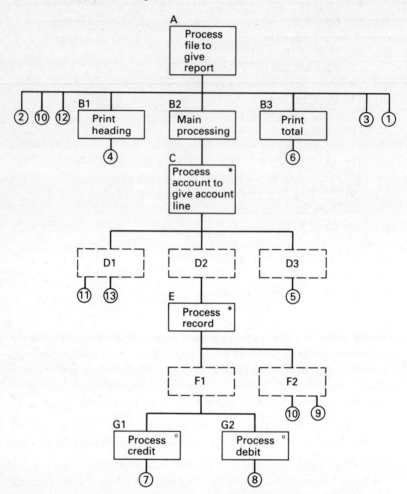

Fig. 4.8 Program structure with operations allocated

general form of schematic logic for the three basic constructs is shown in Figure 4.9.

Specification of the last selection condition is really redundant in that, from the structure diagram, if the choice is not 'B' or 'C' then it can only be 'D'. The choice of 'while' or 'until' in specifying iterations really depends on the target implementation language; 'while' is certainly better as far as ALGOL, CORAL 66 and PL/1 are concerned but 'until' is preferable for COBOL. Whatever the choice, usage should be consistent. From the list of operations and the detailed program

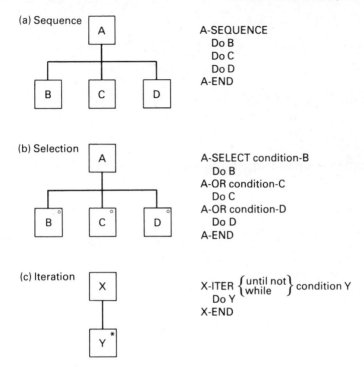

Fig. 4.9 Schematic logic (general form)

structure in Figure 4.8, the schematic logic for the example can now be written as:

```
A–SEQUENCE
    Open FILE, REPORT
    Read FILE record
    TOTAL:=0
    B1 –Print title
    B2 –ITER until end of file (FILE)
*       C –SEQUENCE
            D1 –ACCOUNT:=0
            Store account number
            D2 –ITER until account number ≠ stored
                account number OR end of file (FILE)
                F1–SELECT credit record
                    G1 ACCOUNT:=ACCOUNT+CREDIT
                F1–OR (debit record)
                    G2 ACCOUNT:= ACCOUNT–DEBIT
```

```
                    F1–END
*                   F2–SEQUENCE
                       Read FILE record
                       TOTAL:=TOTAL+ACCOUNT
*                   F2–END
              D2–END
              D3 Print account line
*          C–END
     B2–END
     B3 Print total
     Close FILE, REPORT
     Stop
A–END
```

The statements marked with an asterisk add nothing to our understanding and have only been included here for completeness; they are invariably omitted in practice.

Techniques

While the same basic five-stage design process is applied irrespective of the type of problem, there are several specific techniques within the overall approach that are worth describing, at least in outline. These relate to:

(1) Error handling
(2) Multiple input files
(3) Direct access files
(4) On-line systems

(1) *Error handling.* The main point to stress as regards error handling is that the initial data structures must be drawn taking possible errors into account. It is quite unrealistic to design a program for ideal data and then hope to graft on error handling as an afterthought. By way of illustration, consider a very simple file that, if free from errors, comprises a T1 record followed by an unspecified number of T2 records and is terminated by a T3 record. The ideal structure, as shown in Figure 4.10(a), allows for the fact that there may be no T2 records since the iteration may be of zero occurrences; however, to cater for the possible absence of the T1 and T3 records as well as the presence of extraneous data at any point, the structure would have to be expanded to that in Figure 4.10(b).

The difference in the level of complexity is quite obvious and equally realistic.

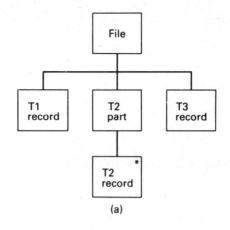

(a)

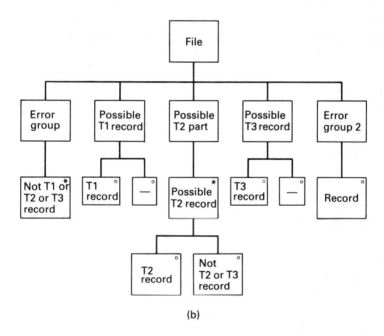

(b)

Fig. 4.10 (a) Structure for ideal data
(b) Structure recognizing possible error data

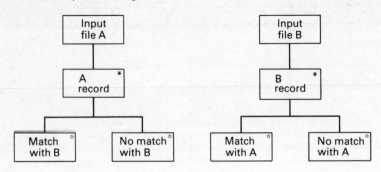

Fig. 4.11 Collating input data structures

(2) *Multiple input files.* The technique for dealing with more than one input file is generally referred to as 'collating'. As far as the methodology itself is concerned, nothing new needs to be added except to recognize the existence of a notional file of 'keys' which relate the input files and draw the input data structures to reflect the matching between records, as in Figure 4.11.

The form of the output data structure is dictated by the program specification. With two input files, there are at most four possibilities, namely:

A+B
A alone
B alone
Neither A nor B

The last case may not generally be of interest but it is a logical possibility nonetheless. The output data structure could then be as shown in Figure 4.12.

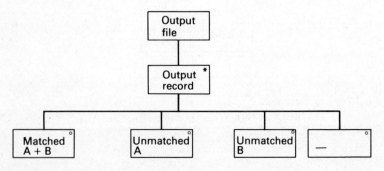

Fig. 4.12 Collating output data structures

With n input files, there could be 2^n selection possibilities on the output data structure, which in turn forms the basis for the program structure. Operations are allocated just as before with the 'read ahead' rule for each input file.

(3) *Direct access files*. Direct access files present no problem at all as far as MJSPD is concerned. In fact, the basic data structure for a direct access file can be represented very simply, as shown in Figure 4.13.

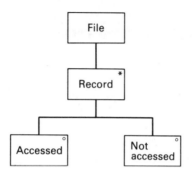

Fig. 4.13   Data structure for direct access file

The convention usually adopted for executable operations is that 'GET' and 'PUT' are used for direct access files and 'READ' and 'WRITE' for serial files. As no operation can be allocated to a 'NOT ACCESSED' function from the above structure, this can safely be omitted from the detailed program structure.

(4) *On-line systems*. On-line terminals effectively generate two files: input from the keyboard and output from the screen. Each of these requires a separate data structure, of course, but they are almost invariably very closely related, with the input largely governing the output. A generalized form of operation to acquire input, such as 'PROCESS KEYED INPUT', allows the 'read ahead' rule to be applied just as before.

The basic advantages of data-oriented design

Data-oriented design, in particular MJSPD, offers a consistent, largely self-validating, machine- and language-independent and eminently teachable approach to program design, tending towards system design at its extreme. There are undoubtedly significant training overheads in the initial stages but, even so, productivity is likely to be at least up to the level achieved with an unstructured approach, and substantially better once full familiarity has been gained. As far as efficiency, in terms of program size and speed of execution, is concerned, consideration should if possible be deferred until the basic design has been completed. Maintenance should be geared to the unoptimized implementation design and it has to be accepted that an optimized implementation runs a much greater risk of having to be redesigned in the event of a change in requirements.

Overall, the most tangible benefit of the data-oriented approach to program design is in the reduction of the time required for testing and integration.

4.4 Coding implications

The structured programming basic constructs of sequence, selection and iteration are particularly suitable for implementation in block-structured programming languages such as ALGOL, CORAL 66 and PL/1 which allow a number of statements to be grouped together and then treated as a single compound statement. While not a block-structured language, COBOL is reasonably practical, although iterations have to be implemented by means of the PERFORM–UNTIL rather than the slightly preferable but logically equivalent DO–WHILE statement. Nesting of IF–THEN–ELSE statements can also prove problematical in COBOL.

FORTRAN and BASIC do not really lend themselves to direct implementation of the structured programming basic constructs, although it can be achieved in nest-free code with the disciplined use of GOTO statements. The obvious risk is the temptation to use them in an undisciplined fashion. Although assembler languages tend to have the same kinds of weakness (in terms of structured programming) as FORTRAN, it is quite feasible to use macros to develop not only DO–WHILE and IF–THEN–ELSE but even BEGIN–END block structure constructs.

4.5 Structured systems design

The very fact that there is a distinction to be drawn between system design and program design directs us towards a top-down, as opposed to bottom-up, approach to system design—for otherwise, how can we tell where to start? Not only this: most people find it conceptually much easier to break down a high-level requirement into progressively more detailed elements, rather than work the opposite way around. It is worth noting, too, that this is a common characteristic of the approaches to program design already described, irrespective of whether the starting-point is function- or data-orientated.

Over the years, there have been numerous attempts to develop a structured approach to system design, which have enjoyed varying degrees of success. Three noteworthy examples are considered below.

4.5.1 The Yourdon and Constantine approach

According to Yourdon and Constantine, most modular systems are centred on certain specific functions, frequently embodied in a single module, the characteristics of which typify the system as a whole. For example, a system may be identified as 'transform-centred', 'transaction-centred', 'procedure-centred' or 'device-centred'. Procedure-centred systems are found generally to achieve only temporal or procedural cohesion that is not as strong as might be desired, while device-centred design is relatively rare outside operating systems. However, specific techniques have been evolved in respect of transform-centred and transaction-centred design.

Terminology
Span of control, or fan-out, is simply the number of immediate subordinates that a module controls. Very high—more than 10—or very low—one or two— spans of control are often indications of faulty design. Low spans can usually be increased either by breaking the element into extra subordinate functions or by combining it with its superordinate. High span is often indicative of 'pancaking' or failure to identify intermediate levels. Figure 4.14(a) illustrates a module, A, with a span of control of three.

Fan-in, as the name suggests, is the converse of fan-out where several superordinate modules cause the execution of the same subordinate, as shown in Figure 4.14(b). While fan-in is desirable in that it may imply that duplicate code may be avoided, it should not be achieved artificially by combining a number of unrelated functions into an incohesive module, which effectively nullifies the benefit.

Depth is nothing more than the number of hierarchical module levels and obviously has some relationship to complexity and size. A simple system, such as that shown in Figure 4.15, is likely to have a depth of 3 or 4; moderate size and complexity are likely to give rise to perhaps a dozen levels; the largest systems can have 50 levels or more. Depth, in itself, is not a particularly valid measure of design quality, but extremes

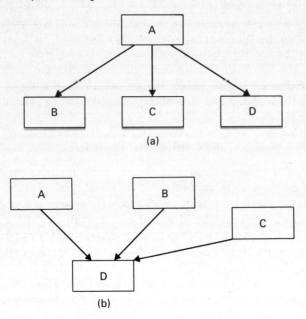

Fig. 4.14 (a) Fan-out; (b) fan-in

such as a depth of 10 in a 100-statement system or a depth of 3 in a 100 000-statement system are obviously highly suspect.

Factoring: if, in an essentially hierarchically organized system, the higher-level modules are predominantly occupied in controlling and coordinating the execution of the lower-level modules which, in turn, are responsible for carrying out the actual system tasks, then the system

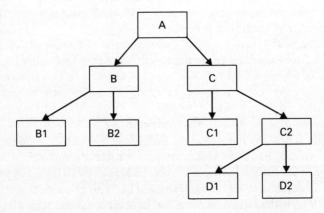

Fig. 4.15 System with a depth of four

is said to be highly factored. At the extreme, the top-level module in a hierarchical system contains only calls to subordinate modules.

Four *types of flow* have been categorized. Where a module obtains information from a subordinate and then, possibly after modification, passes it upward to a superordinate, this is called an 'afferent flow' of data, so the module itself is designated an 'afferent module'. The converse of this is described as 'efferent flow', which gives rise to an 'efferent module'. The third situation where incoming information is modified and then passed back to the original source is called 'transform flow'. 'Coordinate flow' occurs where information received from one subordinate module is routed to another subordinate module. The four

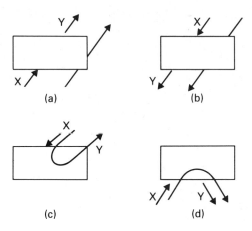

Fig. 4.16 Types of flow: (a) afferent; (b) efferent; (c) transform; (d) coordinate

types of flow are illustrated in Figure 4.16(a–d), where the flow of data is from X to Y.

Transform-centred design

Transform analysis, or transform-centred design, tends to generate systems with low development and maintenance costs because transform-centred designs are usually highly factored. The main design objective is to identify the primary processing functions of the system, together with the high-level outputs. A hierarchy of modules within each of these functions is then created to perform the respective tasks. Transform analysis comprises four basic steps, namely:

(1) The problem is restated as a data flow diagram.
(2) The data elements are identified.

(3) First-level factoring is carried out.

(4) The branches are factored.

Data flow diagrams. The first step is to restate the problem as a data flow diagram. The notation of data flow diagrams is very simple. For instance, the transformation of data item A into data item B is as shown in Figure 4.17(a). If two adjacent data streams are required as input for

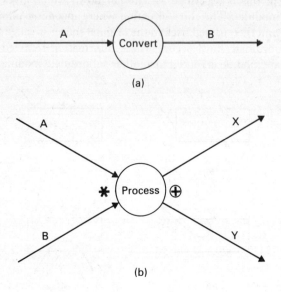

(a)

(b)

Fig. 4.17   (a) Transform A into B
            (b) Conjunction and disjunction operators

the process to be performed, this is shown by drawing an asterisk (*) between them; this is equivalent to an 'AND' operator. Similarly, the symbol ⊕ indicates disjunction, i.e., an 'OR' operator. Figure 4.17(b) shows that input A, when processed with input B, produces either output X or output Y.

A data flow diagram for a simple process can usually be drawn intuitively; for complex systems, it is really a matter of knowing where to start. The usual approach is to start either with the physical inputs and work through successive transforms to the physical outputs, or vice versa. An alternative is to start with a single 'bubble' representing the entire system in terms of inputs and outputs and then progressively break this down into a number of separate transforms. One thing that a data flow diagram should never show, however, is control logic; the arrows represent the flow of the data, not control.

Identifying data elements. Afferent data elements are those high-level elements of data that are farthest removed from physical input and yet can still be considered as input to the system. They are identified by starting with the physical input and moving inward on the data flow diagram until a stream is identified that can no longer be considered as input. This is repeated for each physical input stream and, although it does represent something of a value judgement, experienced designers rarely disagree significantly in practice as to where the afferent transforms end. Beginning, then, at the other end, with outputs, the afferent transforms are next identified in similar fashion. This usually leaves some uncharacterized transforms in the middle; these are designated the 'control transforms' and they carry out the main work of the system in transforming the major inputs into the major outputs.

Factoring. Once the afferent and efferent data elements have been identified, a main module can be specified which, when activated, will perform the whole task of the system by causing subordinate modules to execute. Separate afferent and efferent modules are then specified as immediate subordinates to the main module for each efferent data element emerging from the central transform, and a subordinate transform module is specified to accept the appropriate output data and then deliver it back upwards to the main module.

Having identified branches by the first-level factoring process, each branch is then itself factored independently. The order in which this is done is immaterial but it is important to identify all the immediate subordinates of one module before progressing to the next.

To summarize, transform analysis is based on the analysis of data flow and the assumption that the resulting system comprises a single hierarchical structure. It still requires judgement to be exercised on the part of the designer.

Transaction analysis

Transaction analysis is applicable where a transform splits an input data stream into several separate output streams, as shown in Figure 4.18(a). This type of structure may occur either within the central transform or in the afferent or the efferent branches.

In Figure 4.18(a) the transform 'B'—which receives data from A to produce outputs X or Y or Z—is designated the transaction as in Figure 4.18(b). The span of control of the 'EXECUTE TRANSACTION' module is potentially quite high, depending on the outputs produced, but the logic is usually relatively simple.

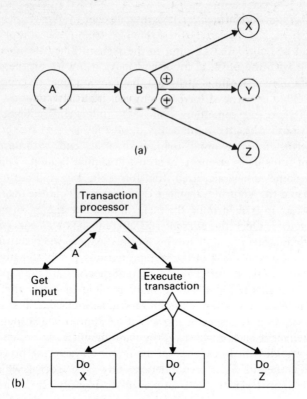

Fig. 4.18 (a) Data flow susceptible to transaction analysis
(b) Factored transaction centre

4.5.2 DeMarco's Structured Analysis and System Specification

DeMarco's approach has a certain amount in common with that of Yourdon and Constantine in that they both use basically the same data flow diagram notation. However, DeMarco has refined and extended the data flow diagram notation and added two further stages which are described below to give a comprehensive picture. He also sees the process of structured analysis as subdividing into seven discrete stages, namely:

(1) Study of the current physical environment and documentation of it as the current physical data flow diagram.
(2) Derivation of the logical equivalent (the current logical data flow diagram).
(3) Derivation of the new logical environment.

(4) Determination of the physical characteristics of the new environment.
(5) Quantification of the cost and scheduling the data for each possibility.
(6) Selection of one option.
(7) Packaging of the new physical data flow diagram plus the supporting documents into the structured specification.

Data flow diagrams
The full notation used is as follows:

(Name)⟶ = named vector to portray the data path
○ = process to portray transformation of data
▢ = source or sink to portray the net originator or receiver of data
⋆ = conjunction operator ('AND')
⊕ = disjunction operator ('OR')

In terms of scope, the data flow diagram should describe the whole environment of the system under consideration rather than just the area of likely automation. This not only puts the area of automation into its proper context but also has the advantage of clearly identifying the man–machine interface.

The recommended way to derive data flow diagrams can be summarized as:

• Identify all net inputs and outputs.
• Work from input to output, from output to input or from the middle outwards, whichever seems easiest.
• Label all the interface data flows carefully.
• Label all the process 'bubbles' in terms of their inputs and outputs.
• Ignore initialization and termination.
• Omit trivial error paths (i.e. where no previous processing has to be undone).
• Never show control flow or information.
• Be prepared to go back and start again.

In practice, there is a physical limit to the number of process bubbles that can be shown on a single sheet without adversely affecting clarity or committing the unforgivable sin of having data path vectors crossing over one another. Six or seven bubbles per page is a reasonable maximum, so a simple diagram might look like the generalized version in Figure 4.19.

It is unlikely that any real-life system is going to be as simple as this,

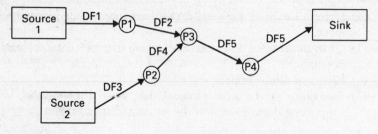

Fig. 4.19 Generalized data flow: DF = data flow; P = process

so DeMarco offers the concept of levelled data flow diagrams whereby each of the processes in the original diagram can be broken down *ad infinitum*. For example P3 may be as shown in Figure 4.20.

Consistency between the different data flow diagram levels is achieved by ensuring that the data flows into and out of the higher-level bubble balance with the net inputs and outputs at the lower level. For instance, process P3 in Figure 4.19 has two input data flows, namely DF2 and DF4, and a single output data flow, DF5. The same is true of

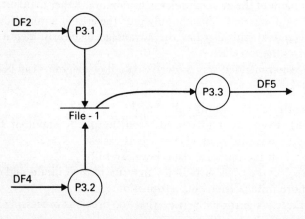

Fig. 4.20 Second-level data flow

the expansion of P3 in Figure 4.20, so the two diagrams do indeed balance. The partitioning process stops:

- when a bubble can be completely described in a mini-spec (see 'Work description' below) of about one page; *or*
- when a bubble has a single input data flow and a single output data flow, excluding trivial error paths, or the number cannot be reduced any further (e.g. as when merging).

The first criterion obviously requires a certain amount of judgement and may give rise to something of an iterative process. However, because the final decision is made, a bubble that is not decomposed into lower-level networks is described as a 'functional primitive' and is the lowest level of process defined.

Two other data flow diagramming conventions are worth mentioning. The first concerns files and the second the indication of the ultimate destinations of data flows. Files are shown on a data flow diagram at the first level where they are used as an interface between two processes. This is why 'FILE–1' appears in Figure 4.20 but not in Figure 4.19. This means that all references are shown at the first level where the file appears. Data flow destinations are shown on the higher

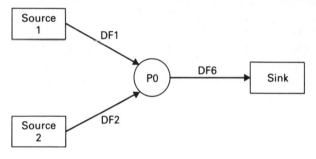

Fig. 4.21   Context diagram

level 'parent' diagram but not on the lower level 'child' where they are held to be redundant.

Obviously, the process can be reversed and the structure in Figure 4.19 may be combined into a single 'bubble' as in Figure 4.21. This 'zero-level' data flow diagram is referred to as the 'context diagram'.

Data dictionaries

Useful though they are, data flow diagrams cannot provide all the information required in specifying a system. In particular, rigorous definitions are required for data flows, data elements (the components of data flows), files and processes, and there is a clear correlation between data flow diagrams and the data dictionary in that there is a separate entry for each unique data flow, each functional primitive. In addition, it is often useful to define subordinate data flows which do not exist in their own right but rather as components of the main data flows.

It would be quite possible to define data dictionary entries in narrative text but, in the twin interests of consistency and conciseness, it has been found preferable to use an adaptation of the Backus-Nauer Form, as follows:

Symbol	Meaning
=	IS EQUIVALENT TO
+	AND
[ ]	EITHER–OR
{ }	ITERATIONS OF
( )	OPTIONAL

The square brackets denoting the selection operator must obviously include at least two options, which can be represented in two different but logically identical ways, i.e.:

$$\begin{bmatrix} \text{Option X} \\ \text{Option Y} \\ \text{Option Z} \end{bmatrix} \qquad \text{[Option X/ Option Y/ Option Z]}$$

Iteration braces can be annotated with upper and/or lower limits, which can again be written in two different but logically identical ways, i.e.:

$$\begin{matrix} 10 \\ 1 \end{matrix} \Big\{ X \Big\} \qquad 1\{X\}10$$

If no limits are specified, this means that from zero to infinity occurrences of the enclosed component are possible.

If we care to do so, we can continue to break down definitions as far as individual characters or digits, as in the following example:

Date	= Day + Month + Year
Day	= First–digit + Any–digit
Month	= [Jan/Feb/Mar/Apr/May/June/Jul/Aug/Sept/Oct/Nov/Dec]
Year	= Any–digit + Any–digit
First–digit	= [0/1/2/3]
Any–digit	= [1/2/3/4/5/6/7/8/9/0]

The value of going this far is at best marginal, because everyone knows what a 'day', a 'month' and a 'year' are—and do we really need to specify the precise format at this stage anyway? Hence, to avoid unnecessary proliferation of data dictionary entries, it is recommended that the process stops at the point where everyone involved understands the meaning without further definition.

Work description
Even after the data flow diagrams have been drawn and the data
dictionary has been created, we still need some unambiguous description of the work carried out by the functional primitives defined on page
103. This is done by writing a separate 'mini-spec' for each functional
primitive. This could, of course, be done in normal narrative text, in
which case the chances of its being unambiguous are remote, to say the
very least. Three approaches, which can be alternative or complementary, exist for defining the transformation of input data flows
into output data flows within functional primitives, namely:

(1) Structured English
(2) Decision tables
(3) Decision trees

(1) *Structured English* has a very limited vocabulary and an equally
limited syntax. The vocabularly comprises essentially:

- Imperative verbs
- Data dictionary terms
- Reserved words for logic formulation

The syntax is limited to the constructs of:

- Sequence
- Selection
- Iteration

Alternative ways of specifying selections and iterations are permitted:

Selection
   (a) If . . .
       THEN . . .
       OTHERWISE . . .
   (b) SELECT . . .
       CASE 1 . . .
       CASE 2 . . .
         .
         .
         .
       CASE n . . .

Iteration
   (a) FOR EACH . . . DO . . .
   (b) DO . . . UNTIL . . .
   (c) WHILE . . . DO . . .

All in all, structured English bears a remarkable similarity to Jackson's schematic logic, but at a system level as opposed to a program level.

(2) *Decision tables.* In the right situation, decision tables are unrivalled in terms of completeness, consistency and compactness. A generalized form of the decision table with two conditions is shown below. The number of rules is simply the product of the number of the possible values associated with each of the decision–variable conditions. Unless an action can be specified for each rule, the policy is incompletely defined.

	Rules
Conditions:	1 2 3 4 5 6
Condition 1 (Y or N)	Y N Y N Y N
Condition 2 (A, B or C)	A A B B C C

Actions:
    Action 1
    Action 2
        .   ⎡ Defined by
        .   ⎢ the policy
        .   ⎣ specified
    Action *n*

(3) *Decision trees.* A decision tree is nothing more than a graphical representation of a decision table. Consequently, the decision table shown above can be represented as the decision tree in Figure 4.22.

4.5.3 LBMS System Development Methodology

The LBMS* System Development Methodology, which has been adopted by the Central Computer and Telecommunications Agency of the UK government as a standard in the government area under the acronym SSADM (Structured Systems Analysis and Design Methodology), is a data-driven approach in six major phases:

(1) Analysis of the current system
(2) Outline design of the new system (including outline processing and overview data model)
(3) User selection of service level for the new system
(4) Detailed data design
(5) Detailed process design
(6) Physical design control

* Learmonth and Burchett Management Systems Ltd.

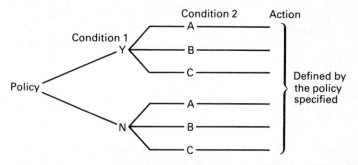

Fig. 4.22 Decision tree (generalized)

The specific outputs produced from the initial starting-point of a feasibility study report are:

- Program specifications
- User procedures
- Operating instructions
- File design or database scheme

Full documentation is built up throughout the analysis and design process using a number of well-proven techniques, such as data flow diagrams for describing the current system and developing the new system, logical data structuring (LDS) for entity modelling, third normal form (TNF) data analysis and system walkthroughs and reviews.

Data flow diagrams
Conceptually, these are identical to DeMarco data flow diagrams, but the notation used is different:

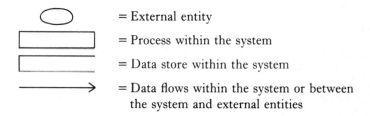

= External entity

= Process within the system

= Data store within the system

= Data flows within the system or between the system and external entities

Entity models
Entity models illustrate real-world relationships between different data items inside the system. They are used to identify entry points and

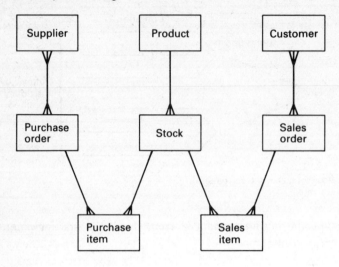

Fig. 4.23 Order processing entity model

access paths to this data. The notation conventions are very simple:

□ = Entity (i.e. data item or group)

↓ = one-to-many relationship (i.e. access path)

Using this notation, an outline order processing entity model could be as shown in Figure 4.23.

Entity models can be developed:

- by using logical data structuring techniques (LDST);
- by using the result of third normal form data analysis and structure rules (TNF structure);
- by combining LDST and TNF strucctures to produce a composite logical data structure.

Transaction history
A transaction history is a representation in chronological order affecting an entity within the system. The notation is identical to that used for the Jackson structured program design methodology so the transaction history for a sales order could well be as shown in Figure 4.24.

Relationships between different views of data
Each of the three different views of data serves a different purpose. Data flow diagrams show how processes and files relate to one another and to the outside world. Entity models demonstrate the relationship

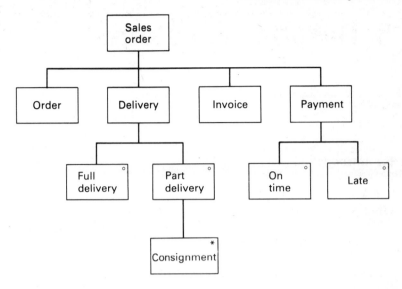

Fig. 4.24 Transaction history for sales order

between different types of data within the system and how it can be accessed. Transaction histories show how entities change with time. There is clear correspondence between entities in the entity model and data stores in the data flow diagram. For an individual entity, there is also correspondence between data flows which affect it in the data flow diagram and the transactions in its transaction history.

4.6 Summary

Several different approaches to structured systems design have been developed in recent years. The three outlined in this chapter are all in practical use. The Yourdon–Constantine approach and that of DeMarco use data flow techniques with very similar notation for diagramming the data flows. The third system, LBMS, is a data-driven approach which uses data flow diagrams and data analysis techniques. Of vital importance is the need for program and system design techniques to be compatible, since the link between them is strong and essential in practice; in this context, both DeMarco and LBMS are compatible with the Jackson method outlined at the beginning of the chapter.

5 Database systems

5.1 Introduction

The present-day data processing manager is under pressure from his organization to satisfy an ever-increasing demand for information. There are two aspects to these requirements. First, there is the growing realization that data is a resource in its own right. This leads to the conclusion that if data which is normally dispersed is brought together, interrelated and made immediately available, there will be considerable benefits for the organization. The requirement is, therefore, to provide management with timely, consolidated and consistent information. The second aspect is concerned with overcoming the problems that plague most data processing departments. The visible effects of these problems are the difficulties which are encountered in expediting changes to existing systems and the length of time it takes to develop new applications.

An increasing number of organizations are implementing database systems in an attempt to come to terms with these problems. The advantages which can be achieved are:

- It is possible to develop an integrated system.
- Maintenance and development costs can be reduced.
- Systems can be developed more quickly and modified more easily.
- The data processing department can become much more responsive to user *ad hoc* demands for information.
- The amount of redundant data can be reduced and as a consequence the information provided by the system will become more consistent.
- It is very much easier to enforce standards and exercise control over both the definition of data and its use.

It is generally agreed that the terminology used in data processing is both inconsistent and misleading. The database area is no exception and if anything it is even more confusing. The following definitions and observations are offered by way of explanation.

Database
Probably the most common definition of the term database is:

A common pool of shared data in which the data is interrelated, where each item of data is stored only once and which is used in a wide range of applications.

In practice, implementations fall far short of this ideal. It is quite common for organizations not to have a fully integrated system but a number of 'databases', each supporting different application areas. Also, redundant data is often included in the database in order to improve processing efficiency.

Database Management System (DBMS)
DBMS refers to a software package which is necessary to support a database and to enable the advantages mentioned above to be achieved. In addition to providing these facilities a DBMS has a language interface with the user of the system. This can be through extensions to programming languages such as COBOL and PL/1, or the DBMS may have its own self-contained language designed to provide an easy-to-use interface for both the programmer and the computer non-specialist. The DBMS will also have utilities to help maintain the database and to protect the integrity of the data it contains.

Database system
A database system is basically any system which has a database (as broadly outlined above) and which is supported by a DBMS (Figure 5.1).

Database approach
A database approach is concerned not only with the techniques that are necessary to set up, maintain and communicate with a database but also with the establishment of the procedures, methods and facilities that are needed to exercise proper control over data. To embark upon a database approach involves a commitment to good standards and firm management. It will also involve the use of a data dictionary to record information about data and how it is used by the programs which comprise the system.

5.2 Data control

It is an unfortunate fact that very few data processing departments have any real control over data. In practice, applications are usually

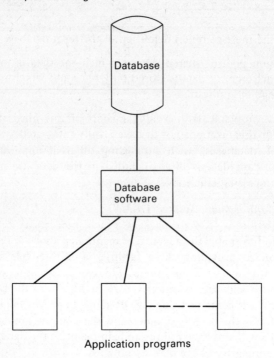

Application programs

Fig. 5.1   Database system

developed under pressure and short cuts are taken which result in standard procedures being bypassed. The situation is made worse by the fact that systems tend not to be documented properly and quite often, even where a documentation standards scheme exists, this is not enforced.

If there is no formal procedure for recording and maintaining 'data about data', programmers are free to choose names and data definitions for the items of data that they use. This leads to a situation in which there is very little knowledge in the data processing department about what data exists and how it is used. The consequences of this are that minor changes to application programs are likely to result in a major rewrite of the programs concerned. Typical of the problems which can occur are: the same item of data may be known by more than one name; the same name may be used for quite different data items; and a data item may have different formats in different files.

There are data processing departments where a centralized control over data has been established for many years and where documentation standards have been rigorously enforced. This has been shown to pay off handsomely and has been particularly rewarding when database systems were introduced. It has quite often been the introduction of a database management system which has forced the data processing manager to look for a better way of controlling data. There are mainly two reasons for this. First, the use of database techniques usually results in a system of far greater complexity and scope than anything previously implemented and this very quickly highlights the need for data control. The second reason is that, where a conversion process is involved, the lack of knowledge about data together with the inconsistencies which are discovered cause major problems which have resulted in budgets being exceeded.

If a database system is to be successful it must be developed within a framework of a well planned database approach. The necessary level of control can only be achieved by establishing a functional responsibility which is supported by powerful facilities. The functional responsibility is provided by the database administrator (DBA) and the most important facility he or she requires is the data dictionary.

5.3 The data dictionary

A data dictionary is basically a centralized collection of definitions, characteristics and interrelationships which describe all the data stored within the system. In addition to providing an authorized source of data definitions, the dictionary may:

- hold a glossary of approved names, error messages and validation rules;
- support the documentation of systems and programs;
- allow the implications of making changes to data definitions to be investigated;
- enable the patterns of data usage to be established;
- result in a simplification in the development of applications, since some of the data required may already be defined in a standard manner;
- enable uncontrolled data duplication to be detected and thereby reduce the risk of data becoming inconsistent;
- allow file and database descriptions to be automatically generated;
- enable security requirements to be specified and controlled.

In practice, a data dictionary may be either a manual system which consists of a set of procedures supported by standard documentation or an automated system supported by software.

5.3.1 Types of data

The types of data that are held in data dictionaries vary quite widely and depend upon the methods and techniques used by individual data processing departments. A department employing traditional methods would, for example, be interested in holding information about files, records, groups and fields. It would also be interested in the interrelationships that exist between these elements and between the programs and systems which use them.

The data processing department that takes a more wide-ranging view of data is likely to have carried out a detailed data analysis and needs to hold data which is concerned not only with the physical implementation level but also with the logical or conceptual level. At the logical level, information is held about the attributes of data items, their logical groupings (entities) and the relationships which exist between these groupings. There is also a need to hold details of the processes to which these elements relate. As part of the design process these logical elements have to be mapped to elements at the physical level and the dictionary needs to hold details of how this was achieved. When a DBMS is used there is an additional requirement to hold details that relate specifically to the database. With a Codasyl system, for example, this includes details of elements such as sets, areas, schemas and subschemas.

5.3.2 Manual data dictionaries

Many of the problems that occur in data processing departments can be solved by means of good documentation standards. This approach does, however, have limitations and it has proved to be only practical for relatively small, simple systems. This is because of the amount of time that must be spent in completing the documentation to the required level of detail and the difficulties that are involved in carrying out the necessary checks for consistency. Also, as systems grow and become more complex they tend to change more frequently and this very quickly results in an unacceptable maintenance load.

5.3.3 Automated data dictionaries

The problems associated with maintaining a manual data dictionary can be eased considerably by the use of data dictionary software. Although the advantages of automated data dictionaries have been recognized for quite some time it is only over the last few years that a range of comprehensive products has become available.

There is quite a wide variation in the facilities provided by the products which are on the market. In general, facilities are provided to enable the data to be created and updated, interrationships between data elements to be automatically maintained, information to be extracted from the dictionary by means of an enquiry language and data descriptions to be generated automatically for each program. The data in the data dictionary will, from time to time, need to be modified in order to reflect changes to the applications. Facilities are usually provided which allow different versions of the data dictionary and its contents to exist so that a test data dictionary can be constructed and the various stages of the development process can be supported.

With an integrated data dictionary system the dictionary database is constructed using the structuring facilities that are available with the DBMS. The current trend is to organize the dictionary to exercise control over all data definitions. This not only includes application programs but also the DBMS, reportwriters and query languages. A free-standing data dictionary system, on the other hand, is designed to be completely independent of any other software. The dictionary database is created, updated, accessed and maintained by a data management system which is contained within the package itself. Specially designed interfaces may exist which will allow the package to operate with a number of different database management systems.

5.4 Database administration

Database administration is a very important function and has received considerable publicity in recent years. There have been numerous publications in which the function has been defined and the implications of establishing it have been discussed. It would be reasonable, therefore, to expect that by now most organizations having a database system would have a well-established database administrator (DBA) who would have the required level of authority. In practice, this has proved to be very difficult to arrange. Many companies have refused to come to terms with the problem and, although there may be someone called a DBA, this is usually a programmer who has no authority to exercise any real control.

5.4.1 Role of the DBA

If it is to be effective the database administration function must have well established interfaces with management, the users, applications development and operations.

The management interface
The database administrator must have the authority to impose the necessary standards and procedures, otherwise analysts and programmers will not take the position seriously. This means that, no matter at what level the database administration function has been established in the data processing hierarchy, the database administrator must have the total support of the data processing manager and preferably also that of the head of management services.

The user interface
The move from conventional data processing systems to a database system can cause problems with the ownership of data. In an integrated system, data may no longer be for the use of just one user but may be shared with several others. In this situation it can be difficult to establish ownership and there is, therefore, likely to be a problem in determining responsibility for data creation and update. There is also likely to be a problem caused by individuals being reluctant to relinquish control of 'their' data to a central body. When these situations arise the DBA will need to be very diplomatic and be prepared to act as an arbitrator.

The database administrator should be responsible for implementing and maintaining access control facilities which satisfy user requirements. Also, in addition to providing the necessary controls, an effective policing system is required which will deter and detect the improper use of data.

The applications interface
An automatic data dictionary system is essential if the DBA is to operate effectively. The dictionary consists of a centralized collection of definitions, characteristics and interrelationships describing all the data that is stored within the system. In addition to providing an authorized source of data definitions, the dictionary allows the implications of making changes to data definitions to be investigated, by answering such questions as: 'If we change the definition of this item of data, which programs will be affected?'

The contents of the dictionary may be changed only under the direction of the DBA and a change to any specification which involves data must be approved by the DBA.

It may be that some systems need to exist outside the database environment but need to have access to the data held in the database, or that during a phased implementation the same data may be required in both the old and the new systems. The DBA should be responsible for the maintenance and compatibility of all the data that is stored in the system.

Another responsibility of the DBA is the supervision of the testing of all new application programs and modifications to existing ones. Testing should be performed against a test database; programs should only be allowed to run against the production database following the DBA's approval.

The operations interface
In practice, the extent to which the DBA becomes involved in the operations area is likely to be limited. Recovery, however, is an area which must be carefully supervised. Errors made in the recovery process can result in data being lost for ever. A member of the database administration section should always be present when the database is being recovered. The DBA should also be concerned with the physical security of the magnetic media which hold log–audit files and security dumps.

5.5 Database design

In most data processing departments, systems analysis techniques and procedures are directed towards considering data from the point of view of a particular application. It is only quite recently that attention has been focused on the need to view data as a resource in its own right. This realization has been brought about by the increasing use of database management systems and has resulted in a growing acceptance of the need to carry out a very much more detailed analysis of the data requirements of the organization as a whole.

The objective of database design is to produce a system that satisfies the needs of a wide range of applications. The first step in this process is a logical database design, the second is the specification of the data management requirement, and the final step is the physical database design (Figure 5.2). It is important to recognize that the design will evolve over a period of time and many of the steps involved will have to be repeated over and over again as changes occur in the user requirement and also as more accurate information becomes available.

5.5.1 Logical database design

Logical database design involves a detailed analysis of the data requirements of the proposed system. This process involves analysis of the

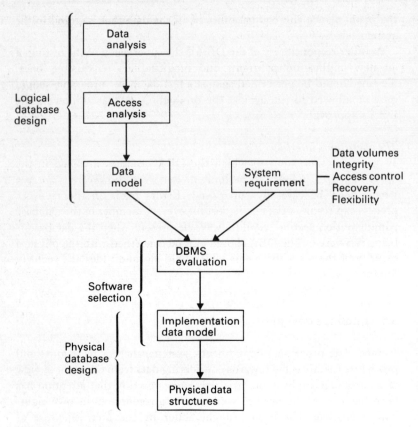

Fig. 5.2   Database design

data and the ways in which it needs to be accessed, using information gathered by the systems analysts. The results should be completely independent of both hardware and software, and should not assume any particular method of physical data organization.

The advantages of approaching the design of the database in this way are:

- It provides a stable base from which to set standards and coordinate the development of the system.
- It provides a data model that is completely free of any implementation considerations and which can be used as a point of reference when either adding to or modifying applications, or changing the components of the hardware or software configuration.
- It provides a specification which can be used in the evaluation of database management software.

- It provides a base line from which an optimum physical data organization can be produced.

A formal approach to database design is vital on a project which is of any reasonable size. There are also considerable benefits to be gained from going through the process on small systems, because it does result in a well thought out design which has good documentation. This will prove to be an even better investment if the scope of the system increases in the future.

5.5.2 Data analysis

Data analysis in theory is concerned with understanding and documenting the nature of all the data which is necessary for a company to conduct its business. However, in the practical world the data processing manager has to work to deadlines and is subject to strict budgetary controls. This means that in reality the objective will be to produce a data model which will satisfy the needs of the applications that are definitely going to be computerized.

The logical data model has three basic components: entities, attributes and relationships. An *entity* is basically anything that is of interest to the proposed system—for example, employee, customer and supplier. Each type of entity can, of course, occur many times. Associated with each entity are a number of properties which describe it and make it unique. These are called *attributes*. For example, an employee entity may have attributes which include such items as name, address and personnel number. In order to be able to identify a particular occurrence of an entity there must be at least one attribute that has a unique value (key) associated with it. In the case of an employee this could be the personnel number. Entities can be associated by means of *relationships*. The types of relationship that may exist in a data model (Figure 5.3) include:

(a) a one-to-many relationship—the number of lines on an order is, for example, a one-to-many relationship between the entities 'order' and 'lines',

(b) a many-to-many relationship—a supplier, for example, may supply many parts and a part may be supplied by many suppliers;

(c) an involuted relationship—within a group of employees there is a management structure and therefore a relationship exists between occurrences of the same type of entity;

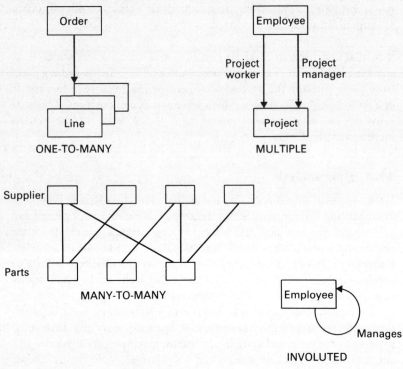

Fig. 5.3 Types of relationship (I)

    (d) a multiple relationship—two relationships called 'project worker' and 'project manager' can exist between the entities 'employee' and 'project'.

Entities can be grouped together to form hierarchical and network relationships (Figure 5.4). In a hierarchy, entities are grouped into a tree-like structure in which no entity can have more than one 'parent' or 'owner'. A customer may, for example, have many orders and each order may contain many lines. A hierarchy usually implies that there is a one-to-many relationship between 'parent' and 'child' but only a one-to-one relationship in the other diretion. On the other hand, in a network an entity may have many 'parents' as, for example, a line on an order may be related to the entities 'supplier' and 'part', in addition to 'order'.

5.5.3 The data analysis process

The first step in data analysis is to study what is sometimes referred to

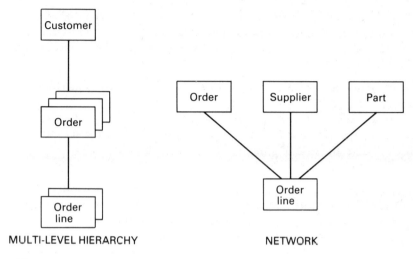

MULTI-LEVEL HIERARCHY   NETWORK

Fig. 5.4 Types of relationship (II)

as the functional specification. This is a document, produced jointly by users and system analysts, which states the user requirement. Consideration of this document, together with discussions with both users and analysts, permits determination of the basic 'things of interest' and hence of the initial entities in the data model. It is important to establish at the outset some idea of the entities that may exist so that a framework can be established that will act as a reference point during the data analysis phase. Although the design process will result in some entities being removed and new ones being identified, experience shows that a large proportion of these 'initial' entities are correctly identified.

The next step is to determine what relationships exist between the entities that have been identified. It is important at this stage to identify all the 'natural' relationships that exist, rather than just those which it is thought may be computerized. An outline data model can then be produced. The finalized version of the model will only emerge following the completion of the access analysis phase.

Following the production of the functional specification, the analyst produces a detailed system specification which identifies processes and their data requirements. This information is used to identify attributes and determine how they should be allocated to the entities previously defined.

The functional and system specifications are the result of lengthy investigations and the data analysis process needs to proceed in parallel with this activity. When sufficient data has been collected, the entities and their attributes should be examined critically to check whether an attribute really does belong to a particular type of entity. This process is referred to as normalization. In simple terms, the normalization process:

- removes repeating groups from the entities and turns them into new entities;
- ensures that attributes are allocated to entities in such a way that each attribute in an entity is only dependent upon the key attribute or, in the case of a multi-attribute key, the whole key.

At the end of the process an entity comprises a primary key and a number of mutually independent attributes, each of which is dependent on the primary key. Although the process of normalization produces a flexible design, it may not result in an efficient system when implemented. There will, therefore, be a trade-off in the final stages of the design process which will probably result in some entities being left in a non-normalized form.

5.5.4 Access analysis

Following the data analysis phase, the next step is to study the way in which data is to be used. For each batch and on-line process the access requirements are recorded in terms of:

- the entities, attributes and relationships used;
- the types of access required to support the various processes;
- the access keys required;
- the frequency of access;
- the response times required.

A composite picture of the access requirement can then be produced by aggregating the above usage statistics. This information can then be used to determine which relationships are required to support the system.

5.5.5 Software evaluation

The logical data model and access requirement do not on their own provide sufficient information to allow the data management requirement to be specified. There must, for example, be a careful investigation of:

- the data volumes that are expected to be associated with each entity;

- the security requirements in terms of integrity, recovery and access control;
- the degree of flexibility required.

If there is to be a choice of data management software, the data model has an important role to play in the selection process. It is important to ensure that the database software chosen will allow an effective implementation of the data model.

5.5.6 Physical database design

The physical database design involves mapping the logical data model to the actual storage devices that are to be used to hold the database; the usage statistics resulting from the access analysis phase play a vital role in this process. Entities and attributes are quite straightforward. The entity becomes a record type and the attribute a field. The way in which relationships are dealt with, however, depends upon which DBMS is used and it will be necessary to produce an 'implementation' data model that is specific to the DBMS. With some types of DBMS, relationships are established explicitly by means of pointers that are stored alongside the data; the programmer is aware of this structure and is provided with commands which enable him to navigate around the database. Some examples of the way in which a model may need to be changed to overcome particular problems (Figure 5.5) are the following:

- Implemention of many-to-many relationships can be achieved by creating an 'intersection' entity to simplify the relation to two one-to-many relationships.
- If the package can implement only two-level hierarchies, it is possible to simulate multi-level hierarchies by introducing additional entities and relationships that link together a number of two-level hierarchies.
- An involuted relationship can be simplified by including an additional entity and relationship: for example, the relationship 'manages' can be replaced by the relationships 'managed by' and 'reports to', linked to an additional entity.
- Two entities linked by two relationships may be simplified by the addition of an extra entity and relationship, so that only one relationship exists between any two entities.

An alternative approach is provided by inverted file and relational systems. With these systems, data is held in files or tables and the structure identified in the data model is implemented implicitly by

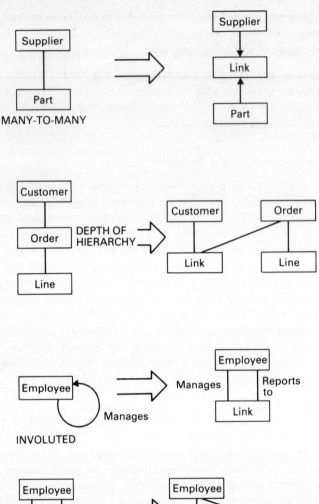

Fig. 5.5 Overcoming structural deficiencies

means of indexes. The programmer does not navigate around the database but issues much more comprehensive commands which, in addition to specifying the data requirements, indicate the relationships involved; the software then makes the necessary connections 'behind the scenes'. If the package does not support some types of relationship, this has to be resolved by programming.

5.6 Database software

5.6.1 Significant developments

The history of database software dates back over twenty years. The early systems were developed by users in order to solve particular problems, and in the mid-1960s the first general-purpose packages started to become available. An important early development took place in 1964 in the USA, where the General Electric Company (GEC) system called IDS (Integrated Data Store) was made available on GEC computers. IDS provided quite powerful facilities which included:

- support for network structures;
- a common database;
- data descriptions that were independent of storage considerations;
- powerful data manipulation facilities;
- an integrated recovery system.

In 1969 a technical group operating under the auspices of Codasyl produced a specification of common database facilities which was strongly influenced by the concepts behind IDS. The Codasyl specification has been enhanced over the years and there are now in existence several database management systems based on the ideas that it contains. These include systems produced by Univac (DMS 1100 and DMS/90), Cullinane (IDMS) and Digital Equipment. IDMS has an interesting background. It was originally developed by a user (the USA chemical company B. F. Goodrich) and was then acquired by the Boston software house, Cullinane. Although initially designed to operate on IBM equipment, it is now available on ICL, Univac, Digital Equipment and Siemens computers.

At about the same time that IDS was being developed, the Space Division of North American Rockwell Corporation was awarded the Apollo contract. In order to handle the problems caused by the size and complexity of this project, a data management system was developed which eventually became a joint project with IBM. With the advent of System/360 this evolved into what is now called IMS. IMS has been developed continually over the years and the present version is a very large and powerful package offering many options. In 1968 Cincom Systems Inc. introduced a DBMS called TOTAL. It was initially implemented on IBM computers but has since become available on most types of computer, both large and small.

In 1966 another significant development took place at the University of Texas. A database management system called Remote File Management

System (RFMS) was developed. This package was based on inverted files and was further developed by the MRI Systems Corporation to become what is now known as SYSTEM 2000. At the beginning of the 1970s another inverted file system called ADABAS was developed in West Germany by a company called Software AG. A number of other systems of the inverted file type have since been introduced, including DATACOM (Applied Data Research Corporation) and MODEL 204 (Computer Corporation of America).

Throughout the 1970s the early packages were enhanced to provide additional facilities and major performance modifications were made. More recently there has been another significant development in the form of the relational DBMS in which the database consists of number of simple tables (files) which are accessed by means of a very high-level language. There is a growing trend towards providing comprehensive easy-to-use languages and most of the suppliers of database software provide facilities in this area.

5.6.2 Data independence

Most of the benefits that can be achieved by the use of database management systems depend to a large extent upon the degree of data

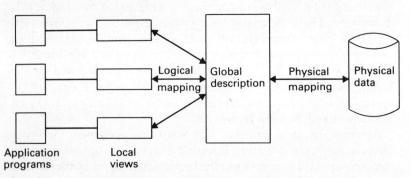

Fig. 5.6 Data independence

independence provided by the database software. The object of data independence is to make the application program dependent only on the data which it actually requires for its processing needs (Figure 5.6). Ideally, if changes occur in parts of the database not actually used by a program there should be no need to make any changes to that program. Similarly, changes to the way data is physically stored and accessed should not have any impact.

In most cases an application program is concerned with only a small proportion of the data in the overall database. At the logical level, data independence is concerned with providing facilities to enable:

(a) a global representation of the data to be created which can be optimized for the application environment as a whole;
(b) a series of local data representations (subsets) to be derived from the global view which will allow a particular program to be independent of the other programs using the database.

The global description of the database is described by means of a data definition language (DDL). In Codasyl terminology this is referred to as a *schema*. In practice, the methods that are used to define a local view fall into two categories. The first allows the database administrator to define, by means of a data definition language, a subset of the global view (a *subschema* in Codasyl terminology). In the second category, the local view is specified in the data manipulation command by the programmer, and the database administrator may restrict this view by means of access control facilities.

At the physical level, data independence is concerned with making the global representation of the data completely independent of the way in which the data is physically stored and accessed. There should ideally be no dependence upon the type of storage device, the storage structure, the format in which the data is stored, or the methods used to access the data.

In practice, database storage structures do require to be reorganized from time to time in order to maintain a satisfactory level of performance. Physical data independence should allow this to be achieved without any impact on the programs using the system.

5.6.3 Data structures

The data structures employed by the database software packages at present on the market mainly employ either record chaining or inverted file structuring techniques. The data is organized almost exclusively on direct access devices.

Where record chaining is employed, relationships are implemented by linking records together using pointers. It is usual to store the pointers with the data to which they relate. In a Codasyl sytem such as IDMS (Figure 5.7) the interrecord relationships are called *sets*. A set is basically a chain of related records consisting of one owner record and one or more member records; next, owner and prior pointers may be used to establish the necessary linkages. A record may be the owner of

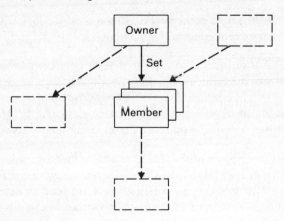

Fig. 5.7 Data structures—IDMS

more than one set and it may participate as a member of more than one set and may be an owner and a member of different sets.

A somewhat different approach is employed in the case of TOTAL (Figure 5.8) where there are basically two types of file in the database: a *master file* and a *variable entry file*. Variable entry files are accessed through a record in a master file. The records in a master file are stored randomly and are accessed through a control key. The relationships between master file records and variable entry files are implemented by means of pointers. Related records in variable entry files are automatically chained together by means of both forward and backward pointers. It is possible for master file record to own more than one variable entry file chain, either in the same or in different files. Also, variable entry file records may take part in more than one relationship.

Another example of record chaining is provided by IMS (Figure 5.9), where the programmer views the database as a hierarchial structure which is made up of a number of data segments (repeating groups). Each hierarchical structure is referred to as a *logical database* and is defined by specifying intersegment relationships in which the segments may belong either to the same or to different physical files. An IMS hierarchy consists of a root segment and a number of dependent segments each of which may have only one parent but may have many children. The physical files are themselves organized in a hierarchical form and linkages are implemented by means of pointers stored with the data.

In an inverted file system the data is held in a series of files and is accessed through an index (Figure 5.10). There is no primary key, since any field in a record may be defined as a key. To access the

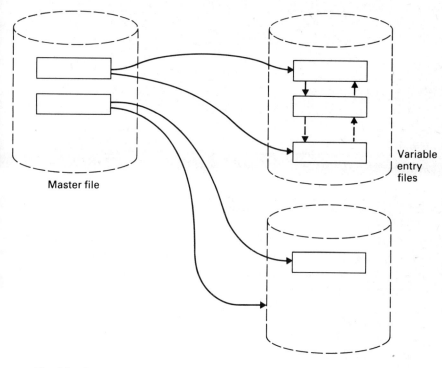

Fig. 5.8 Data structures—TOTAL

database the user specifies a command which contains the necessary selection criteria. Complex queries are resolved in the index and it is only when the appropriate symbolic addresses have been identified that the data in the database is actually accessed. Queries which refer to more than one file are usually resolved by comparing lists of symbolic addresses which have resulted from searches of indexes for individual files. In the case of ADABAS, however, the indexing system can be used to relate files in such a way that the user may access more than one file in the same command.

5.6.4 The programmer interface

The programmer's traditional means of communication is a procedural language such as COBOL or PL/1. Languages of this type are known as host languages and have to be enhanced with special data manipulation language (DML) commands before they can interface with a database management system.

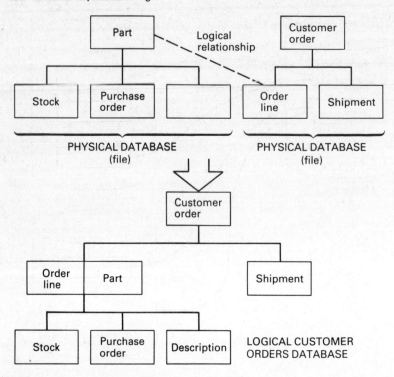

Fig. 5.9 Data structures—IMS

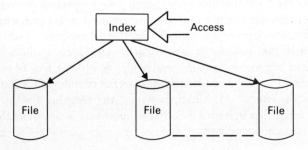

Fig. 5.10 Data structures—ADABAS

Two different approaches are used in specifying the host language interface. In one method the user embeds the DML commands in his program. The program is then processed by a preprocessor (precompiler) which converts the DML commands into host language 'CALL' procedures. The resulting program can then be compiled in the normal way. The other method requires the user to write the necessary 'CALL' procedures, which contain the DML commands together with the information required for their operation. In most cases the parameters of the 'CALL' procedure point to locations where the commands and related parameters are to be found.

5.7 Summary

Database techniques are widely used by organizations throughout the world. Experience has shown that the companies that have the most success have the following characteristics in common:

- a long history of successful data processing;
- the existence of good standards and procedures which are strictly enforced;
- previous experience in implementing integrated systems;
- a corporate commitment to using database management systems for all systems.

The following problem areas are those most frequently identified by people who have implemented database systems. They are based upon the experiences of several hundred companies in the USA and Europe:

- Implementation costs are likely to be higher than expected.
- The demands made on hardware resources (CPU, main memory and disk space) may force the company to acquire extra equipment in order to produce a satisfactory system.
- Claims by DBMS suppliers may be exaggerated; it is advisable to check with existing users.
- Tightening up existing procedures and introducing new ones can take longer than expected.
- Staff need to be retrained in order to take advantage of the new techniques; the time it takes for them to become fully effective can affect project time-scales.
- In changing over and interfacing with existing systems it is very easy to underestimate the amount of effort required.

The benefits arising from the use of database systems are now unquestioned and the development of microcomputer database system such as dBASE II clearly emphasizes the value of applying a database approach in systems design.

6 Distributed processing

6.1 Introduction

To get some idea of the nature of distributed processing let us invent a medium-sized manufacturing company and trace a typical history. In so doing we shall see how computing needs have grown and how these needs are currently being satisfied.

The Peters Petroleum Products Company (PPP) makes specialist lubricating oils and entered the data processing field in the early 1960s with an invoicing system running on a small computer. The majority of orders were received by post each morning and were typed onto punched cards for subsequent input to the computer in batches. The computer system was responsible for producing packing lists for the warehouse and for printing invoices. The system worked quite satisfactorily in batch mode for several years, having enough spare capacity to handle a modest increase in trade.

As the company prospered and grew, new computer-based systems developed and a payroll package and an accounting system were added. Both new systems ran in batch mode on a regular scheduled basis, the payroll being run once weekly and the accounting package once per month. It was soon realized that the computer files held a lot of important information which, if organized properly, would be of enormous value to the company's management. A statistical package was therefore added so that, at the end of each monthly accounting run, detailed breakdowns of orders, cash flow and sales were made available to management. By this time the computer system was fully utilized.

During this period of rapid growth it became clear that the warehousing side of the business would also benefit from computerization. A stock control system was needed. Rather than overburden the existing computer system (now running at full capacity) or replace the existing computer at high cost, it was decided to purchase a special stock control computer. The new machine had its own backing store for inventory details, a slow printer for outputting stock-holding details and a keyboard for data entry; information about stock movements was entered at the keyboard by a single operator. Only one operator was necessary because of the small size of the machine and the fact that it was used for only one application. All stock files were kept on-line so that the computer could provide an up-to-the-minute account of all stock levels in the warehouse. A byproduct of this system was the printing of consignment labels—an easy task because all details of orders leaving the warehouse were already entered into the machine.

Thus, the company had two separate computer systems, each dealing with essentially independent business functions. At the time such a system would have been thought of as a distributed system even though the two machines were located at two totally different sites. Both machines held important company data but, so long as there was no need for any interaction between the computers, all worked very nicely.

The batch processing system did, however, have one main drawback from the company's point of view. It could not quickly provide answers to telephone enquiries about customers' accounts. Such queries had to be answered manually from paper files. Although these files were computer generated and maintained, the company could not guarantee that the information they contained was completely up-to-date. The company was forced, therefore, to consider changing its data processing system for one that could provide on-line processing. This was a time of considerable change: VDUs appeared in offices, orders were input directly into the computer as soon as they were received, making modifications to existing orders easier, and telephone enquiries could be dealt with efficiently. Office clerks now had computerized work-stations—a VDU connected on-line to the main computer—and managers were able to call for up-to-the-minute reports on orders, sales and invoices.

But the situation was by no means perfect. It was impossible to respond quickly to enquiries about stock holdings because clerks handling on-line enquiries did not have access to files held on the stock control computer. This problem was partially solved by creating a copy of the stock file in the main data processing computer. Unfortunately, the updating of this file could only take place at the end of each day's work, as this was the only time that the stock control computer was not being used for its primary purpose. The method of transferring data from the stock control computer to the data processing machine also posed a problem. The backing store of the stock control computer used disks incompatible with those on the data processing machine. The solution was to use punched paper tape. It was possible to connect to the stock control computer a punch which punched out paper tape that could be ready by a paper tape reader on the data processing machine!

Not the fastest method of working, but since the transfer took place essentially overnight there was no reason to look for a faster method.

The company continued to expand and opened distribution branches in other parts of the country. It was then decided to regionalize sales so that each branch would deal with orders originating in a particular region and, moreover, would satisfy those orders from its own warehouse, and each branch was equipped with its own data processing computer to handle sales. The opportunity was also taken to include the stock control application on the same computer. The original company location became head-office and used its data processing computer for company-wide payroll and accounting applications; however, to coordinate successfully the distributed nature of the new company, the head office needed access to the data held by the individual branch computers. The ideal solution was to link each branch computer to the computer at head office for the purpose of exchanging data. This was eventually achieved by the use of private communications links. At the end of each day's transactions each branch would initiate a transfer of data files to the head office, and each morning would request an update to its files. Thus, the branches operated autonomously during the business day but coordinated their actions with head office during the night via the regular transfer of data files; the data files held by branches were the responsibility of each branch.

Software maintenance for all branch and head office computers was the sole responsibility of a central computer group at head office, to ensure compatability of all systems. All hardware procurement was dealt with by the same central facility.

The position in which our company now finds itself is complicated by the rapid growth in the use of computers throughout its industry. Many of its larger customers have their own computing facilities and want to communicate with PPP directly by computer. After all, it makes economic sense to transfer data directly rather than have one computer print an order, only for that order subsequently to be input to another computer. But the problems of direct computer communications are many. The communicating firms have to agree on a standard of file or record that both computers can cope with, and hardware has to be compatible for the data transfer to be physically possible. Moreover, a firm does not know in advance who it will be doing business with and hence does not know what kinds of computer system it will have to communicate with. It is, therefore, in our firm's best interest to develop its computing facilities in a way that will make it easy to communicate with other computing systems, by adopting universally accepted standards for data exchange.

It is clear, therefore, that any company may find itself in a position where not only is its own computing facility physically distributed but its computers have to communicate with other firms' computer systems which are themselves distributed. In one case the company has control over distribution (its own computers), but in the other it is faced with communicating with devices over which it may have no control whatever. The lesson to be learned is that a systems analyst's first responsibility is to satisfy his firm's own business needs, but he also must be aware of possible future developments in the area of distributed processing.

6.2 Centralization versus distribution

The initial trend in the use of computers in business was towards large centralized facilities. Hardware was located on one site and all computerized business functions were executed by this single machine operating in batch mode. In fact there was little alternative as these were the only machines available. There are, however, many advantages to centralized computing, not least being the simple but effective management structure required to oversee what is, in reality, a very expensive and scarce resource. Indeed, centralization often comes about for the very reason that a resource is scarce and therefore requires to be used economically. This implies that careful control must be exercised over it and it is easier to exercise control over a single facility than over a distributed one. A single department can be made responsible for the procurement, maintenance and management of all hardward, software and data.

The situation today is very different. There is a choice between centralized and distributed systems in which cost no longer favours the former, and there is no need for the computer to dictate the way in which the business is run. It is really the advent of on-line use of the computer that has revolutionized business practices, and the distribution of processing is simply an extension of this. The location of a terminal does not depend on the location of the computer, and there is no necessity to batch up transactions. This frees the analyst to design systems that use workstations (facilities enabling an operative to store and manipulate data) for carrying out business functions and which put computer power where the people are. This includes the possibility of distributing not only the terminals (typically VDUs), but all the other components of a computer system—central processor, peripherals, data files and software. The emphasis then is on solving business problems without being restricted by technical limitations. The analyst can concentrate on finding the best solution to the business problem in the knowledge that there will be a cost-effective technical solution.

For present purposes, so that we can evaluate the advantages and disadvantages of distributed systems, let us define a distributed system as one consisting of several separate computer systems cooperating to satisfy the business needs of a company.

6.2.1 Benefits of distributed systems

The benefits of distributing computing facilities between sites are many. A distributed system can be built up in stages, offering flexibility in terms of finance and development. Each local system can be tailored to local needs, which will vary because different locations will, in general, be responsible for different business functions. A corollary to this is that a local system has to be as complex only as local needs dictate (compare this with a central system which has to cater for all needs), and any reduction in complexity is a benefit since it improves the ease with which the system can be maintained. Business efficiency is also improved through local control, although it should be remembered that local control must always be accompanied by local responsibility. In short, a distributed system offers the analyst flexibility of design and gives flexibility in use.

A distributed system can also be a more effective solution to a business problem than a centralized system because:

- There can be a more rapid response to local needs;
- Flexible solutions can be devised, since all sites do not have to accept the same rigid solution;
- A more robust system can be designed.

The robustness lies in the fact that, in the event of a local system failure, it may be possible for the remaining parts of the system to continue processing. It is the reduced complexity of a local system which limits the effects of a failure and makes it easier to recover from such a failure.

6.2.2 Overheads

Large centralized machines often carry the overhead of a large operating system, and many diverse applications have to be catered for which increase the complexity still further. The result is that the operating system consumes more processing power and thereby reduces the power available to applications. The interface between applications and the operating system typically will become more complex. Any reduction in complexity, however, reduces application development time and thus reduces costs and the number of staff required to support the application when it is finally running. The fact that in a distributed system several computers are working in parallel implies that a greater throughput of transactions should be achieved. It is the potential for less complex local systems which makes distributed systems so attractive.

There are, however, arguments in favour of retaining a degree of centralization. Duplication of work and costs can be avoided by developing application programs common to several departments within a company. A single data processing department can take advantage of economies of scale and can provide support for smaller parts of the company. There are also advantages in standardizing equipment and it is easier to apply system design quality control with a centralized facility. There is one overriding factor which supports centralization, however: the need to share data. It is unusual for different divisions of a company to be so independent that they never need to exchange data. Centralization avoids the problem of data duplications in terms of consistency and accuracy between copies of the data. Also, centralization offers security in that data can be kept under tighter control and recovery from mishaps can be better managed.

In a similar way, there will always be some parts of the hardware which need to be shared—perhaps specialized or expensive peripherals which are not used often enough by individual units to warrant the purchase of more than one unit.

In conclusion, it is apparent that the better, i.e., the more flexible, less complex and more apt solutions to business problems are afforded by distributing computer power; however, it must always be remembered that there will be applications that demand some central facilities. Experience shows that a mixture of distribution and centralization can often provide the best solutions to business problems.

6.3 Location of data files

The location and management of data files in a distributed system are perhaps the most important issues to be resolved. In some situations a single central file is the answer—as, for example, in an airline booking system. For a company with independent divisions it may be best to have a separate file for each division. Current database management philosophy also stresses the importance of avoiding data duplication which tends to suggest that a single centralized database is the best way to hold a company's data. Indeed, centralized files are better understood and are easier to manage than complex data networks.

It would be a mistake, however, simply to keep a copy of the whole database at each site. This is because more data is stored at each site than is required to support the local processing. Storing more data than is absolutely necessary means that more physical storage is required and access to relevant data will be slower. Keeping copies of a database makes it difficult to maintain consistency between copies, especially when new data is inserted and existing data is updated.

Notwithstanding the advantages of centralized files, there are good reasons for distributing individual files (as opposed to complete database) throughout the system:

- The system as a whole becomes more robust in the sense that, if parts of the system fail, the remainder of the system can still continue useful processing.
- Modularization of data can lead to a reduction in complexity, with a resultant improvement in understanding, management and maintenance of the data.
- Data files are more secure, because there need not be any single point in the system giving access to more than a subset of the data.
- Bottlenecks in file access are reduced, thereby increasing overall throughput.

In general, therefore, there is a wide range of choice when it comes to distributing data, from a single centralized system to a fully distributed file system. The only way to resolve the difficulty of deciding upon the location of data files is through a good understanding of the business needs of the organization. This means that, for a given application, it is necessary to determine (a) who owns the file, (b) what speed of response is required from the system, (c) what the likely volume of transactions is going to be and (d) what the degree of interaction with other systems will be.

Distributed processing means wide access to the computer and its data files, but the responsibility for them cannot be distributed. It must be clear who is responsible when things go wrong. It should be possible, on purely business grounds, to decide who has (or should be given) responsibility for a given file. For example, in an organization with several branches each branch should be responsible for its own customers and hence be responsible for the corresponding customer files. If the same organization has a central accounts department, this department should be responsible, for example, for all sales ledger transactions. The rule to be followed is that a file should be held locally to the section responsible for its accuracy.

Other rules for the location of data files can be drawn up in respect of response time, volume of transactions and the interaction with other systems. Data files should be held close to where the fastest response times are required and to where the largest volume of transactions is to be found. Clearly, these may be conflicting requirements in practice, but it is up to the analyst to resolve these problems by first working out what is desirable before taking into account the practical difficulties. For example, a new system that will have to interact with another should first be designed in isolation, to ensure that it can satisfy the business needs for which it is being built, before the interactions are taken into account.

It is important, therefore, to identify clearly the main files of any system and then decide on their ideal individual locations. This will inevitably lead to conflicts, so alternative distributions should be drawn up and evaluated against each other. At this stage the secondary issues, such as the constraints imposed by interaction with other systems and the investment in existing computer equipment, can be used to resolve any remaining conflicts.

In practice, it is also acceptable to split individual files between sites and, furthermore, data may be replicated. When it is felt necessary to do this, it is vitally important that the relationships between parts of a file and, indeed, between individual files be maintained and that, for replicated data, the master copy is clearly identified. This means that careful management of data files has to be exercised and procedures for resolving difficulties following failure have to be set up, and for this purpose there must always be one copy of the data acknowledged as representing the true state of the business application.

The availability of on-line and distributed systems has enormously extended the range of solutions to business problems. In so doing it has widened the scope for mistakes. The systems analyst can reduce the incidence of mistakes—first, by fully understanding the needs of the business and, second, by reducing the complexity of the solutions. The more complex an area, the more difficult it is to get it right; there is a useful lesson to be learned from software design, where it has been found beneficial to split up a problem and analyze each part independently in order to develop a quicker and more reliable solution. This solution is also more likely to be correct and can be more easily maintained. As a general rule, it is always best to look for solutions which are modifiable in the light of changing requirements.

Modularization is the key to such solutions; distribution is often the implementation of such a strategy.

6.4 Access to files

For a given application it is possible to adopt a file strategy that is totally centralized, or one that is totally distributed (only local files exist in the system), or to use a mixture of central and local files in which centralized files are used for central applications and where users need access to a common resource, while local files are used for independent processes.

The fact that files are centralized need not imply that the whole system is centralized. Workstations can be widely distributed but still access central files. In so doing, however, there is an additional overhead to be taken into account—communications costs. A remote workstation accessing a centralized file incurs the cost of using some communication link, and it would be wrong to conclude that these costs can be reduced by replicating the files at each remote site. The inherent centralism of the system implies that each local update must be communicated to all other sites if all files are to be consistent at all times (crucial in a seat reservation system, for example), and to achieve consistency requires a great deal of communication between sites—far more than is required for the original centralized file system. A much better solution is to modularize the application and determine which aspects have to be dealt with centrally and which can be handled locally. For example, it may be possible to edit and validate input data locally and use the communication lines only for central file access. Output reports can likewise be handled locally.

Access to a central file from a remote workstation is essentially the same. From the user's point of view, it does not matter whether the file he is accessing is local. Similarly for the analyst. The problem is one of several terminals accessing a single on-line file. There is still only one computer system to be considered—a familiar and well understood problem. The difficulties arise when an application is a mixture of local and remote processing, where a workstation may have to access different files residing in different computer systems. For example, in the case of a customer requesting a product which is temporarily out of stock at a branch, it would be useful to be able to access the stock holdings of other branches to determine whether or not the order could be met quickly.

Just as it is foolish to localize inherently central data, so it is to centralize inherently local files. The result of placing independent files at a central location is the unnecessary addition of communications costs.

6.4.1 Mixed access

Solutions to the problem of mixed access come in three broad categories and depend on the nature of the mix of local to remote processing.

If the interaction among sites constitutes a major proportion of all transactions, there will be a high degree of communications traffic. The probability is high, therefore, that it will be economic to centralize all relevant files, thereby reducing the problem to one that we have already seen is solvable. Here there will be one copy of each file, to which all remote sites have access for interrogation purposes but which just one site is responsible for updating. If the application is not dependent on having totally up-to-date information, a reduction in communications can be achieved by updating the centralized files on a periodic basis—say, overnight.

The secondary category of mixed access is where local processing predominates over remote access. Again, the solution is to reduce the problem to one that is familiar. Files are considered to be totally local. To access another site's data, one site acts as a customer and telephones the enquiry in the usual way. If this system is too slow, a terminal (possibly with dial-up facilities) at one site can access the computer system at the other site. Thus, all local systems are independent, they each allow sites to access their files, but there is no direct interaction between local computers.

The third category comprises situations in which there is significant use of both local and remote files at each site. The best solution is to allow both local machines to operate independently of one another but to have the facility of sending messages to each other. The simplest implementation of this strategy consists of a single central processor acting as a switch. That is, all local machines are connected directly to the switch, which simply reroutes messages between the different sites. By prefixing a message with the address of another site, the switch is able to send that message to the appropriate destination; as far as each local system is concerned, it simply receives messages (typically requests for file accesses), whether those messages originate from a terminal or come from the switch. The local system replies to each message by sending the requested output back to the requestor. If the message came via the switch, it is up to the switch to ensure that the reply is routed back to the local site which created the original request.

The use of a central message switch is suitable only when the total distributed system is under direct control. The switch, the format of messages and the local hardware configurations can be designed as an integrated system. However, it may not be feasible to add new sites to such a system or to replace existing computers without a great deal of difficulty; a much more flexible solution is required if the system is to cope with future expansion and change. This flexibility can be accomplished through local area networks (LANS).

6.5 Local networks

The need for distributed computers to communicate has brought about a great deal of research into computer networks. Networks are sets of interlinked computers which pass messages from one to another. In some networks some of the computers are used solely for message switching and such computers are known as switches or switching nodes. Other computers, known as host computers, can then be connected to the network of switching nodes to communicate with other hosts to achieve the business needs of a company. A switching node does not have to be connected to all other switches—messages can be routed between several switches in order to travel from one host to another. It is quite common for such networks to be based on the principle of packet switching. In packet-switched networks messages are broken up into smaller units (packets) which are individually routed through the network, finally being brought together at their destination to form the complete message.

The low cost of microcomputers coupled with the development of packet-switched networks has led to the production of local area networks. Typically, a group of micros is connected in a ring (Figure 6.1). In addition to being a switching node of a ring, each micro acts as an interface or entry point to the network. It is possible, for example, to connect a VDU to one of the micros so that any message generated in the VDU will be split into packets (by the micro) and, accompanied by an address, will be shipped off to the designated destination micro.

One use of such a network is to connect a VDU to each micro, to allow users to communicate with one another over the ring. A more sophisticated use is to connect other computers, file stores, printers, etc., to permit users of workstations to have access to computing power while still retaining the communication ability.

The local area network, designed for low-volume data transfer over relatively short distances, offers companies an extremely effective

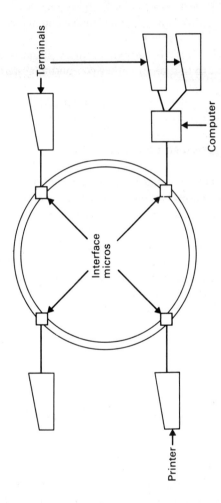

Fig. 6.1 The ring

management tool. All managers and secretaries can be interlinked and able to send memos and reports to one another; they can have quick and easy access to data files, and can have access to the outside world by connecting a telex facility to the ring. Such management information systems can also be equipped with text processing facilities to provide secretarial help. Local area networks represent low-cost communications equipment that can provide management with precise and up-to-date information about the state of the company. It should be realized, however, that the design of these systems needs to be as carefully planned as that of any other computing system and to satisfy business needs to the usual standard. The communication aspects of their design are considered more fully in Chapter 7.

6.6 Standardization and protocols

We have made the point that in the wider context there is a need for independent and dissimilar computer systems to intercommunicate. It is not a simple matter to arrange for any two machines to cooperate to solve a business problem, but there exists a good way to tackle the problem. If messages are to be transmitted between machines, there needs to be an agreed set of rules and procedures governing what is sent and how it is sent. The agreed set of rules and procedures is called a protocol. A protocol has to be adhered to by both communicating partners if each is to 'understand' what the other is talking about.

Much current research in this area aims to establish a standard set of protocols (several are required for general computer-to-computer communications) so that every computer system can be equipped with the required software to make cooperation possible.

6.7 Examples of distributed processing systems

6.7.1 A bank

For checking accounts, a bank uses a mixture of batch and on-line processing. Each evening, after the close of the day's business, the bank's mainframe computer at its head office is used to update the customer accounts master file. Batch processing is the technique used and takes several hours to complete. However, there is sufficient time left for the bank to send the computer output (customer statements and account details) by courier to all branches by the start of the next day's business. This means that branches have correct details of their customer accounts at the start of each day but do not have access to update information throughout the day. Currently the bank feels that this system is sufficient for its needs.

Naturally, millions of transactions take place during the course of each day and these have to be used to update the master file each evening. Transaction details are input to the head office computer via 'back office' terminals located in branches and connected on-line to the head office computer. These terminals are used throughout the working day for data input. Data about transactions is collected in random order on a transactions file on disk. This transactions file is first sorted into sequence corresponding to the ordering of records on the master file so that it can be used in the batch update process.

The bank's master file is held on magnetic tape (and currently fills 22 tapes). The speed of the batch update process is sufficiently fast (even using magnetic tape) to meet the bank's requirements for daily account updating. The fact that the master file is physically held on separate tapes has resulted in several benefits. As far as the batch system is concerned, it is dealing with a modularized file. The bank has so arranged the master file that the remote branches are held on that part of the file which is processed first, while accounts in branches closest to the head office are processed last. In this way the maximum amount of time is available to transport the computer output to the farthest branches. The partitioning of the master file also means that the system is more robust than one which attempts to update the whole of the master file at once. Effectively, there are separate batch update runs for each part of the file, making recovery from error much easier and less time-consuming.

The hardware at head office has been made robust by installing two identical mainframe computers and two communications computers. When one computer fails there is another standing by to take over. When a branch terminals fails, transactions have to be taken to other branches for input.

Thus, the bank's computing system uses centralized data files and centralized processors; only terminals (workstations) are distributed. The advantages to the bank of a mainly centralized system are:

- Security—data is under tight control.
- Robustness—duplication of hardware.
- Simplicity—an uncomplicated, well understood and easily maintained batch updating process.

The main problem with the current system is the difficulty of adding in new business functions. Overnight batch processing is available, but it would be difficult to expand the on-line activities without changing the file system.

6.7.2 ACP 80

ACP 80 (Air Cargo Processing in the 1980s) provides air cargo processing facilities for Heathrow and Gatwick airports in the UK. There are three participating groups within ACP 80: agents who are responsible to customers for the shipment of goods by air, airlines who provide transport for freight, and the British Department of Customs and Excise who are responsible for the determination and collection of duty and taxes. All three groups (there are about 30 airlines and 300 agents) have a vested interest in the collection, storage and manipulation of data about air freight. They all need accurate up-to-date information and they need to access the information quickly and easily.

Here we shall look at the part of the system that deals with goods arriving at an airport from another country. These goods may be destined for an address within the UK, in which case they may well be subject to import controls, licensing requirements and excise duties, levies and taxes, HM Customs and Excise being responsible for ensuring that all statutory requirements are met. Some of the goods are stored temporarily in sheds at the airport, either for re-export or because they are *en route* to another UK destination. All the information about cargo destined for Heathrow or Gatwick or currently held in a shed has to be collated and managed. ACP 80 uses a centralized computer system to do this. Inventory data about imports is held in a large file called the Communal Consignment File (CCF), which is continually updated on-line as the consignment processing reaches various stages. Members of the three groups access this data frequently during their daily operations. The CFF and the software for accessing and maintaining it are held on one computer.

The aim of the import inventory in ACP 80 is to record the state of a consignment of goods from the time it first arrives at the airport until it eventually leaves the airport. Consignment records are created by airlines and are updated in various ways until the record indicates that the consignment can be released for delivery. Three conditions must be met before a consignment can be released for delivery:

(1) The agent must have checked that the number of packages expected for a consignment equals the number of actual packages received.

(2) The airline must be satisfied as to the creditworthiness of the consignee.

(3) Customs must have granted clearance for the goods.

All three groups have to input data to the computer, indicating that their responsibilities with regard to these conditions have been met. The computer uses this data to update the CCF.

With such a complex system, discrepancies are bound to occur. For example, more packages may be received than were expected, or some of the packages making up a consignment may not be received within a reasonable period of time. It is up to the computer system to keep track of the goods and produce reports on discrepancies; it is the responsibility of the airlines, agents and HM Customs to ensure that the information is accurate and up to date.

The ACP 80 bureau consists of the CCF and software to create and maintain the records relating to inventory control. The ACP 80 bureau can be accessed via terminals sited in airline offices or sheds, in agents' offices on or off the airport, or on HM Customs' premises (Figure 6.2).

Besides access to the CCF, the ACP 80 system also provides software for the individual agents and airlines to perform their own inventory functions. In general, the software for agents is different from that for airlines and HM Customs has its own separate system. Thus, ACP 80

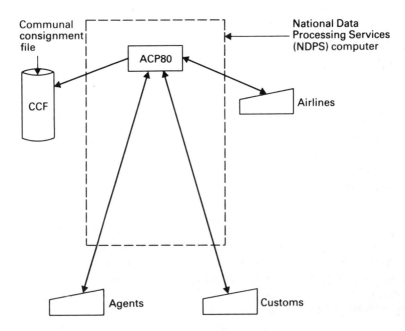

Fig. 6.2 ACP 80 in outline

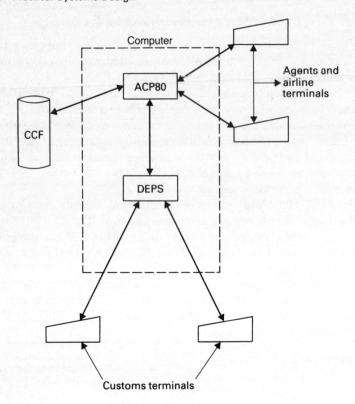

Fig. 6.3 Separate software systems

relies on two separate software systems: ACP 80, dealing with inventory control, and HM Customs' own Departmental Entry Processing System (DEPS) (Figure 6.3).

ACP 80 has been designed to allow HM Customs to access the inventory control information required by the DEPS system for checking the status of a consignment. The two systems interact (or communicate) via the common data file (CCF).

The story is further complicated by the fact that six of the ACP airlines have their own computer systems. Moreover, these airlines are concerned with goods at airports other than Heathrow and Gatwick. ACP 80, therefore, also interacts with six other independent inventory systems. These six systems transmit inventory control directly to the CCF.

There are thus seven different computer systems (excluding HM Customs DEPS) all cooperating to provide an inventory control mechanism for Heathrow and Gatwick airports (Figure 6.4).

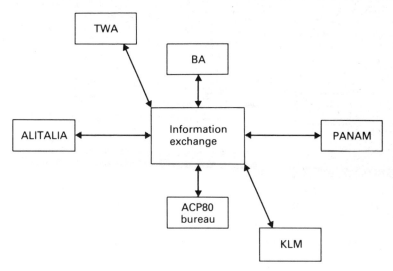

Fig. 6.4 Inventory control system users

The information exchange is the public switched network (PSN). Once a computer is connected to PSN it can send data to any other computer. It simply tells PSN the address of the computer for which the message is destined: PSN does the rest. Thus the whole ACP 80 system can be represented in Figure 6.5

The fact that each of the six airlines has its central mainframe in a different part of the world means that the whole ACP 80 system is widely distributed. The consequent problem of information exchange has been solved by two devices:

(1) a common data file which holds up-to-date information of relevance to all the participants in ACP 80;

(2) a computer network which allows the remote users of ACP 80 (the six airlines) to communicate with the common file.

The lessons to be learned from this example apply to a wide range of computer systems, not necessarily as large as ACP 80.

- Common data has been centralized (as the CCF).
- Other local systems exist independently of the central ACP 80 bureau for their own processing needs.
- The central system offers a service to those partipants who require computing facilities but have none of their own.
- Computerized work stations are located in the most appropriate

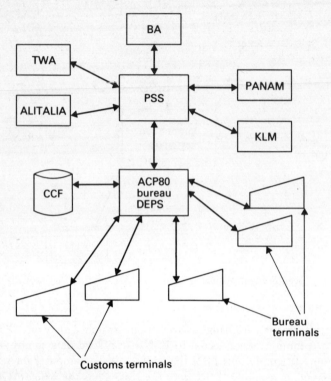

Fig. 6.5 ACP 80 complete

places (airline sheds, agents' premises both on and off the airports, HM Customs' buildings).
- Communication between the independent airline and the central ACP 80 bureau uses an existing communications network (PSN).

6.7.3 A tobacco company

The company has two central computers—one for manufacturing and accounts, which is housed in Belfast, the other for distribution and sales in London. Goods reach retail outlets via six branches, each of which receives goods from the factories, stores them and then meets orders captured by the salesman attached to that branch. Each branch has a minicomputer, to deal with its local processing, which is connected to the central computer in London (Figure 6.6).

Orders gathered each day by the salesforce are sent to the branch for processing. They are then entered into an order file on the branch's minicomputer. The data entry is performed on-line and basic validity

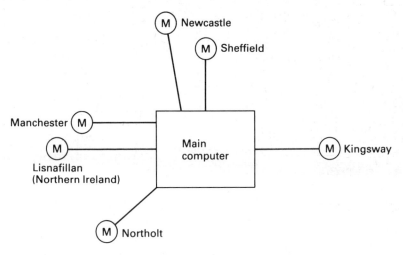

Fig. 6.6 The network: M = Minicomputer

checks are carried out. All the orders for one day are processed that day, in batch mode. Each branch maintains its own database, containing, among other things, the customer details. The minicomputer is responsible for preparing the invoices and advice notes. As a further part of the order processing system, the computer prepares the packer's notes which are used in the warehouse to put each order together.

The two largest warehouses maintain their own second computer for stock control.

Sales are coordinated centrally, all customer accounts being held in the main computer at the London distribution headquarters. The sales ledger and marketing database are also kept at headquarters and are updated daily, using data transmitted from the branch minicomputers after the local processing of orders has taken place. In a similar way, the local databases, which are abstractions from the main headquarters database, are updated daily by data transfers from the main computer to the branch minicomputers (Figure 6.7).

Branch minicomputers and the main computer in London communicate by sending data over fast telephone lines. Data thus flows between temporary update files, which are subsequently used to update the appropriate part of the database on the relevant machine. A similar data transfer is used between factory minicomputers and the central production computer at Belfast. The two central computers exchange information directly via leased telephone lines.

Salesmen send in completed order forms to their branches for

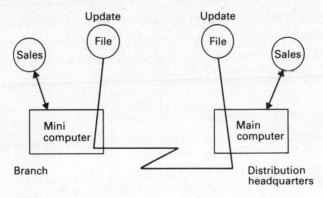

Fig. 6.7   Sales

subsequent input to the minicomputer. However, an experiment is being carried out on a new salesman system, by distributing the computing even further. Instead of an order form, the salesman now uses a hand-held microcomputer. This computer holds information about standard products and thus allows the salesman simply to key in the quantities ordered by each customer. Each day, the salesman visits a predetermined set of customers and records their orders on his micro. Each evening, the salesman calls up his branch computer by telephone and uses a modem to let his micro communicate with his branch mini. The small file of data about orders is then automatically transferred from the micro to the mini's order file. In return, the mini enters data into the micro concerning the salesman's round for the following day.

The use of the hand-held micro clearly speeds up the order entry process considerably and at a lower cost but it also has other advantages. The micro has, for example, a small facility to validate orders and thus avoid some of the errors associated with written orders. It has further pieces of software which help with the salesmen to keep their own records up to date.

The local database of the branch computer system enables it to satisfy many customer enquiries. Enquiries come in by telephone to one of a number of operators, each of whom is equipped with a VDU. All queries about current orders can be satisfied from the data held in the local database. However, queries about customer accounts have to be satisfied by the central London computer. This problem has been solved by providing each branch mini with software that can distinguish between queries answerable by the local database and those which require the services of the central system.

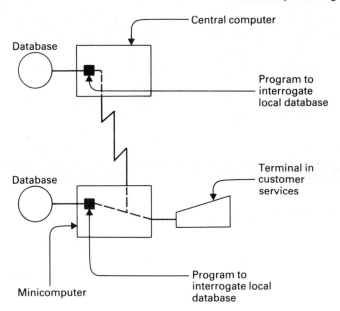

Fig. 6.8 Enquiries

The systems are thus widely distributed, the local computers holding sufficient information in their databases for their own local needs, while central computers are used for centralized business functions. Information is exchanged between the local and central computers to update the various databases (Figure 6.8). The databases are distributed and the major part of their data occurs in two places—in the central databases and in the appropriate branch database.

The firm has a customer-services department at each branch which interrogates both the local and central databases. Although the company's computing is distributed, there is a need for the machines to cooperate by exchanging data.

This example illustrates many of the important points about distributed computing:

- Local needs are met by local systems (at all levels—headquarters, branch and salesman).
- Each local system has its own files holding sufficient data for its own purpose.
- Customer services VDUs, order entry VDUs and salesmen's micros are examples of computerized workstations in which computer power is put where it is needed.
- Each computer site operates independently of all others.

- Where it is necessary to communicate between systems, a simple file transfer takes place; thereafter, the local computer system continues to work independently.
- Although the data files are also distributed, it is quite clear that the master files are kept at headquarters and, in fact, each branch has a new copy of its local database abstracted from the main database every day to ensure consistency of data.
- The system is robust in that, in the event of a line failure or central computer malfunction, a branch can continue the bulk of its processing by using its own database from the preceding day.

6.8 Summary

Distributed systems offer many advantages in the solution of business problems not previously realizable through centralized systems. In particular, local needs are met through local systems and centralized information can be collected for corporate or head office needs. Local systems create a local identity, giving increased responsibility for the accuracy and integrity of data. The application systems developed offer a robust service to their users and provide immediately available local data for the business.

7 Real-time systems

7.1 Introduction

Real-time systems represent a growing part of the systems developed today as computers are increasingly used to interact with their environment—to listen and respond, sometimes to control. No one-sentence definition will suffice to encompass just those systems we would like to label as 'real-time', but the following covers the majority:

> 'A *real-time system* is one in which the actions or outputs are derived from its inputs in a time frame determined by and related to those inputs'.

The following examples illustrate the range of systems that are covered by this definition.

(1) An airline reservation system should respond to seat booking requests at about the same speed as a human conversation. A request from a customer for information on seat availability is converted by the operator into a request on the terminal. Once the request has been made, both customer and operator wait for the computer to reply with a confirmation. When this has arrived the conversation continues with a customer request for a booking, and so on. The time frame for the system's response is similar to that of a normal conversation.

(2) When he uses a cash dispenser, a bank's customer holds a simple conversation with the system, a conversation with a small repertoire of questions and answers. The speed of the system should be related to the medium of communication—button-pressing to 'speak', reading a small screen to 'listen'. Again, the time frame involved is determined by the customer's conversational speed in this situation.

(3) A radar tracking system at an airport receives a constant flow of information from its radar antenna. It must analyze this flow fast enough to present the aircraft speed, heading and height data in a form

usable to air traffic controllers. To be usable, this data must above all be available in time for the operators to make use of it to control the movement of aircraft—this defines one time frame of response for this real-time system. But there is another time frame—the radar antenna itself needs to be controlled so as to look at the aircraft as it rotates. The system must therefore generate other antenna-control outputs within the time-frame determined by the rotation rate of the antenna. The system will therefore be working with at least two outputs of quite different time frames. Both relate to the same input data but the two actions require different speeds of response.

(4) By coordinating the operation of traffic lights in an area of a city, a computer system can significantly improve traffic flow. Such a system will receive traffic flow information from a variety of sensors in the region and immediately outside it. To regulate the flow, the incoming data must be used to derive optimal settings of the traffic lights in the subsequent seconds and minutes. These required settings then need to be transmitted to the lights themselves while they can still have the desired effect and before they get out of date. The system can be said to be working within a time frame determined by the 'death-date' of the commands it produces.

(5) At the supermarket checkout the items purchased can be deducted immediately from disk-held stock levels, thereby allowing closer control on stock ordering and hence removing the cost of maintaining unnecessarily high stock levels and the risk of running out of popular items. A customer paying by credit card has his credit status checked—the checkout till calls the card company's computer automatically—and his account is debited in favour of the super-market.

(6) New interactive information systems such as Prestel allow subscribers to access central databases via viewdata computers. Those computers are dealing with numerous calls simultaneously.

(7) Robots on a car assembly line 'interact' with the car components they are welding together through sensors that constantly monitor the position of the components relative to the welding arm as it moves through its welding sequence.

(8) New electronic telephone exchanges contain real-time computer systems that perform the high-speed routing of calls needed to satisfy the throughput requirements.

These simple examples all show systems interacting with their environments. To be successful, those interactions need to take place at an appropriate speed—this is the key property of a real-time system.

7.2 Characteristics of a real-time system

In this section we take the crude definition given in the introduction and identify in detail the characteristics which collectively are common to those systems we would label 'real-time'. Taken individually, these characteristics are not exclusive to real-time systems; a system exhibiting a number of them, however, will generally benefit from being called real-time and being dealt with accordingly.

7.2.1 Producing timely output

One key feature that can be seen in the above examples is the speed of the system's response. It is not the *absolute* speed that is the critical factor; what is important is the speed of response *relative* to the arrival of input, or, to put it another way, the speed with which the system interacts with the larger system in which it is embedded. In his book *Design of Real-time Computer Systems*, James Martin expresses this idea by defining a real-time computer system as 'one which controls an environment by receiving data, processing it, and taking action or returning results sufficiently quickly to affect the functioning of the environment at that time'.

There is in all of this more than a hint of the idea of feedback. A real-time computer system frequently 'closes the loop' between the output and the input of a larger system (Figure 7.1).

Our traffic lights system example clearly shows up the problem of making decisions fast enough to control the environment correctly. Traffic flow data goes stale very quickly and needs to be used to control

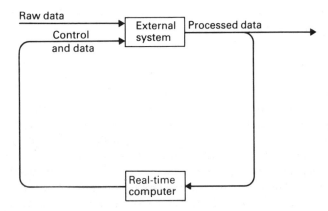

Fig. 7.1   The feedback element in a real-time system

the lights before the situation on the roads has changed appreciably and invalidated the decisions made.

'Timeliness', we have said, is a relative matter. In the example of the airline reservation system a response within 50 ms would be acceptable but unnecessarily fast, since the interacting system—here a human operator—needs about one second to prepare mentally for the reply's arrival in text on the screen. A response time of one or two seconds is all that is necessary for most requests. We can identify a 'real-time window' during which a response is required from the system. In this case we could define it as being the period between one and three seconds from the transmission of the reservation request by the depression of the ENTER key on the operator's terminal.

In the real-time radar system the computer deriving tracking data for objects within sight of the rotating radar antenna will be working with much smaller windows. For instance, it may need to activate certain acquisition hardware between 10 and 20 ms before an object is illuminated by the antenna and then read the returned signals within 5 ms of that illumination. Here the windows are measured in milliseconds, and such a system may have to work with very many windows at the same time, very often in a cyclical fashion.

7.2.2 Keeping a record of the past

In common with other control systems, a real-time system frequently needs to act upon input data not simply in isolation but also in the context of what has happened in the past. The radar system derives from successive radar returns the tracks of the aircraft it is following. These track histories are used to predict where the antenna should search for each aircraft on the next scan. When that scan's returns are received the histories are updated and so on.

Typically the track histories can be held in a computer's memory, as they are not large. An airline reservation system, on the other hand, needs to remember the results of all reservation 'conversations' with its booking clerks for the airline's flights for a year ahead—a massive amount of data, requiring high capacity disks for its storage.

Similarly, the traffic light control system would give the appearance of simply changing lights at random if it controlled them purely on the basis of the last set of inputs from its traffic sensors. It needs to remember, probably in a digested form, what has been happening over the last few minutes—what the trends are—if it is to develop a 'strategy' for preventing the build-up of traffic in particular area. In addition to these short-term trends it can also be designed to record data about the trends during the day, by different days of the week and even over different times of year. In a sense, this reaction to longer-term trends is a form of real-time behaviour, now with a time frame extending to 12 months.

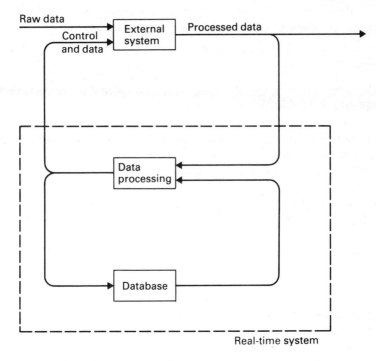

Fig. 7.2   The internal feedback in a real-time system and its place in the larger loop

This is all indicative of another feedback system—this time an internal one. Figure 7.2 shows it in isolation and as part of the overall feedback loop.

7.2.3 Handling concurrent input processing

A common feature of real-time systems is that they need to process more than one set of inputs simultaneously. The airline reservation system receives many requests from terminals at the same time. At any given moment each request is at some different point in the processing cycle and the real-time system has to meet a different set of windows for each request. Since the requests arrive asynchronously the windows also are asynchronous and it becomes necessary for the computer to handle this.

The same requirement exists in the radar processing system. A number of aircraft may be being tracked by the system, each being illuminated at a different point in the antenna's rotation. So their respective antenna–control windows are not related in time.

7.2.4 Competing and cooperating processes

The situation is generally made more complex by the fact that concurrent processes are rarely totally independent, even though they are initiated by asynchronously arriving inputs and have different and unrelated windows. They inevitably compete for resources and/or need to cooperate in some way or other.

Whether the system is a single processor or a multi-processor, processes will compete for processor time. Some want small amounts often, others large amounts infrequently. Some require high priority and get processor time when they ask for it—others may be prepared to wait.

Competition for memory occurs as independent processes request memory for messages arriving on communications lines or for data being read from disk. Competition also occurs for disk space, the use of direct memory access (DMA) channels, bandwidth on communications links, access to lineprinters and so on.

On the other side of the coin, processes may well need to cooperate to produce the required outputs. In our radar tracking system example, a process requesting the illumination of a target during that window needs to know the precise position of the antenna and its rotation rate so as to predict the exact time of illumination. It will rely perhaps on a separate process for this data, a process responsible for monitoring the motion of the antenna and acquiring its position and rotation rate on behalf of other processes.

Any competition requires an arbitrator and real-time systems are no different. One of the real-time designer's tasks is to determine the scale of this competition—who the competitors are, how many they are, what resources each wants, how much of each, when, how often, and what they want to happen to them if the resource they require is not currently available.

The required level of cooperation also needs to be established—process X cannot operate without the results of process Y's calculations, process Z needs a positive acknowledgement from process W before it can activate process V.

7.2.5 Coping with failures

An important question that needs to be asked about a real-time system is how the system is to respond to failures within itself and in other systems with which it interacts: how resilient the system is to be.

It may be sufficient for a FORTRAN program to abort abruptly if it makes the mistake of dividing by zero during the arithmetic. It is rarely acceptable for a real-time system to collapse so crudely in the event of error. Some level of resilience to error is generally expected and is one of the most important requirements to be established. This level of resilience will have a fundamental influence on the hardware configuration and software design and can have a major effect on the total system cost. The level of resilience that can be afforded will often be determined by the cost of failure to the user should it occur, and consequently this needs to be established with the user.

Resilience to failure can take a number of forms from complete recovery to complete collapse. With the high cost of failure in, for instance, banking systems, air traffic control systems and command and control systems, there is an increasing amount of commercial hardware and software that offers continuous service despite failure of critical components—processors, master file disks, communication lines and so on.

Partial recovery can consist of a combination of reduced performance and reduced functionality.

If the disk file holding the traffic trend data in the traffic light control system is corrupted, the computer will have to continue to operate the lights and will be obliged, say, to work with a less ambitious strategy that does not require daily trend data. This level of reduced performance may be satisfactory until the trend data can be restored.

Reduced functionality can also take many forms. If the note-dispensing machinery in a cash dispenser becomes jammed, the dispenser may still be able to offer its other services such as chequebook ordering and current balance reporting.

In all these examples the system has fallen back to a state where the service is in some way reduced. Such fallback states may be reached quite automatically by the computer system itself, or with the help of manual intervention or control. Fallback may not only require human intervention in being attained but may also involve human activity in supporting it once it has been attained. What would otherwise be automatically controlled switches may need to be operated manually if the control hardware fails and the computer can only notify an operator of how he should set the switches.

If complete closedown is an acceptable or unavoidable response to failure it is often necessary to shut the system down 'gracefully' rather than halt the machine abruptly. This may involve disconnecting calls on communications lines cleanly, closing disk files, unloading magnetic tapes or sending apologies to terminal users before logging them off the system.

7.2.6 Providing a reliable service

The question of resilience leads directly on to another important consideration for implementers of real-time systems: what level of reliability is required? That is, how susceptible to failure can the system be?

Invariably, greater reliability implies greater cost, since the increased comprehensiveness of validation means more effort, more time and— unavoidably—more money. This applies to hardware and software.

7.3 Defining the special requirements of a real-time system

When the need for a real-time system is first identified, its purpose is often stated in high-level strategic terms appropriate to the organization's requirements:

- To improve the speed of service at our cash dispensers
- To increase the traffic flow in our city centre
- To provide track data to operators at the local airport
- To guide a missile to a designated target

The expansion of gross objectives like these into a set of detailed targets and constraints sufficient for system design is possibly the most critical activity of the development of the real-time system. The thoroughness with which it is done will have a major impact on the success of subsequent development work. The characteristics of good systems work apply to all systems, batch, real-time and office automation. We note here those factors which need special consideration in real-time systems design and which will steer our choice of design strategy.

7.3.1 Defining the system outputs

What are the different datasets output by the system?
What are the size and format of each dataset?
What speed of response is required for each dataset?
- Related to arrival time of an input dataset
- Related to some other event

How are the different output datasets related?
- Deriving from common input datasets
- Independent
- Relying on a common database

How are the output datasets derived?
- From input datasets
- From a database of fixed information
- From a database of past events
- Historical data
- Using such-and-such algorithms

What windows are available for the output of datasets?
Do the windows vary for different situations?
What are the output channels to be used?

How is the system to respond to different types of failure (besides those on input and output channels)?
- Failures in subsystems directly or indirectly connected to it
- Failures in itself
    in applications software
    in the operating system
    in hardware components (disk, memory, printers . . .)
- Overloading
- Speed and extent of recovery required

What fallback mechanisms are to be available in the event of failure?
- Automatic/manual/manually assisted
- Fallback in performance/functionality/both
- Variation with type of failure
- Data recovery to be supported

What action is to be taken on complete closedown?
- Operator initiated/system initiated
- Closing of databases
- Alarms
- Final state of devices (e.g. cash dispenser vandal screens and hydraulic rams on a test rig)
- Notification to users/callers/operator

7.3.2 Defining the system inputs

What are the different datasets input to the system?
What is the size and format of each dataset?

What is the arrival pattern of each input dataset?
- Frequency of arrival or sampling rate
- Maximum and minimum rates
- Random/fixed/cyclic patterns and trends

Within what window is the data available and valid?
- Indefinitely
- For a fixed period after arrival
- Until acknowledged
- Until another data set arrives
- Until some other event occurs

How will the arrival of data be detected?
- By interrupt
- By the setting of a status register on the interface
- By polling the device concerned

At what speed will the data arrive?
- As controlled by the computer
- As controlled by its originator

How is the system to respond to loss of input data?
- By ignoring the fact
- By re-polling or re-requesting
- By extrapolating on the basis of past history
- By closing down the interface/call/conversation

How is the system to respond to corrupt input data?
- By extrapolating
- By re-requesting
- By ignoring it

What notification to the outside world is to be given of corrupt or missing input data?
- Log records locally/remotely
- Notify operator/user/caller

7.4 Problems of real-time processing and their solution

7.4.1 The situation so far

In Section 7.2 we identified the properties that characterize a real-time system. These can be restated more positively as problems to be solved in the development of a real-time system:

(1) The system must respond to inputs within the appropriate time frame(s).
(2) The system must keep an accessible record of the past.
(3) The system must handle more than one set of inputs simultaneously.
(4) The system must allow different activities to share common resources.
(5) The system must respond appropriately to different types of failure.
(6) The system must achieve a certain level of reliability.

There is no simple categorization of real-time systems and it will be no surprise to note that there is no single solution in software or hardware to the problems they raise. The designer needs to be aware of a range of solutions and to decide which is appropriate to his problem. In this section therefore we look at some techniques available and we begin with the effect of microcomputers.

7.4.2 Single process system

As an example we start with a system that is to echo the movements of a stylus in the hand of a user by drawing a line on a screen. As the stylus is moved across a sensitive tablet the line is drawn to follow its movements. This falls clearly under our definition of a real-time system—the line needs to keep up with the stylus.

Such a system, designed for a single user, has the very simple processing path shown in Figure 7.3(a). The path is short enough to rely on sampling the stylus position as soon as drawing to the last position has been completed, to give the impression of 'keeping up'. Thus we could implement this system as a single program looping around that path, running on a microprocessor with an input channel for the stylus position from the tablet and an output channel for vectors to be sent to the graphics terminal. The program never waits for anything, it simply goes as fast as it can.

Suppose we now add a refinement to the requirements of our system. We fit the stylus with an 'up/down' switch that allows the user to indicate whether or not drawing is required, so that he can move the stylus from one part of the screen to another without getting a line. The logic could now take the form shown in Figure 7.3(b). This system has two loops. The right-hand one is the loop it cycles around when the stylus is down and is essentially the same as Figure 7.3(a). The left-hand loop is cycled around as long as the stylus is up. It effectively

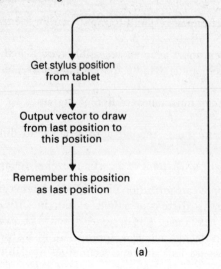

(a)

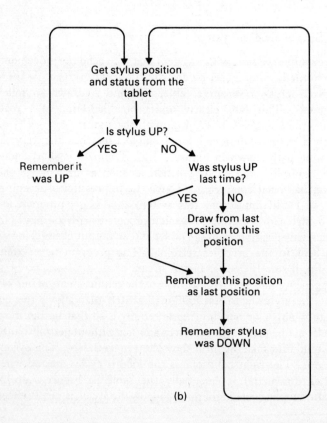

(b)

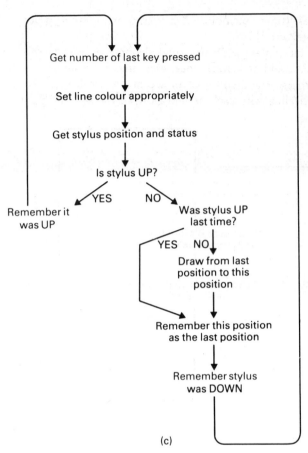

(c)

Fig. 7.3 (a) Following a stylus with a line
           (b) Following a stylus with an up/down switch
           (c) Following a stylus with an up/down switch and controllable line
               colour

polls the stylus, waiting for it to come down so that line drawing can begin again.

This form of polling—looping waiting for something to happen—is acceptable in a system that has nothing else to do, but will definitely not do for more complex systems, as we shall see later.

The important point is that our tracing system is 'single-threaded', that is, there is a single process controlling the system, with uninhibited access to data, resources and I/O channels. It has the luxury of not needing to coordinate its actions with those of other processes, to share resources (time, memory, disk space) with other processes or to cooperate with them.

How far can we push our single-looping process in this way? For instance, could we attach four such tracing terminals to the single microprocessor and still give an acceptable service to their users? By simply dealing with each user in turn, in the style of Figure 7.4, the

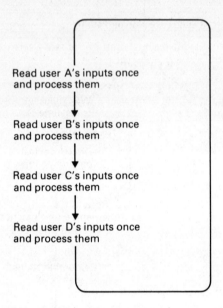

Fig. 7.4   Serving four drawing users

answer is 'Yes'. However, could a four-user system be further extended to support the storage and retrieval of traced pictures on 'diskette'?

On the single-user system this could still be achieved with our single program. During the storing or fetching of a tracing it would not poll the stylus or the keypad as this would be meaningless. It would instead go off and single-mindedly retrieve the picture. The user would wait for this to be completed. On our proposed four-user system however, users A, B and C are unlikely to be prepared to wait while the system forgets them to fetch B's picture. Another approach is needed.

7.4.3 Multi-process systems

Our single-process system of stylus movement was successful when it dealt with one user. To be successful with N users we need N

independent processes, each dedicated to one user. But, given that the processor of our computer can only do one thing at a time, what does it mean to talk of N processes running on one processor? Clearly they must take turns in some fashion. But would it be necesary to have four copies of the program code? If not, what exactly would a process be?

Definition of 'process'

The concept of the process is clearly central to consideration of real-time systems and it is important to be clear what is meant by it. We start with a rather abstract definition of this term: a 'process' is something that possesses data and has a number of rights:

(1) the right to 'use'—execute—certain pieces of program;
(2) the right to use the computer's CPU occasionally;
(3) the right to have data—to use parts of the computer's memory;
(4) the right to access peripherals—to perform transfers of data with the outside world.

In the one-process example the process concerned had all these rights without restriction. In a multi-process system the processes are entities known to some form of operating system and it is this operating system that reconciles the conflicting rights of the processes under its control.

The term 'process' is by no means universally used. 'Activity' and 'task' are common synonyms. Each operating system will have its own term, some simply using the term 'program' where each process can be identified with a single piece of code.

Types of multi-process real-time system

Our definition may seem over-abstract, but it does capture the various sorts of real-time system that are possible, in particular:

● Systems in which some processes use the same program
● Systems in which each process has its own program
● Systems in which some processes share data
● Systems in which each process has its own data

The multi-user tracing system could be implemented as a multi-process system with one process per user. Each process uses the same program but has its own data—my-last-pen-position, my-last-pen-status, my-last-colour, my-channel-number etc. The processes still have to share access to peripherals—in particular, to the disk that holds the drawings for all the users—and to the processor itself.

From this description it should be clear that a process is not simply the code it might execute, since that code may be shared by a number of processes. On the other hand, under our definition, each process in a system may have its own code—code that only it obeys—and the processes may share data. It is this sort of real-time system that is common in transaction processing and which we now discuss.

Typical multi-process system

As an example, consider a cash dispenser withdrawal clearance system. Such a system receives requests from cash dispensers for clearance of cash withdrawals being requested by bank customers. One way to handle this would be to create a new process for each withdrawal request as it arrived and for that process to push the request through the system, executing such code as was needed on the way. There would be common code shared by all processes, while each process would have its own relating to the request it was processing. This 'parallel stream' solution would look much like our four-user tracing system. The individual withdrawal processes would compete for resources quite independently, leaving it up to the operating system to sort out the allocation of resources and make sure that they all got through the system. Indeed, this is the mechanism frequently used inside operating systems themselves.

However, it is generally advantageous to turn this scheme on its head and to have a number of processes each responsible for a different stage in the processing of a withdrawal request from a cash dispenser. A request now traverses the system in the form of a dataset that is passed from process to process. Figure 7.5 shows diagrammatically the difference between the two approaches. In the parallel streams case, the processes are related to individual withdrawal requests. In the waterfall case, the processes are related to individual processing steps. In the parallel case, the flow through the system is a flow of processes traversing fixed code. In the waterfall case, it is the datasets that traverse the fixed processes.

In the waterfall case there is now only one process at each stage, but many datasets (or transactions) wishing to go through that stage, so each stage-process becomes a resource for which datasets must queue. With each stage-process we associate a queue of datasets waiting their turn and we can draw such a transaction-processing system as a flow diagram showing the network of paths along which datasets can flow. This is covered in more detail later.

7.4.4 Speed and how it is achieved

The speed required of a system is usually expressed in terms of its throughput, e.g.

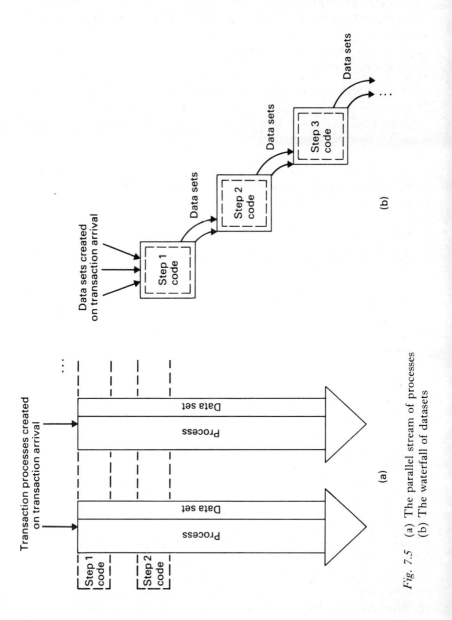

Fig. 7.5 (a) The parallel stream of processes
(b) The waterfall of datasets

- The system shall respond to an enquiry within three seconds of receipt in 90% of cases for a sustained enquiry arrival rate of four per second, and within 10 seconds in all cases for the same arrival rate
- The system shall support up to five drawing stations operating concurrently

The area of loading and throughput calculations is a large one, relying heavily on the application of statistical theory. In this section we restrict our attention to the factors that affect the speed of a system and over which the designer has control.

Speed usually means cost; speed for its own sake is therefore an expensive luxury. The designer must identify precisely where speed is required to prevent bottlenecks, for example—and spend his resources there where they will have their best effect.

The processor and host operating system

The sheer speed at which the processor can execute instructions is always of interest, though it is not necessarily critical. A great many real-time systems are constrained more by the speed of their peripherals—particularly disks—than by the processor's speed. A system processing cash dispenser withdrawals, for example, will do little arithmetic but many disk file operations, so the speed of floating point divisions is of no interest.

Data transfer in and out of memory

It is becoming increasingly common for the burden of controlling peripheral devices to be taken off the central processor and placed instead on dedicated processors—generally microprocessors—in peripheral controllers. Transfers between memory and these peripherals then take place via Direct Memory Access (DMA), typically at speeds around 1 Mbyte/s. The central processor needs only to request the appropriate controller to perform the transfer. Once the transfer is complete, the controller notifies the central processor.

Real-time systems frequently interface to specially built exotic devices. To allow such devices to be handled efficiently, manufacturers generally provide some form of general-purpose DMA interface card. This supports both data and control signals from an exotic device and may even have room on the card itself for users to add their own logic. The precise DMA capabilities of the computer to be used must be checked—some have none, some allow two channels that are allocated dynamically, some allow many more.

Optimizing code
Despite the efficiency of modern compilers for high-level languages
(HLLs), some measure of greater speed can always be obtained by the
use of assembler languages. However, given that HLLs allow much
higher programmer productivity than assemblers—they keep programming costs down—there is a trade-off to be made between the two.
Since most programs spend most of their time in relatively small
sections of code, the balance is generally best struck by identifying
those areas and hand-coding them in assembler: device drivers are often
handled in this way.

An option available on a number of minis and mainframes is that of
microcoding critical code. Often the instruction set visible to the
normal user is treated by the processor as an HLL. Each assembler
instruction causes the execution of a number of smaller instructions—
microcode instructions. Thus, an assembler instruction to add two
numbers might be executed as the following sequence of microcode
instructions:

- Fetch first operand
- Fetch second operand
- Add operands
- Check for overflow
- Store result

On some computers, users are given access to the processor's microcode, often via a 'Writable Control Store' (WCS). Since the opportunities for optimization are great in microcode, the designer should consider this option for highly critical sections of code or for operations that
are repeated with high frequency—special bit-level manipulations
performed on buffers of characters, for example.

7.4.5 Producing a resilient system

In addition to the built-in reliability, a real-time system will generally
be expected to cope to a greater or lesser extent with failures in
itself—its hardware or software—or in devices to which it is connected.

Detecting failure
Handling failure adequately first requires that mechanisms for detecting it are provided; fault detection mechanisms can exist or be placed:

(1) in the computer system;
(2) in the operating system;
(3) in the applications software.

In a computer system we should look for

- Watchdog timers
- BITE—built-in test equipment
- Memory protection
- Program failure detection mechanisms by interrupt
- Peripheral checkout and autodiagnostic facilities

A *watchdog timer* is typically a device connected to both halves of a redundant system, such as two processors either of which can carry out the system's operation. At any one time, one processor is the master— the active processor—while the other is in 'warm' or 'hot' standby mode and able to take the load should the master fail. Both processors must send a signal periodically to the watchdog timer to indicate that they are still operating. The intersignal period is generally programmable and is typically measured in units of 0.1 or 1.0 s, often being related to the time frames within which the system is working. Should one processor fail to signal in time, the watchdog timer will notify the other by interrupt, possibly also ensuring that shared peripherals are switched over to the new master processor. These could include disks, terminals and communications lines.

BITE is commonly incorporated in purpose-built hardware and is designed to allow that hardware to exercise itself periodically in order to check for errors or to allow an operator to get the equipment to self-test on demand. Ideally, BITE should operate without affecting normal operation. By its very nature it is designed into the system.

When the designer builds his real-time system he can identify which processes have access to which resources in the computer, and in particular their access to the various parts of memory. *Memory protection* mechanisms allow him to exploit this knowledge. The hardware is told, usually via memory-held tables, which processes have access to which areas of memory. Should a faulty process (or the code it is executing) attempt to access a memory location in a way for which it does not have the necessary authority or privilege, the hardware will generate a special interrupt. This can be identified as such by the operating system, which can take appropriate recovery action.

Similar *interrupt mechanisms* are generally available in the case of processes attempting to execute illegal or invalid instructions. Such violations are also notified to the operating system.

The computer hardware and peripherals often have built-in *self-test facilities* along the lines of BITE in special hardware, or sometimes in the form of diagnostic software that can be run periodically to check particular components during periods when no other processes are active. Typical examples are memory diagnostics that write and read test patterns around the memory, searching out faulty memory, and disk diagnostics that do the same thing on disk packs.

All of the mechanisms described have one goal: to detect errors in a controlled fashion so that controlled recovery can take place. It is this that is now discussed.

Handling failure

Recovery techniques are available in both hardware and software. They are not exclusive and are generally complementary, each requiring support from the other.

Considerable advances have been made recently in fault-tolerant hardware, particularly in commercial data processing, with manufacturers offering computer systems designed specifically for resilience. Typically, key components such as disks are duplicated and extra hardware is incorporated to allow automatic or programmable switchover in the event of the failure of the active component in a pair. This may extend even to having duplicate computer buses, but the essential point is that duplication is at the component level, rather than at the system level as has been the case traditionally with warm- and hot-standby systems in which a failure in a component in one system leads to a switchover to another system entirely.

At whatever level duplication takes places it invariably requires support from the software, at least from the operating system and sometimes from applications software. Manufacturers offering resilient hardware generally make available middleware that gives this support by, for instance, handling the switchover, supporting mirrored databases on duplicate disks, providing checkpointing of transactions and so on, on behalf of applications programs.

Where an error is detected in software the principal problem is that of confinement. This generally means keeping interfaces between software components as small as possible, reducing shared data, exploiting hardware protection mechanisms, restricting the privileges granted to individual software components to the minimum possible and generally putting up barriers against contamination.

7.4.6 Producing a reliable system

If resilience is about what needs to be done when things go wrong, reliability is about what needs to be done to stop things going wrong in the first place. An operational system can do nothing to improve its own reliability. It is either reliable or unreliable, assuming we take reasonable care of the environment of its disk and tape decks.

Reliability in hardware

Off-the-shelf items from hardware manufacturers generally come with a mean-time-between-failures (MTBF) value. The equivalent MTBF for a collection of items assembled as a single configuration can be calculated from component MTBFs.

It is important that this theoretical system-MTBF is treated as an optimistic estimate. Failures as seen by the user include the transient faults or 'glitches' that would not number in MTBF figures for components and the practical MTBF figure of the system in use can turn out to be smaller than the theoretical value.

However, where reliability is a critical requirement these calculations should be done as they give the best figure that will be attained. Where the computer system makes use of the high-resilience features discussed in Section 7.4.5, the reliability of the system can be expected to be greater.

Reliability in software

This is the area where the real-time system developer has the greatest control over reliability. Reliability hangs on verification at every stage of software development. As we have said elsewhere, design techniques should be adopted that, through their formalism, improve (or even guarantee) the likelihood that the design is correct. Precisely the same can be said for the coding and testing phases—either automatic or manual checking must be done at each stage: production of code, production of test cases, running module tests, integrating modules into subsystems and systems, testing against simulators and so on. In this sense real-time systems are no different from any other system: reliability must be built in both at a technical level and through managerial control.

The special difficulties of testing real-time systems stem from the following factors that are not found in non-real-time systems:

- The presence of interfaces to specially engineered equipment, rather than off-the-shelf only components
- The need for multiprogramming and multiprocessing
- The unpredictability of input arrival
- The extra level of reliability required
- Complex relationships between processes

These difficulties can be handled in a number of ways. Where an exotic interface is to be supported, the designer should consider the use of a simulator during development of the software that will meet that interface. This could take form of a specially engineered piece of hardware that emulates the exotic device at the interface but allows a user to see and control the data crossing the interface. This can be particularly useful in testing special device driver software and for exercising that software against the entire range of error conditions and rarer peripheral actions that might be extremely difficult to set up with the real device. A software simulator of the exotic device should also be considered. This would again emulate the device but now co-reside with the software under test. Software simulators are generally easier to build and more flexible than hardware counterparts but do not, of course, allow electrical interfaces to be checked out.

Simulators are also of use where variable loads from, say, communication lines are to be tested. Again, hardware and software simulators should be considered. Whichever is chosen it should allow a user to control closely the instantaneous loading and its profile so that the performance of the system can be monitored.

Testing of a system for correct multiprogramming, multiprocessing and relationships between processes generally is an especially difficult problem. Once again, simulated loading can be used but this will only show that the system did not fail during a test and cannot show that a system will not fail, and that it is correct. Correctness can only be achieved through design and it is important that the designer establishes the correctness of his design before committing it to the concrete of code.

7.4.7 Keeping historical records

We have seen that the sort of feedback control involved in a real-time system generally necessitates the storage of past inputs and outputs for future decisions. Early in system design it is necessary to calculate just what are the total real-time storage requirements of the system, what degree of accessibility is required for the various types of data, and how shared access is to be controlled where it occurs.

7.4.8 Operating system support

Most of today's computers are supplied with an operating system by the manufacturer—VME for ICL's 2900, VMS for Digital's VAX, RTE for Hewlett-Packard's 3000 and so on. In some cases, particularly with microprocessors, operating systems are also commercially available.

Although all these operating systems share a common purpose—to support user programs—they vary greatly in the level and nature of that support.

Possibly the best way of seeing the operating system's overall purpose is to look upon it as a master program that takes control of the entire physical machine but that, at the same time, allows user programs to 'imagine' that they are running on a more powerful 'virtual' machine, richer in facilities than the raw hardware. The value of an operating system to a real-time system designer can then be judged by the quality of the virtual machine it offers.

The following facilities that are of interest to the real-time system designer can be expected in some measure in most operating systems:

- Process creation and deletion
- The controlled sharing of memory and program code between processes
- Communication between processes via messages of some form
- Process scheduling—the allocation of processor time according to priorities and quotas
- Queueing facilities: creating queues, adding and removing entries
- Process coordination allowing processes to cooperate
- Semaphores and critical region access
- Interrupt handling
- Timing functions

It must also be emphasized that a real-time system, as well as getting the benefit of the above facilities, needs to retain some level of control, especially in exceptional situations. In particular, often it does not want the operating system to handle peripheral transfer failures and time-outs, attempts to take entries from empty queues, unsuccessful semaphore reservations or even invalid service requests and program failures. It may instead prefer to be notified of these events so that it can itself take action appropriate to the real-time situation.

In summary, a suitable operating system will support the process concept, cooperation between processes (coordinating their activations and exchanging data) and competition between processes for resources, at the same time allowing the process to retain a level of control.

Timing functions
These are crucially important for real-time systems. In the opening sections we identified the importance of catching windows and cited as an example a radar system having to request input from an antenna within 5 ms of radar illumination of an aircraft. Any system operating

with windows of this sort requires a real-time clock. This is a peripheral device that generates a hardware interrupt at a regular interval. Typical clock rates are 1 ms, 10 ms and 100 ms.

A real-time system frequently requires some or all of the following functions in order to handle windows and time frames:

- Activate process X after time t from now
- Activate process X at time T in the future
- Activate process X regularly at intervals of time t

Process creation and deletion

An operating system generally allows one process to create or 'spawn' another, giving it a name or identifying number and a priority level and specifying the code at which it is to start execution. In some cases, a process will correspond exactly to a program held in a file on disk and 'creating a process' will in effect be the same as making the name of this file known to the operating system.

Conversely, a process will be able to delete itself and to have itself removed from the ken of the operating system. It is unusual for one process to be able to delete another because of the obvious dangers. When this facility is provided it is often restricted to processes possessing a special privilege.

Memory sharing

The operating system often provides not only a mechanism for processes to obtain and release memory for their own purposes but also to allow processes to share data and to access common areas. Where this is possible it is usually complemented by the provision of semaphores or some other mechanism that allows a process wishing to access shared data to prevent other processes from accessing the data until it has finished. This is particularly important in critical regions of code during which a data structure is temporarily in an inconsistent state and hence cannot be accessed by another process. A typical example of a critical region is code adding new entries to a queue or removing entries from a queue.

Code sharing

We shall see later in this chapter, when we look at methodologies and languages, that a frequent requirement in real-time work is for processes to share common code. This generally requires cooperation both from the language—which must allow re-entrant code to be written—and from the operating system—which must allow re-entrant code to be executed by different processes.

Communication between processes

It is especially important in real-time systems for processes to communicate, either by mutual activation or by exchange of data (as in the example of the cash dispenser system). Exactly how this is supported varies. One common mechanism allows process A to request the activation of process B—or, more strictly, the placing of process B on the list of processes ready to run—possibly passing some data to B carrying an indication of why it has been activated. When B is actually run will depend on the scheduling algorithm being used by the operating system.

It is increasingly common for operating systems to support queueing of messages on behalf of processes wishing to communicate data in this way. Thus a process can direct a message to the specific queue of the process that is to read it.

Process scheduling

At any one time the operating system arranges for one of the processes to be using the processor while the other users' processes are dormant. A record is kept for them, to show where they were in the program when they were stopped, together with the contents of the computer's registers at that point. This process–specific information is known as the process's 'context' and the operating system maintains its own data structures holding the contexts of the processes it is running.

The operating system also operates some mechanism for ensuring that each process gets a fair crack of the whip: the processes time-share. There are many algorithms for allocating processor time among processes. Large operating systems employ quite sophisticated techniques that take a great many factors into account, such as:

- Relative priority as set by the user
- Time since last activation
- Processor time used since process was started
- Ratio of peripheral transfers to processor time used
- Amount of memory required

When looking at the operating system on the machine he is to use, the real-time system designer needs to check carefully that the strategy used suits his purpose in allowing his process to behave as he wants them to.

Interrupts and the control of peripherals

The real-time system designer should look for the following facilities in the virtual machine offered by an operating system:

- Synchronous and asynchronous transfers: the ability to initiate a peripheral transfer and to opt either to wait for it to complete or to continue while the transfer proceeds
- Notification of a transfer failure to the requesting process
- Return of a peripheral's status to a requesting process
- Ability to specify a maximum duration or timeout period for a particular peripheral or peripheral transfer and to notify the requesting process when a peripheral fails to complete the transfer in the timeout period
- Ability to incorporate into the operating system special peripheral handlers or drivers, such as drivers to handle special communications lines or specially built hardware

7.5 Languages for real-time systems

There have been a number of attempts to produce a programming language appropriate for real-time systems, in particular CORAL, RTL/2 and Ada®. All three have their roots in ALGOL and embody the principles of structured programming. In this respect all three are valuable in real-time work—as they are anywhere that reliable software is required. But they vary in the specific real-time qualities they offer.

A designer should not assume that these are the only three languages that can be used for real-time work. In the right environment and with correct handling most languages can be used, though some will hinder more than help, and in some cases the designer may not have the luxury of choice. The ability to write re-entrant code stands out, however, as an essential feature if processes are to share code.

7.5.1 CORAL

Pure CORAL contains no constructs relating to processes, their scheduling and coordination, semaphores or any technique related to real-time architecture as such. However, it has five features that give it some claim to being of use to real-time workers in particular.

(1) It is designed to allow efficient compilation and the compilation of efficient code. The relative lack of richness in syntactic structures (compared, say, with Ada) is balanced by the fact that the constructs

---

®Ada is a registered trademark of the US Department of Defense, Ada Joint Program Office.

that are present transform cleanly onto the order code of modern processors.

(2) Parts of a CORAL program can be written in assembler. This facility has two important consequences. Firstly, it gives the programmer direct access to the memory by absolute addressing (to get at peripheral I/O ports, for instance), to the instruction set of the processor (to execute semaphore instructions, peripheral control instructions and so on), and to the host operating system (if the compiler does not provide libraries giving CORAL programs access to operating system facilities). Secondly, it allows critical sections in programs to be hand-coded in assembler without having to be removed from their logical home.

(3) So-called 'anonymous references' allow CORAL code to reference absolute locations in the computer memory without using assembler. Again, this allows access to special ports and registers.

(4) Real-time work frequently requires data structures such as lists, queues and tables, and the ability to work at bit and byte level as well as with words. CORAL allows data items consisting of one or more contiguous bits—part-words—and data structures in the form of 'tables'.

(5) Generally CORAL compilers allow re-entrant code to be generated. This is particularly important where code is to be shared by processes.

7.5.2 RTL/2

Two main aims of RTL/2 were to achieve a good compromise between efficient code and re-entrant code, and to enable the effective description of multi-process systems without actually constraining RTL/2 programs to run under a particular style of operating system.

Like CORAL, therefore, RTL/2 has no mechanism relating to processes. However, it shares CORAL's positive features regarding efficient compilation, reference to absolute memory locations, insertion of assembler, data types and re-entrancy. As in CORAL, re-entrancy is generally achieved by giving each process its own independent work space in which its data is kept and can be manipulated by the shared code. The most common mechanism is a stack for each process.

7.5.3 Ada

Both CORAL and RTL/2 could be said to be appropriate to 'deeply embedded' software systems rather than exclusively real-time systems.

In the USA, the Department of Defense has specified the Ada language, again specifically oriented to embedded software systems. In contrast to the relatively simple syntax of CORAL and RTL/2 and their lack of specifically real-time control features, Ada presents the programmer with an extremely rich set of features. One of the consequences of the above is that an Ada compiler is significantly larger than one for either CORAL or RTL/2.

Ada has been described as the first language likely to be widely used that has contained embedded facilities for process-oriented work. It is possible in Ada to declare 'tasks' which can execute, conceptually at least, in parallel with other tasks. Mechanisms are provided that allow tasks to be activated, to communicate data, and to synchronize. Further mechanisms allow a task to suspend itself for a given interval.

7.6 Transaction processing

In Section 7.4.3 we introduced two ways of dealing with systems handling streams of independent but concurrently processed transactions. In this section we start with these two extreme types of transaction processing system and develop a more general model of such systems.

In the parallel-stream system, each incoming transaction is carried in a dataset and this dataset—probably in a block of memory—is associated with its own process. This process then traverses the code appropriate to the transaction, independently of all the other transaction processes currently in the system. The code traversed naturally has to handle the coordination between the processes, while the operating system is used to handle the competition between them.

In the more common waterfall system, each incoming transaction is still carried in a dataset but this dataset itself now traverses a number of fixed processes, each process having its own code and performing a particular operation. As an example we consider what might happen in the central clearing computer controlling a number of cash dispensers. If we used this strict waterfall model we might design a system such as the highly simplified one in Figure 7.6. Each ladder-like object represents a simple FIFO (first in, first out) queue of datasets, while circles represent the processes removing the datasets and processing them.

On arrival from the cash dispensers the datasets containing withdrawal requests are 'posted' on to the WR-queue. When a WR-transaction reaches the head of this queue, the WR-process logs its

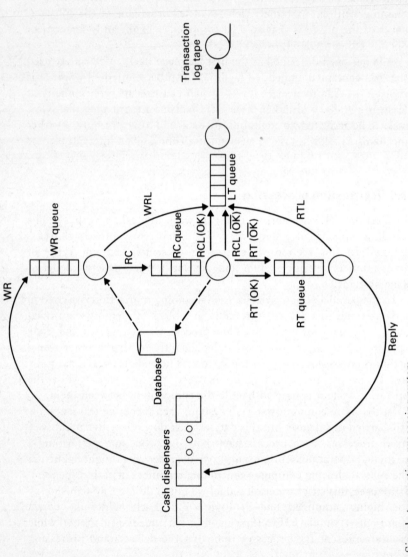

Fig. 7.6 Simple transaction processing system
WR = Withdrawal request; RC = Ready for checking;
RT = Ready for transmission; LT = Log transaction

arrival by creating a new WRL-transaction and posting it to the Log Transaction queue. It then appends customer data from the database to the WR-transaction and converts it to a Ready for Checking transaction before posting it to the RC-queue.

The RC-process checks whether the request can be approved. If it can be, it creates a new RCL(OK)-transaction and appends it to the LT-queue, updates the database and converts the RC-transaction to a Ready for Transmission (OK) transaction which is posted to the RT-queue. If the request cannot be approved, an RCL (not OK)-transaction is posted to the LT-queue and an RT(not OK)-transaction is posted to the RT-queue.

Such a simple system is clearly inadequate for the real world as it has no means of handling failures on the database, failures on retransmission, flow control into the system, guaranteed logging and so on. Nevertheless, it does demonstrate the principles:

- The processes remain fixed while datasets (transactions) flow between them via queues. A real-life system may have perhaps hundreds of transaction types with far more complicated flow paths. Datasets queue for the attention of processes.
- Each process handles one queue. Some processes (e.g. WR) expect only one transaction type, others (e.g. LT) several types. Types are brought together on to one queue wherever common or coordinated processing is required for them. Thus, since there is only one log tape, it is made the 'property' of one process whose queue (LT) collects all transactions to be logged. This also ensures correct time ordering on the log tape.
- When a process's queue becomes empty it must wait until something arrives. This means that whenever a transaction is posted to a queue it must be ensured that the relevant process is woken up if necessary. The operating system may provide a message-queueing facility of precisely this type for communication between processes.

While some groups of transactions, such as log transactions in our example, can benefit from a separate queue and process, simplicity can often be achieved by collapsing a number of processes into one where such combination does not affect any other considerations. Thus, in Figure 7.7 we have combined the WR- and RC-processes while retaining the different transaction types. We have also asked the LT-process to generate the RC-transaction from the WRL-transaction and return it to the WC-queue. This will ensure that receipt of the withdrawal request is logged before further action is taken—an often important property that was not present in Figure 7.6.

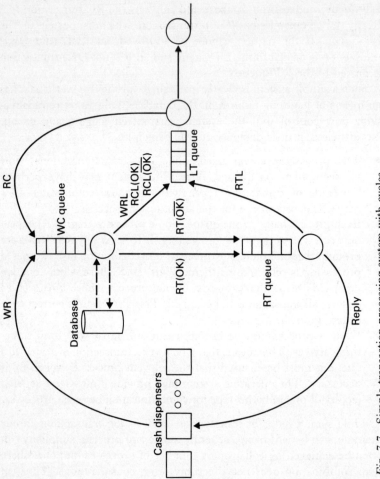

Fig. 7.7   Simple transaction processing system with cycles

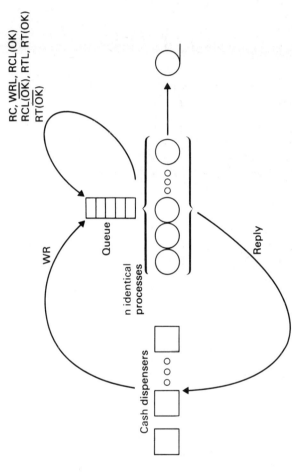

Fig. 7.8 Single-queue, multiple-process transaction processing system

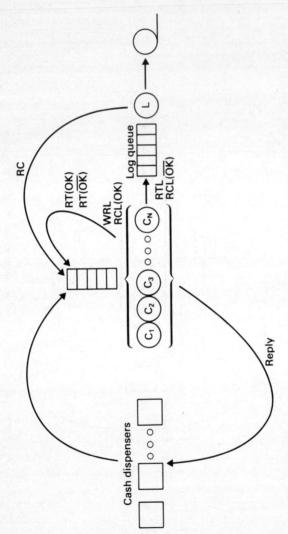

Fig. 7.9 Multiple-queue, multiple-process transaction processing system

This collapsing process can be taken to the limit, leaving a single process with a single queue operating in FIFO mode. This has a clear disadvantage in that the system will be unable to do anything else while the single process is waiting for a peripheral transfer to finish on behalf of the transaction at the head of the single queue. We can handle this easily, however, by having several independent processes all taking transactions from the single queue. With N processes we can handle N transactions concurrently. Each process is quite general in that it will process any transaction type and hence can traverse any of the system code. In such a system these identical processes are usually all given the same priority level. This is a common technique in transaction processing. It allows both simplicity and control. Under this regime our simple system would look like Figure 7.8. The number of processes used would depend on the amount of concurrency that could be achieved, instead of on the amount required—i.e. it would not depend on the throughput required.

This single-queue, multiple-process mechanism brings with it a number of problems. Since the processes are now independent, the queue may no longer be dealt with in strict FIFO fashion. This may not be important in many cases, but in others it may be critical. For instance, the order in which updates are made to a database may need to be carefully controlled if the database is to be kept consistent. If this is so we need to compromise our simple solution by reinstating a separate queue and process for transactions requiring strict temporal processing. Figure 7.9 shows our simple system with the logging queue reinstated to ensure that log records appear on the log tape in chronological order of their generation. Figure 7.10 shows in time-order the progress of the transactions that result from the arrival of a valid withdrawal request. It can be followed through against Figure 7.9. The waterfall nature of the mechanism is now evident.

We have reached the point with our simple example where we can identify the form of the general transaction processing system. It consists of a network of queues between which transactions flow. Each queue is serviced by one or more processes depending *inter alia* on whether strict chronological processing is required or not. Each queue also has related to it the code that is required for processing the transactions that appear on that queue. A process for a queue traverses the part of that code relevant to the type of the transaction it is dealing with at any one time.

A great many real-time systems can be dealt with in this way— particularly those offering the same service to a number of simultaneous 'users'—people, other computers, traffic lights, aircraft and so on.

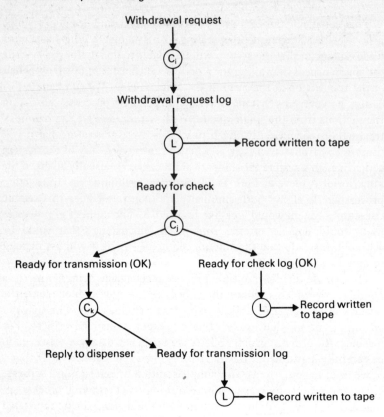

Fig. 7.10 Cascade of transactions

7.7 Summary

In this chapter we have dealt with some of the detail of real-time systems and this has in some cases meant getting down almost to a programming level. This should not, however, distract attention from the wide variety of real-time systems in common use and the essential characteristics of real-time systems: the production of timely output, the recording of what has happened during system operation and the ability to cope with system failure and provide a reliable service.

8 Data communications

8.1 Introduction

Data communications traffic is increasing by an estimated 35% per year, as more and more organizations establish links among an enormous range of devices. Systems analysts find themselves becoming increasingly involved with projects utilizing different hardware and software to enable these links to be established.

In this chapter we examine the data communications considerations that the analyst must take into account when charged with the task of designing a system that will transport data from one place to another. The different hardware devices will be covered individually before we see how they can be linked to create, or become part of, a network. In addition to covering the different networks and modes of transmission for remote devices, we also examine the interconnection of local devices to form a LAN (local area network).

Systems utilizing data communications often need a considerable amount of applications programming effort. However, this task has been eased considerably in recent years with the advent of systems software products such as data communications monitors, network control programs, database management systems, etc. We will be investigating the functions of these software aids and the impact they have on the systems analyst and the applications programmer.

8.2 Systems design considerations

The design of data communications systems requires an analyst to consider a range of new systems factors. These should cover at least:

(1) *Method of transmission.* Does the amount of data to be transferred, and the speed with which it must be transferred, necessitate the use of telecommunications links at all? If the system is not particularly time-critical it may be feasible and very much cheaper, to transport the

input and output via road or rail, using one of the many different postal and courier services available. Most business organizations already have telex equipment which can be utilized to transfer data and, although telex operates at a slow speed (some 300 characters per minute) and has a limited character set, some of its newer features mentioned in Chapter 9 make it a worthwhile practical proposition for some applications. If a telecommunications link is required, do the speed and volume of transmission require a conventional dial-up link, a leased line or a faster wideband circuit? All of these questions are examined in more detail later in this chapter.

(2) *Currency of information*. How accurate and up-to-date must be the information that the system provides? If terminal users are to access data for enquiries, what problems will arise through data being last updated the night before, or at the end of the previous week? If the end-users are given the facility to access an on-line system for both enquiries and updates, what different problems may this cause?

(3) *Input and output*. How will data be collected for input? Collection and batching of data for transmission at the end of the day is a cheap and easily implemented solution, but will it really enable us to meet the user's needs? If each item of input data is to be entered as soon as it becomes available, this will entail higher costs and require a more sophisticated solution, but may meet a user's needs more closely. What medium is required for the output? With an on-line system, the amount of output is usually small and displayed on a VDU screen; is hardcopy of the output required instead of, or in addition to, a display? With a batch system, the amount of output may be large and a printer of some description may be essential. If so, careful thought must be given to the speed of the device itself and also the interface equipment which will facilitate its attachment to the processor.

(4) *Ease of use*. Much importance is now placed upon designing systems that are 'user-friendly'. A system that is to be accessed by an end-user who may be a clerk or a storeman must be much easier to use than the on-line systems typically used by programmers and operators in the normal course of their duties. Instructions and responses need to be in plain English with facilities provided to help the user if he gets stuck. Good back-up documentation must be provided which includes an explanation of the correct connections and switch settings for the hardware devices at the user's end (typically the modem, telephone, control unit and the terminal device itself).

(5) *Response time*. We have already examined the question of the currency of information but we also need to determine the response time the users will need. This is defined as the time interval from

entering a transaction at a terminal to receiving the generated response at that terminal. Poor response times from a bank's computer system, for example, may result in a long queue of frustrated and angry customers at a cash dispenser.

Response times depend on terminal type, modem type, circuit, system software, central processor speed and workload and, while a good response time may be available at 8.30 a.m. when six users are connected to the system, the situation may be very different at 10.30 a.m. when fifty users are accessing the system frequently.

(6) *Reliability and flexibility.* The impact of different hardware and software failures upon the users must be accurately gauged. Some computer installations have on-line systems which can be reconnected almost instantly to another processor should the first one fail, thus the problem at the central site is transparent to the user. However, failure of the central processor often means that no service at all can be provided for the end users until the fault is corrected; this may mean a delay of ten minutes due to a complex hardware malfunction.

The failure of a control unit may render a cluster of terminals inoperable, whereas a modem or terminal fault may only affect one user. Duplication of all components of the network would obviously make for a highly resilient system but the cost would be prohibitive, so the areas where reliability and flexibility are most needed must be carefully studied. Some of the systems implications are considered in Chapter 6.

(7) *Security and integrity.* Initial access to a central computer from any remote device usually entails a number of checks performed by the system software to ascertain whether the user has a valid identifier and password. However, a system designer must also consider the need to restrict access by authorized users, to ensure that each user may access only the files and tape/disk volumes that contain his data. It may also be desirable to restrict certain transactions to authorized users only; for instance, a storeman in a warehouse may have 'read only' access to a database whereas his supervisor can make updates. Back-up copies of files must be made at appropriate intervals so that if disaster strikes it is possible to recreate both files and complete databases within a reasonable time span. Fortunately, many of these requirements are now catered for automatically by system software.

8.3 Terminal devices

The hardware devices available to permit data transmission via the PTT networks are many and varied and need careful selection.

Consideration must be given to such factors as:

- Volume of data to be transmitted
- Line protocol to be used
- Pattern of data transmission
- Speed of response desired
- Reliability required
- Flexibility desired
- Cost
- Transmission code to be used

Interactive terminals may be either synchronous or asynchronous in their mode of transmission. Synchronous transmission is often referred to as block transmission, as a complete block of data is transmitted in one single operation. Asynchronous transmission is often referred to as 'start-stop' because only one character at a time is transmitted.

8.3.1 Synchronous transmission

Synchronous terminals must have the ability to insert control characters at the beginning and end of each block of data to facilitate message routing and error detection and recovery. To support this mode of transmission the modems at either end of the telecommunications link are synchronized. This is usually achieved through a timing mechanism incorporated in the modems, enabling the receiving station to sample the line at the correct time intervals to receive the incoming bits and assemble them into characters. Consequently the modems are relatively sophisticated and thus expensive, but synchronous transmission enables the user to make use of more sophisticated facilities such as full screen editing. Many of the terminals in this category emulate the IBM 3270 range of VDUs, typically operating in the speed range of 2400 to 9600 bits per second. These devices are connected to the modem via a separate control unit, which can support several VDUs and thus enable a number of terminals to share one telecommunications link (Figure 8.1). Synchronous terminals typically employ a 7- or 8-bit code such as ASCII or EBCDIC.

8.3.2 Asynchronous transmission

Asynchronous terminals are simpler and cheaper than their synchronous counterparts and can be attached to the telecommunications network via an acoustic coupler or a slow-speed modem. An acoustic coupler consists of two rubber cups into which the two ends of a

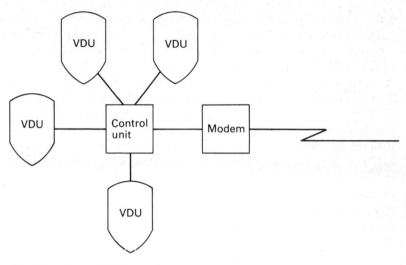

Fig. 8.1 Several VDUs sharing one telecommunications link

telephone receiver can be placed, thus making an acoustic connection rather than the hard-wired connection which a modem requires. However, asynchronous terminals using acoustic connections are easily affected by even minimal interference on the telephone line. The terminals in this category may be VDUs or printer/keyboard devices. Many of the cheaper, slower terminals employ the 8-bit teletype code and work at speeds as slow as 110 or 300 bits per second. The terminals will support editing capability, though not as sophisticated as the full screen editing of synchronous devices, and can usually buffer a number of pages of output. The printers usually utilize either a thermal print mechanism or an impact mechanism (e.g. daisy wheel or golf-ball). The thermal printers are quieter but require specially treated paper which is more expensive. Some impact printers have the advantage of being able to produce multiple copies when fed with multiple-part stationery. Typical printer speeds in characters per second are:

Golf-ball	15 cps
Daisy wheel	55 cps
Ink jet	90 cps
Dot matrix	180 cps

8.3.3 Batch transmission

Batch terminals, or Remote Job Entry (RJE) terminals as they are often called, typically consist of a card (or diskette) reader and line printer with an integral control unit. They typically support 80-byte card image input and 132 characters per line printer output. They are all synchronous devices which usually operate in a speed range between 2400 and 9600 bits per second. Each batch terminal connected to a central processor requires a parameterized system set-up which enables the user to 'sign on' to the system using a unique identifier. Most batch terminals can be used only for job input or job output at any given time—not both simultaneously. However, a 'multi-leaving work station' may have both card reader and line printer functioning simultaneously because of intelligent interleaving of line traffic and use of buffer storage areas. The speeds which can be expected of the line printer depend on the quality of the data communications line, the type of print line to be produced and the printer character set; a rule-of-thumb guide with speeds shown in lines per minute is:

$$2400\,\text{bps will drive a printer at } 120\text{--}180\,\text{lpm}$$
$$4800\,\text{bps will drive a printer at } 260\text{--}340\,\text{lpm}$$
$$9600\,\text{bps will drive a printer at } 600\text{--}700\,\text{lpm}$$

So far we have confined our discussion to conventional interactive and batch terminals, but many other devices (which may be dubbed minicomputers, microcomputers, distributed processors or even word processors) may function as terminals for all or part of the time.

The physical connection of a terminal device to a modem should not pose any problems as practically all of these devices adhere to the V24 (or RS232 in the USA) interface. This is a CCITT recommendation which ensures that standard cables and connection sockets are used between terminals and modem.

8.4 Interfaces for data communications

Telecommunications links between hardware devices may consist of:

- A dial-up telephone line
- A leased telephone line
- A high-speed wideband data link
- A satellite link

For the majority of applications the choice lies between a dial-up or leased line telephone connection. Although many users are under the impression that heavy terminal use is essential before a leased line becomes cost-justifiable, a leased line can be cheaper if the average use is as little as 90 minutes a day; a simple calculation can be used to work out the cost. A leased line should also be of better quality and thus support faster data transmission and many modems can be provided with dial-up backup capability in the event of the leased line being out of action.

8.4.1 Multiplexer

Another way to reduce line costs is to employ a multi-port modem or a multiplexer. Up to four terminals can be connected to a multi-port modem and thus share one telephone line, but the combined speed of the terminals attached cannot exceed the modem's maximum speed rating; for example, four 2400 bps devices could be attached to a 9600 bps multi-port modem, or two 4800 bps devices could be attached,

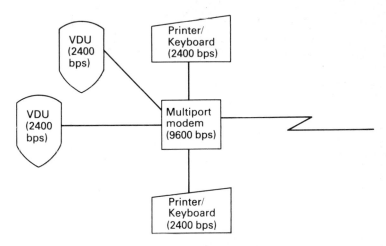

Fig. 8.2 Four 2400 bps devices linked to a 9600 bps modem

or even one at 7200 bps plus one at 2400 bps. Figure 8.2 shows four 2400 bps devices linked to a 9600 bps modem.

Multiplexers have more extensive line-sharing capabilities and may support a large number of devices of many different types. Multiplexers are often sited at remote branch locations of a business organization and linked to a large central mainframe. Thus devices may be attached to their nearest multiplexer by a local dial-up connection and so reduce the cost of a long-distance call. A multiplexer is also required at the CPU site to bring together outgoing signals and demultiplex input signals. This is shown in Figure 8.3.

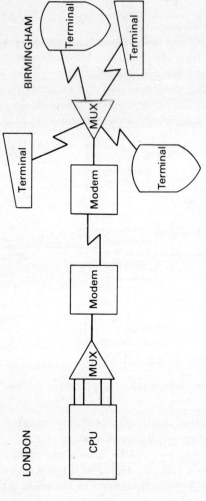

Fig. 8.3 The multiplexer at the CPU site brings together outgoing signals and demultiplexes input signals. Note that further modem links are needed at the remote location, between multiplexer and terminals

Multiplexers enable devices to share one high-speed link, either by dividing the bandwidth into different frequency ranges or alternatively by dividing the enter bandwidth into time slots—known as frequency division multiplexing (FDM) and time division multiplexing (TDM) respectively. One problem with non-intelligent TDM multiplexers was that if a connected device had nothing to transmit when it was sampled, the multiplexer would pad out the time slot for that terminal with 'idle' bits. Statistical multiplexers have enough intelligence to switch quickly to the next terminal and make the best possible use of all the time slots. Thus, transmission time is allocated only to channels that have data to be sent and the multiplexer can support a number of terminals whose combined bit rate is greater than that of the communications link. If at any time data traffic exceeds the capacity of the link, excess data is temporarily buffered within the multiplexer.

8.4.2 Concentrators

A concentrator also has certain line-sharing capabilities and is often employed as a 'store and forward' device. It can be sited at a location

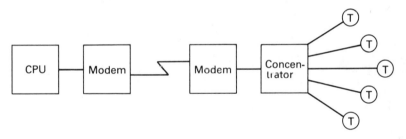

Fig. 8.4   A concentrator disseminates to multiple terminals a message received from the CPU

remote from the central computer and can disseminate a message received from the CPU to multiple terminals, as shown in Figure 8.4. This makes it an excellent device for message-switching systems.

8.4.3 Front-end processors

To ease the workload on the CPU most networks employ a front-end processor, sometimes referred to as a communications controller. This device may be purpose-built to control the communications network or it may be a standard minicomputer which is employed solely for this task. The predecessor of the front-end processor was a hard-wired box called a transmission control unit (TCU) which had only physical control of the lines in the network; more sophisticated functions such as error checking, code conversion, polling and addressing were supported by the CPU. The FEP now performs these functions and consequently the CPU is free to concentrate more on processing user programs (see Figure 8.5).

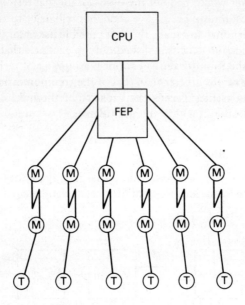

Fig. 8.5 Front-end processor: M = modem; T = terminal

Where multiple CPUs exist in a large network the FEP may be employed to decide which CPU should handle input from a terminal and then to establish a connection between the appropriate CPU and terminal. This method is commonly employed in large international time-sharing networks.

8.4.4 Data encryption

Because of the dangers of unauthorized tapping of a telecommunications link, data of a confidential nature can be scrambled by a data encryption device before transmission over the public network and then unscrambled at the receiving end. The position of the data encryption device in the network is shown in Figure 8.6.

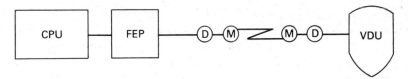

Fig. 8.6 The position of the data encryption device (D) in the network; M = modem

8.5 Data communications networks

Having covered the different hardware devices which comprise most data communications links, we can examine some of the different methods available for connecting these devices into networks of different types.

8.5.1 Conventional services

Most large mainframe computer users employ a supervised network, where the CPU is in overall control of the entire network; although it may delegate certain functions to both local and remote communications controllers, this type of network will often utilize just one powerful CPU and may have hundreds, or even thousands, of terminals connected to it. Alternatively, a large organization may have a number of CPUs in different geographical locations which are linked to form a multi-tier network. This can be used to enable terminals to link in to their local CPU for most applications and also to link to another CPU if necessary, which may support a different operating system as well as different applications. A simplified example of this type of network is shown in Figure 8.7.

A simpler network may consist of two communicating computers linked by a point-to-point link, or a number of communicating computers comprising a multi-point network. Instead of operating as a supervised network, a multi-point set-up may operate in contention mode. Consider the example shown in Figure 8.8 where four minicomputers are linked together. None of these minicomputers is in overall control of the others: they operate in contention mode—meaning that when one wants to communicate with another it sends a signal down the line to 'bid for the line'. It is possible for each of these devices to communicate with the other three even if there are not direct connections between A and D, and between B and C. If A wishes to transmit to D it can send the data to B and request B to forward it on to D.

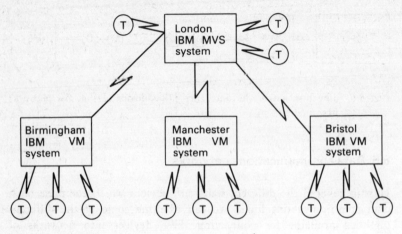

Fig. 8.7 Multi-tier data communications network

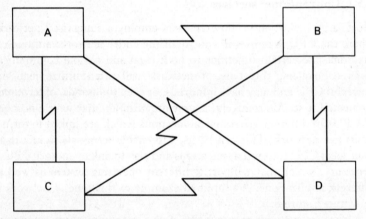

Fig. 8.8 Four minicomputers operating in contention mode

All of the networks mentioned thus far typically utilize, in the UK, the conventional British Telecom Datel services, using either dial-up or leased lines or a wideband circuit. However, considerably more flexibility can be built into a network by the use of a packet switched network or viewdata.

8.5.2 Packet switched services

The Packet Switched Service (PSS) involves the sending of data over 48 000 bps trunk circuits in 'packets', each containing up to 128 characters, plus an address code and a sequence number for error checking and correction purposes. British Telecom estimate that this will bring the service to within local-call range of some 60% of the users of the Datel services. There are now packet switching exchanges (PSE) in London, Reading, Bristol, Birmingham, Cambridge, Manchester, Leeds, Slough, Liverpool, Newcastle, Glasgow and Edinburgh.

In operation, a user makes a connection with his local PSE and enters his data, which is assembled into packets at the PSE and forwarded to its destination's nearest PSE. The packets are transmitted between the PSEs at high speed and different packets may travel via different routes depending upon line availability. The PSE at the destination end ensures that the contents of each packet have been transmitted successfully and that all packets are in the correct sequence before they are transmitted to the receiving station.

Packet switching provides advantages in both flexibility and price. Terminals can transmit data at their optimum speed regardless of the speed of the receiving device. Price is important because the charges are based primarily not on the duration of the connection or the distance over which it is made, but on the volume of data transmitted. It is said to be particularly economic over long-distance telephone links greater than 56 kilometres.

Figure 8.9 represents four terminal devices transmitting data to a mainframe computer centre.

The first packet switched network was DATAPAC, which was opened in Canada in June 1977 and established the now internationally accepted X25 standard. This CCITT recommended standard permits interconnection between packet switched networks and opens up tremendous scope for the users to link to many different services around the world.

France introduced TRANSPAC in 1978. EURONET, as its name implies, is a European network with nodes in London, Paris, Rome and Frankfurt and access points in Dublin, Brussels, Amsterdam, Copenhagen and Luxembourg. In the USA, two mainly privately operated PS networks are in operation: TELENET and TYMNET; several others are planned for implementation.

8.5.3 Other networks

Some networks are offered by computer system manufacturers which are not based on X25. This locks the user into one manufacturer's product list until other suppliers can provide protocol emulation. IBM's System Network Architecture (SNA) is a classic example of this.

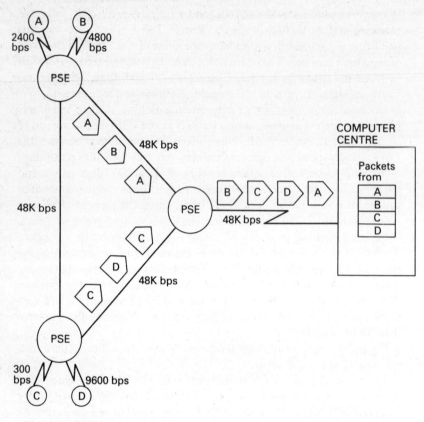

Fig. 8.9 Packet switching: four terminal devices transmitting data to a mainframe computer centre

SNA provides a number of potential benefits to a large IBM user:

- It allows any terminal in the network to access any application program in the host mainframe.
- It frees the user from many communications management responsibilities.
- It provides for reconfiguration of the network during normal use.
- It centralizes network control.
- It allows several host mainframes to be serviced by one communications controller.
- It allows terminals using the Synchronous Data Link Control (SDLC) protocol, and accessing different applications, to share communication lines.

- It provides for automatic reconfiguration of links in the event of a failure.
- It enables remote modem diagnostic tests to be made from the host site.

GATEWAY enables a conventional PRESTEL (British Telecom's VIEWDATA service) user to be connected via the PRESTEL computer to an external private computer. The link between PRESTEL and the external computer is provided by the Packet Switched Service (see Figure 8.10). Access to computers via GATEWAY means that

Fig. 8.10 GATEWAY: a PRESTEL user connected via the PRESTEL computer to an external private computer

television sets can be employed as low-cost terminals to permit access to a myriad of applications and huge encyclopaedic databases.

8.5.4 Local area networks

There is an increasing requirement to link together a range of devices for intra-office communication and this is now possible with the use of a Local Area Network (LAN). These LANs (see also Chapter 9) are not dependent on a powerful central processor and can handle data transfer rates far higher than those possible over an ordinary telephone connection.

A LAN consists of a piece of cable—which may be coaxial, a twisted pair, a ribbon cable or a fibre optic link—which runs around a building with connection points at regular intervals and is similar in concept to an electrical ring main. It may form a continuous loop—a ring, in networking terminology—or it may start at one end of a building and finish at the other. LANs are not necessarily limited to one building: the cable can link buildings and there are more advanced links that enable LANs to bridge the gap between tall buildings in close proximity.

LANs are technically capable of carrying data, text, voice and video traffic and although the initial installation costs for the wiring are extremely high, adding devices to the link is easy.

Inter-company communications are also possible, enabling one company's LAN to link to another via the public network, although one obstacle to this is the wide range of different transmission protocols that may be used by different equipment. However, a considerable amount of effort is being put in to the development of protocol converters which would enable a wide range of different devices to communicate regardless of the fact that they spoke different languages.

8.5.5 Digital communications

The networking limitations currently imposed by our aged analogue communications network will be alleviated by the advent of more sophisticated equipment which will facilitate digital transmission. This huge project of equipment replacement will take many more years and consume vast sums of public money; it will be well into the next century before the whole of the UK has been converted, but a phased transition is already well under way. The user will benefit from higher transmission speeds and lower equipment costs. Modems will become redundant and a much simpler interface will be employed.

In the UK, British Telecom is having to become more 'marketing-oriented' now that its monopoly has been relaxed and it is having to compete with aggressive competition from the private sector. BT are thus introducing a package of proposed digital services collectively called X-Stream. Five services are proposed for introduction by 1985 in most of the major UK cities. Kilostream will offer 64K bps data transmission via leased line. Megastream will support voice transmission speeds of up to 8M bps. Switchstream One is the existing PSS. Switchstream Two will provide System X facilities such as multi-party connection, automatic call re-routing, etc. Finally, Satstream will support high-speed voice and data transmission routed via satellite between dish aerials at the subscriber's premises.

8.5.6 Network control and programming

Whatever type of network is employed, control of that network is essential. In a large supervised network there is usually a network control section at the mainframe site. This provides a central 'help' facility for users who are having problems in communicating with the mainframe, since users may have little or no knowledge of their own terminal equipment and how it is connected to the computer.

The programming of a data communications system is obviously somewhat more complex than that of conventional batch processing systems. Some of the problems the communication systems programmer must consider are:

- Different terminals with different speeds will access the computer.
- Different data codes may be used by different terminal devices.
- Good error detection/recovery procedures are needed.
- Messages from terminals may need queueing, routing and priority scheduling.
- Input may arrive at random intervals.
- Input and output may be of variable length.
- Terminals may need polling and addressing for I/O operations.
- Terminals/computers may need automatic dialling and answering capabilities.

To cope with all these highly complex programming requirements a wide range of software products is available both from computer manufacturers and independent software suppliers. The use of these products allows the application programmer to concentrate on the application programs required to solve a given communications-oriented problem.

In early networking systems the programming capability usually remained entirely in the host CPU but these days the software is often distributed between the CPU, the front-end processor, the terminals and their controllers. We need to examine, therefore, the following categories of communications systems software:

(1) Telecommunications access methods.
(2) Network control programs.
(3) Data communications monitors.
(4) Database management systems.

(1) *Telecommunications access methods* simplify and reduce the amount of user programming necessary to enable terminal users to access a user application running within the computer; they are part of the operating system. To use the access method, the application programmer simply issues the appropriate read or write instruction. This automatically generates the appropriate I/O instructions. The facilities of the access methods are incorporated into the operating system at the time it is generated (tailored to meet the user's needs) and loaded into his system.

The access method software makes it easier for the programmer:

- to define the communications system;
- to activate and deactivate the system;

- to provide dialling and answering on switched lines;
- to send and receive messages on switched lines;
- to poll terminals and receive messages on switched lines;
- to address terminals and send messages on leased lines;
- to perform code translations;
- to manage buffer storage areas;
- to detect and handle errors.

(2) In most modern systems the *network control program* is a software product which resides in the front-end processor. We have already seen that the FEP exists to free the CPU from much of the routine work involved in supporting a data communications network. The network control program provides such functions as:

- Communication line time-out control.
- Error checking.
- Character assembly on input.
- Character disassembly on output.
- Control character recognition.
- Polling and addressing terminals.
- Control character insertion for output.
- Control character stripping for input.
- Performing code translation.
- Dynamic buffering.

Note that some of the functions of the access method and the network control program are the same; this illustrates just how the FEP can take over work which would otherwise have to be done by the CPU.

(3) *Data communications monitors* and (4) *Database management systems*. Although the databases are covered in detail in an earlier chapter it is appropriate at this stage to review the data communications software which permits access to databases.

To enable remote users to access a database it is necessary to provide 'database/data communications' software (DB/DC). This software provides an interface between the operating systems and the application program and isolates the application programmer, as much as possible, from the details of data handling and communications control. This enables application programs to be more immune from the effects of changes in the format of the data and changes in the hardware devices used. It thus has the additional benefit of reducing application program maintenance requirements to a minimum.

The DB/DC software is usually provided by some form of data communications monitor and a database management system. Perhaps the best known DC monitor is IBM's Customer Information Control System (CICS), which provides support for on-line systems in much the same way as the operating system supports batch processing work, the information updated through on-line transactions also being available to batch processing programs. It provides for relatively quick implementation of new applications and can handle changes in the volume of on-line transactions, database organization and terminal configurations. A DC monitor such as CICS permits access to resources by maintaining a number of tables which hold detailed information on:

- the terminals allowed to access the system, their address, type and priority;
- the transactions which may be invoked, their priority and security identification;
- the programs valid for execution within CICS, their location and source language.

When a user signs on to the system these tables are used to verify his authorization by checking his identification and the password provided. CICS can further check his authorization to enter a particular transaction, or to use a particular program or file, and will determine an overall priority for a transaction by checking the individual priorities of the operator, terminal and transaction. The data integrity features ensure that only one user has access to a given section of data at a time. Common database management systems (DBMS), such as IDMS, TOTAL, IMS and ADABAS, look after the data handling, access, updating and security of the database itself. As business organizations implement more databases, there is a need to relate data in one with data in another; to facilitate this, it is possible to use a DB/DC data dictionary which provides for unique definition of data in a number of databases through the use of one common data dictionary.

The process of accessing database via DB/DC software can be broken down into a number of steps as follows (see also Fig. 8.11):

(1) A user keys in a transaction through a terminal.
(2) The transaction is written to a log file on tape or disk.
(3) The transaction is scheduled for processing according to priority and placed in a queue.
(4) The transaction is examined to determine which application program is required.
(5) The application program is loaded into main storage and given control of the system.

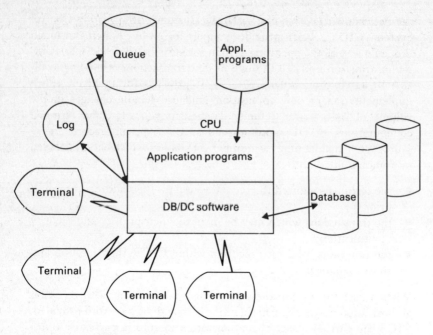

Fig. 8.11 DB/DC interface between operating systems and application
program

(6) The program acts upon the transaction; any data transfer to or
from the database is handled by the DBMS.
(7) If the database is to be updated, a 'before and after' image of the
updated record can be stored on the log file.
(8) The appropriate response is sent to the terminal which origin-
ated the transaction.

The log file, which contains all the transactions in chronological
sequence, and a copy of the database, which is taken at regular
intervals, can be used to recreate the database in the event of a disaster
such as 'head crash' on a database disk.

8.6 Summary

The continuing growth of on-line systems makes it essential for the
systems analyst to appreciate fully the special considerations relating to
communications between users and applications. The type of hardware
required at the user's end is often dictated by the type of hardware

already installed at the processing location. However, a number of options are usually available and, having decided upon the type of terminal (or processor) and modem, etc., there is a very wide choice of equipment from many different manufacturers. Much of the communications system programming is automatically handled by systems software products such as telecommunications access methods, monitors and network control programs.

The programming effort required from applications programmers is now made considerably easier by the advent of sophisticated data communications monitors. These products allow the user to generate a specific system configuration and define the environment in which it is to take effect. Such software aids obviously reduce the costs of implementing an on-line system, simplify installation and maintenance, and should provide tight security and good response times.

The range of data communications users, and the speed of data transmission, will increase dramatically in the next few years with the advent of more and more high-speed digital links, satellite services and System X facilities. These will further fuel the growth in data communications traffic as the feasibility of on-line solutions to an enormous range of problems increases.

9 Office automation

9.1 The challenge of office automation

Explosive growth is occurring in the application of computing technology to 'office systems', as opposed to 'data processing systems'. As people costs increase and equipment costs fall, it becomes increasingly attractive to use more capital equipment and to employ fewer people making better decisions. Implicit in this dream is that fewer people will be employed and that they will make better decisions: not necessarily the case. Equally implicit is a belief that such change can be accomplished. Right now, no one knows where the office of the future lies—apart from in the future! Equally, the role the systems analyst will be called upon to play is emerging with as much pain as did his original incarnation in the 1950s and 1960s. In this chapter we can do no more than point to some of the directions which could be followed.

Trends
The cost of staff is increasing more quickly than the gains in productivity available with old technology equipment. Fortunately the cost of new technology information processing equipment is falling. In communications, the use of satellites and optical fibres replaces copper at a fraction of the cost; in processing, more powerful computers are available at substantially less cost than the products they replace. The newer electronic storage devices are becoming less expensive and will probably eventually be cheaper than paper as a medium for mass storage.

Many office technology devices such as the telephone and facsimile copiers only fulfil their function if they are connected to similar devices, and to be effective they require an adequate population of compatible devices and a communications infrastructure with agreed international standards. For the same reasons, facsimile transmission has suffered from the small number of installations and the incompatibility of different suppliers' equipment. However, recently introduced international standards are resolving the problem of compatibility. The installed voice telephone networks have also been used for data communications between computers, but in general terms the communication of other than voice messages has been held back by the absence of adequate communications infrastructure and common standards or protocols. This is changing quite dramatically.

European PTTs (telecommunications authorities) are now rushing to introduce Packet Switched Networks, which are ideal for the occasional user who wishes to send low volumes of data or messages to other users of the network. Unlike telephone charges, the tariff is not based upon distance: for the cost of a local telephone call one uses a service charged by volume, i.e., the actual number of 'packets' sent. There are now also agreed standards for a new network Teletex which will supersede Telex, and this standard will clearly be observed by a wide range of equipment suppliers.

These developments, together with the liberalization taking place in the UK, significantly improve the prospects for the effective use of new information technology.

Office activities

There is considerable confusion and disagreement about how office workers—clerks, secretaries or managers—spend their time. Consequently the areas of activity in which productivity improvements through automation can be made are far from clear. This is not to say that improvement cannot be made, merely to emphasize that we simply do not know what happens in offices and that the use of productivity gains in factories as a yardstick may be misleading. What we do know—and most surveys show this—is that managers spend 40–50% of their time in spoken communication. Can office automation yield productivity gains here? Surprisingly, it can, since a quarter of this time appears to be wasted in telephoning people who are not there and consequently communicating with them in another way or adopting an even less efficient alternative. Other surveys have shown that half of all communications are internal to the organization; instead of speeding these up by automation, perhaps the systems analyst should be eliminating some of them. Similarly, surveys show that there has been little investment in improving office productivity. It would appear that pressures to reduce overhead costs have merely generated containment exercises rather than thoroughgoing reviews of office activities and systematic investment plans designed to introduce new and improved office technology-based systems.

There are, however, two kinds of improvement which are now beginning to be made in increasing numbers. These are concerned with cost displacement and added value. Applications that reduce the cost per unit of output, either by reducing total costs or by avoiding cost increases, are termed cost displacement systems. They focus on improving the efficiency of routine information processing tasks, either through providing better tools (mechanization) or by delegating tasks to the computer (automation).

The areas that have most commonly benefited from improved productivity are administrative typing support and administrative filing support. The former have been found to yield efficiency gains of the order of 20–50% time saving, the latter perhaps not so great but still providing significant space cost reductions. One organization, for example, was able to dispense with 5000 four-drawer filing cabinets previously occupying 32 500 square feet of expensive floor space—an attractive saving!

Applications that improve professional and managerial effectiveness and allow the organization to perform functions that were not formerly possible are termed value added systems. These applications can reduce paperwork, expedite communications and improve information gathering. They benefit the business through an improved quality of service, increased competitiveness and better decision-making.

9.2 The analyst's approach to office automation projects

The systems approach to problem solving is common to data processing and office automation systems. In this section we highlight some of the particular aspects of office automation projects.

9.2.1 Establishing functional requirements

Not surprisingly we are concerned first of all with what the users want from their system. In the main, the information gathered will be qualitative, based on interviews with a considerable number of potential users. However, with office automation projects it is as important to discover user attitudes towards a new technology and to find out on what experience these attitudes are based.

A recently conducted investigation resulted in the following functional requirements being identified. The technical solution in this case was to provide the entire executive board of a large engineering company with management workstations—an advanced application. The designed solution was required to provide:

- an internal correspondence in-tray for the receipt and review of reports, board papers, board minutes, memos and messages;
- authoring facilities for the origination, checking and revision of correspondence and reports;
- voice annotation of documents;
- internal messaging providing the facilities to send text or voice messages and internal documents between users of the system. This would avoid circulating papers, notes on memo pads and the need to remember to pass oral messages, and would address the problem of infrequent contact between busy and much travelled executives;
- appointments diaries with the provision for common access to arrange meetings;
- bring-up files to serve as automatic reminders;
- the maintenance of personal files with good indexing and retrieval facilities;
- common access to telephone directories, contact lists (names and addresses) and other useful index information;
- password-based security facilities to maintain the security and privacy of information;
- self-teach facilities;
- simplicity in use.

9.2.2 Data collection

The collection of data complements the information obtained from interview and is used to confirm the opinions expressed. Also it helps to 'size' the system requirement. Possible ways of collecting data in these circumstances include direct measurement, logging of activities and subjective recall of activities.

Direct measurement
The most comprehensive method of directly measuring office activities is to use a trained observer who keeps a record of the nature and duration of each activity and can add comments about external factors that influence the completion of an activity. The problem with this approach is that the presence of the observer is intrusive and may change work patterns and inhibit the conduct of certain activities. It may in general terms be unacceptable to the person being observed and sometimes the industrial relations climate in an organization may preclude this approach.

Other forms of direct measurement can be found, however, in the form of logs or procedures applied by the organization itself. These can include automatic telephone logging at the exchange (rentals can be arranged for once-off surveys), mail books recording mail arriving at or being sent from a central mail room, typing and telex records, and so on. Examples are as follows:

- *Automatic telephone logging.* Calls made, time spent on telephone, number of unsuccessful calls. Programmed exchanges now provide comprehensive information in this area.
- *Mail books.* Volumes of mail incoming and outgoing by department or individual. Occasional information by destination (e.g., internal van delivery used).
- *Telex records.* Copies of telexes to show length, destination and author.
- *Typing records.* From central pools on typing volumes and throughput, plus possibly an analysis of the mix of letters, reports etc.
  Copies of letters sent kept in files will show average length, destination etc.
- *File/library requests.* Where information is stored centrally, documentation on file movements shows the liveliness of the file, time out from central records etc.

Logging of activities
Activity logs require the user group being studied to keep a record of events as they occur. There are several variations to the logs:

- *Simple event logs* in the form of tick-sheets: these record the frequency of, for example, telephone calls within each of a number of set time periods (hours, days, weeks) or the number of interruptions by unscheduled visitors, colleagues etc.
- *Detailed activity-specific logs.* These can be used to collect rather more detailed information. Using the same example, they can be used to record the time and duration of telephone calls, whether they are incoming or outgoing, and some information on the content of the call.

- *Daily logs.* The purpose of a daily log is to record all of the events occurring in a day in order to gain a picture of the activity pattern of the clerks, managers or secretaries under investigation. The level of detail recorded against each activity may vary but, if the material is to be conscientiously collected, the amount of detail required should not become too onerous.

- *Project logs.* One way of gaining more detail about a range of activities without overburdening the respondents is to log activities related to specific and identified projects, rather than all activities in a day. Logs applied to specific projects also make it easier for the evaluator to follow through a sequence of events and identify sources of problems and frustrations associated with the completion of a task.

- *Tags.* The tag is a variant on the logging of an activity which is suited to pieces of work that pass through a number of stages. The tag is attached to the piece of work (e.g., a typing draft, invoice, order etc.) at the start of its processing within the office, and is completed at each step by whoever holds responsibility for that step (e.g. correcting a draft, retyping). The tag samples pieces of work rather than the activities of individuals.

Overall, the use of logs and tags can be a valuable source of data but should not be overworked. It may be necessary to collect data by using a series of logs for specific activities rather than attempt to collect all the sought data at one time.

Subjective recall of activities

Directly asking respondents how they spend their time and what are their main activities is the most straightforward way of gaining data about activities. However, comparisons of subjective recall with direct observation and logging techniques have shown that managers and other office workers substantially mis-estimate their use of time on specific activities. In particular, they underestimate time spent in discussion and on the telephone, and overestimate time spent reading and writing. More reliable data can be obtained if the subjective opinions are linked to some form of objective data, such as a simple log of events. The log can then be used as an *aide-mémoire* to the respondent in recalling and describing events.

9.2.3 Establishing the shape of the technical solution

It was implied earlier in this chapter that a recurrent theme of modern office automation is 'convergence' or integration. Consequently, one outcome of a strategy study must be a statement of the future overall 'shape' of the organization's processing, which will provide an understanding of where the processing centres should be, of the applications they should serve, and of where and how the data will be held. The shape is often affected as much by company style and politics as by technicalities. Where systems will rely on 'proven technology', establishing the technical shape can be fairly straightforward. Where there is doubt, however, about the technology, because it is very new and changing quickly, some technological cornerstones must be laid down before the technical shape can be ascertained.

The main point to be aware of is the wide variety of options now becoming available and the need to choose wisely. Not only must the equipment meet the company's needs, it must be cost-effective, secure, sufficiently reliable and have sufficient flexibility to meet changes in company organization. When addressing such questions it is very important to select a range of equipment that is compatible with both the current network and the network of tomorrow. For example, terminals initially intended to use normal modem connections may later be required to connect to a packet switching network or a local office network. A terminal that could preserve the user interface during the technical transition from one network to the other would obviously be of immense benefit.

Where a processing technique is novel and the techniques to install and use it are lacking, it is essential to run a pilot system to gain experience. The technical shape of processing will still have been conceived first, but can be regarded as provisional until proven by this means. The pilot experiments will be subsets of a realistic solution to the whole problem, and used to refine the technical strategy at each review. The aim will often be as much concerned with testing people's reaction as with learning about the technology itself.

9.2.4 Pilot trials

A pilot trial is an excellent way of evaluating opportunities and resolving technical issues—provided that it is managed properly. It can be an *ad hoc* exercise or part of a research programme to back up a strategic office automation plan. The following approach can be used:

- Identify new technology and significant opportunities within the business.
- Select appropriate versions of the technology and meaningful ways of evaluating it within the business.
- Cost justify a pilot as a research trial.
- Establish success criteria and monitoring methods in advance.
- Manage the pilot trial to evaluate:
    the performance of the technology
    the likely effect on the business
    its effect on people.
- Identify cost–benefit justification.

Pilot trials need not be expensive. The size of the trial can be kept to a minimum and suppliers are often willing to arrange special one-off deals. In some cases a bureau service can be used even though an eventual implementation might be assumed to require in-house invest-ment. Sometimes the trial can be simulated on existing hardware using rented software. Interfaces and peripheral functions can be temporarily patched together at minimal expense without invalidating the veracity of the main functions.

One pilot trial carried out by an analyst compared the use of word processing with the original methods for producing a standard range of company documents such as letters, memos, financial statements etc. (Table 9.1). The trial showed where the greatest savings could be made and what overall savings the company could expect.

Table 9.1   Percentage time saved by use of a word processor
Column 1: % reduction in time for each document type with use of word
   processor
Column 2: % typist time with use of original method
Column 3: % reduction in time achievable (i.e. 1 × 2)

Type of document	Original production method	1	2	3
Letters/memos	Electric typewriter	23	22.1	5.1
Reports	Electric typewriter	27	14.2	3.8
Standard letters	Magnetic card typewriter	66	41.5	27.4
Preprinted forms	Electric typewriter	30	15.2	4.6
Financial statements	Magnetic card typewriter	80	7.0	5.6
Total				46.5

9.2.5 Organization for office automation

It is clear that a profound change of attitude has been taking place since 1980. Office technology used to be seen as a specialist activity (provid-ing word processors for typing services etc.) and there was little awareness of the subject at general management level. Yet recently many organizations have established office automation steering groups. In some cases a senior management services manager is coopted, but the majority of members are usually senior managers with line responsi-bility. The existence of such a body certainly helps, provided that the group (a) recognizes the danger of spending too much time trying to learn about the technology and (b) concentrates its energies on the more important task of identifying business needs and opportunities. A steering group is no guarantee of progress, unfortunately: often the most difficult part is getting to the point of action—of actually getting started.

At a recent conference in New York one American executive recounted the following, highly pertinent story: 'We had this office automation steering group, which was extremely diligent. For nearly two years we evaluated this technology and considered that one, but without coming to any conclusion as to which way to proceed. Fortunately at this point the president issued a dictate—get off your fat butts and do something'. These words had the desired effect and the group proceeded to implement what appeared to be the best of a number of options. This was an electronic mail service linking the various factories, offices and sales branches. To the group's amazement, the company now has 900 regular management users, who each pay their own bills and who solidly endorse the cost-effectiveness of the system.

The analyst working without the support of such a steering group may have little chance of success or may be confined to low-level work. With the right backing, doors are opened, information gathering becomes possible and the technical solutions identified by the analyst are subject to immediate management scrutiny which, if favourable, will more easily lead to a full management commitment to implementation.

9.2.6 Company style

A key question to be considered during the planning is whether a particular strategic option best suits the style and experience of the organization. Naturally, every effort should be made to avoid duplication; we want to design a freeway, not just a series of unconnected bypasses. Unfortunately, this is not simple. In office automation some of the strategic options are fundamentally different because the range of functions is infinitely greater, and there is an ever-increasing number of specialist suppliers. However, a number of the established data processing suppliers have confirmed that they intend to remain in the much greater market for office automation equipment. Thus communications networks, word processing, document storage and retrieval voice messaging, viewdata, graphics etc. feature prominently in their product releases and promised future options.

Staying with a preferred supplier is a principle that commends itself to many managers, since it builds on existing relationships and avoids that 'head on the block' feeling which is inescapable when making a substantial commitment to a new supplier's equipment and software.

But reliance on a famous name is no substitute for a cool assessment of the company's own needs and opportunities, and a critical evaluation of what the market has to offer. For many organizations this may mean establishing a strategic office automation system from a different supplier, but one which can coexist with the previously implemented data processing systems.

Again, the organizational style of the company is important. The role played by the office and its relationship to other parts of the company vary enormously and need to be reflected in the design of appropriate information systems. In some cases the stimulus is provided by what competitors are doing.

9.2.7 Problems to overcome

Although it may seem to be straightforward to identify the opportunities and select the solution, the following checklist highlights some of the down-to-earth practical problems of implementing office automation systems.

- *Organization change.* Technology may facilitate a wider span of control and a flatter organization structure. It may encourage more working from home, more flexible working hours, and dispersal of office locations. Staff may come to expect more investment in the office design, style and equipment of the workplace.
- *Education.* Managers usually care about the efficiency of operations and of clerical activity. They seem to be complacent about their own effectiveness. They need to be re-educated into the systems approach and their own responsibility for it—for the last 20 years they have abdicated responsibility in favour of technologists. The key is to get an understanding of what is possible so that business needs are solved by technology and not vice versa.
- *Two 'cultures'.* There are those who take advantage of technology and those who reject it. This may lead to a polarization within an organization between 'haves' and 'have-nots', based upon age or educational differences.
- *Dehumanization.* Is the job of the person using the new technology enriched or dehumanized?
- *Fears for privacy and security.* Does the use of technology increase or reduce the privacy and security of information? Not least, does it lead to a transfer of control to new sets of people?
- *Ownership of information.* Most people's position and influence depend upon the information which they 'own' in their heads and

'bottom right-hand drawers'. Will the automated office lead to a loss of 'ownership', and hence be a threat to people's positions and prospects?

- *Management of expectations.* Some people are impatient and expect change to happen 'yesterday', they will have to be restrained. Other people do not want change and will have to have their expectations raised.
- *Job change.* 'Does it make my job more or less easy/interesting/useful/powerful/rewarding?' 'How will I learn to use the new technology?'
- *Commitment/coordination.* There needs to be a long-term commitment and a coordinated programme. A good analogy is with a freeway—developed piecemeal and only part completed it has limited value.
- *Phasing of implementation.* The office of the future will not happen with a 'big bang'. There will be a long period of partial and imperfect systems coexisting with well-developed people-based and paper-based systems. Both will exist alongside traditional DP systems which will not be fully integrated with office automation systems for some years.
- *Existing investment.* Existing paper and computer systems are complex and have been developed at high cost over a great many years. These are not to be lightly discarded.
- *Generalized housekeeping rules.* A common dependence on office-wide electronic systems may necessitate rules and standards for the entry, storage and disposal of electronic material.
- *Technical system management.* A quality information system which facilitates the easy retrieval of relevant information will necessitate powerful and complex 'behind the scenes' systems management. This will depend upon information specialists, hardware and software.
- *Union attitudes.* Some union opposition to the introduction of technology in offices has already arisen and has concentrated either on job redundancy or on the supposed health hazards from visual display units. If, however, some pundits are correct and the information revolution will have bigger and more profound impact than the industrial revolution, union attitudes may well assume greater importance. Some unions in the UK have well-thought-out new technology policies and negotiating positions.
- *Legislation.* In the UK the British Telecom monopoly restricts some of the options available, although this is becoming relaxed. In other countries legislation has been enacted which prescribes the

storage and/or communication of certain types of information. Legislators like to legislate and this may increase—encouraged by popular fears.

9.3 Components of office automation

This section deals with the components of office automation. It covers text, voice and image information, and gives a brief résumé of some of the new communications systems.

9.3.1 Text processing

Word processing
Word processing is the most fundamental change in the basic mechanism of the typewriter since its invention a hundred years ago. It takes advantage of microprocessor technology to provide improved keyboard facilities to the typist, secretary or author and electronic storage for text held prior to printing. This separation of keying from printing provides the bulk of the productivity gain because stored text can be corrected, revised and incorporated as standard paragraphs or standard letters without rekeying. Printing is usually performed on 'daisy wheel' letter quality printers at speeds of 500 words per minute; dot-matrix printers produce draft copy at considerably higher speeds. Depending upon the mix of work, the productivity gain will certainly be 10% and may be many hundreds of percent. Most word processing operators react strongly to any suggestion that they might return to conventional typewriters because they appreciate the improvement in working efficiency which the modern system represents. According to some classifications, there are seven different types of word processor ranging from 'blind' systems without screens, to others with a 'thin window' display, and finally full screen displays. It is the last type which commands the most attention because of the benefit which follows from being able to see the layout of the text displayed prior to printing.

Screen-based word processors are commonly classified as:

(1) Stand alone   A single system which is provided with keyboard, display, processor, backing storage and printer.
(2) Shared logic   A system in which a cluster of keyboard/displays share a common access to storage and printers via a central processor.

An authoritative study of word processors has identified over 80 salient features which are potentially important in the selection decision. Table 9.2 gives a few examples that illustrate the range of features possessed by different word processors.

Table 9.2 Typical features of word processors

Storage capacity	Mini diskettes holding 38–40 pages each. Diskettes holding 60–100 pages each. Disk drives holding 800–32 000 pages each.
Screen size and type	Thin window display of e.g. 40 characters. Display screen 80 chars × 24 lines. Display screen 80 chars × 64 lines (A4).
Vertical scrolling	Facility to 'roll on' text when the bottom of the screen is reached.
Printer character pitch spacing	10, 12 or 15 char/inch (i.e. PICA, ELITE, etc.). Proportional spacing (i.e. professional print quality).
Right justified margin	Ability to produce columnar text as in a newspaper (usually in conjunction with proportional spacing).
Temporary margins	Paragraph indent and tabulation control.
Automatic file merging	Variables, standard lists, standard paragraphs, etc. can be easily composed into finished documents.
Block move	Ability to move whole paragraphs, etc., around within a document.
Column delete	The system deletes the first column, then automatically moves all other columns to the left, e.g. on a monthly accounting report.

Text retrieval

The importance of text-based information systems may be of new significance to systems analysts concerned with office information, but for others—librarians, research scientists, lawyers—it has long been recognized. The importance to such people of bibliographical storage, indexing and retrieval led many years ago to the development of computer-based systems appropriate to the characteristics of text and user requirements.

It is important to recognize at the outset that data is precise and definable and that text is imprecise and open-ended. The difficulty with text is that content and context together make up meaning.

Most systems for text storage and retrieval have their basis in three files:

(1) *Word list:* a complete list of all words contained on the data bank. This is used at 'edit' time to identify the occurrence of new words on the input documents.

(2) *Inverted index file.* This can be regarded as a direct access alphabetical index of all words with cross-references to all documents containing each word. It is common to have a 'stop list' of words that are not to be so indexed (e.g. the, and, not, for, by etc.).

(3) *Document file:* a file containing the actual documents, abstracts, summaries, etc.

The editing of input documents and updating of the inverted index of every word not on the 'stop list' is a heavy processing task which is typically performed in batch mode overnight or at weekends. In contrast, searching of the inverted index file for occurrences of combinations of words is a relatively trivial task which tends to impress the onlooker with the speed and power of the system.

A number of packages are available which basically conform to the above description but which follow one or other of two schools of thought. This description is quite apt because the pros and cons are debated with academic intensity by their advocates.

(a) *Free text system.* This is basically as described above and is relatively easy to set up and operate. Examples are STATUS (developed at Harwell) and STAIRS (developed by IBM), both available as mainframe packages with powerful on-line search capability. STATUS is also available on many minicomputers and in the UK as a bureau service.

Opponents of such systems would, however, allege that the quality of retrieval efficiency suffers from a 'Garbage in, garbage out' approach to information handling, and that information tends to be entered in a relatively unselected way.

(b) *Free text system with thesaurus.* This is as (a) but with the added burden of responsibility for maintaining a thesaurus in which word meanings (including synonyms and antonyms) and word relationships (e.g. 'Cod' is a member of 'fish' family) are established for all words that are to be indexed. This implies greater quality control scrutiny at input stage and it is common to 'extend' the text of a document with added terms or keywords which in the opinion of the indexer will improve retrieval efficiency at search time. An example of such a package is ASSASSIN (developed by ICI); thesaurus options are also available with STATUS and STAIRS.

The thesaurus can be used at search time as follows:

- If insufficient material results from the first search, reference to the thesaurus will suggest ways of 'broadening' the search.
- If too much material results from the first search, reference to the thesaurus will suggest ways of 'narrowing' the search.

A microprocessor-based version of ASSASSIN has recently been released under the name HOMER.

Electronic mail

Telex and the public mail service are being challenged by new technology which will transport documents from point to point faster and more efficiently. This includes the latest facsimile transceivers capable of unattended operation and a speed of approximately 35 s per page.

A number of organizations are already using word processors for electronic mail, either linked to the existing Telex network or else communicating directly with similar compatible word processors via telephone links. The opening of the Packet Switched Service (PSS) network by British Telecom has provided a powerful stimulus to this approach and links to international networks will benefit many organizations. The favoured option for future electronic mail is commonly supposed to be a mail-box service which has at its centre a computer capable of interacting with a particular terminal (word processor, teletype, telex etc.) that stores the resultant message or document and then forwards it to the mail-box of the addressee. Such mail-box services have been widely used for some time on the USA common carrier data service and more recently the first systems have been launched in the UK—COMET by BL Systems, and BT GOLD by British Telecom.

Videotex

The distinguishing feature of Videotex systems is the use of a modified domestic colour television for text-based information systems.

Teletext. This generic term describes broadcast television services which use spare bandwidth to broadcast news pages to modified domestic televisions. For technical reasons the capacity of such a system is limited to about 200 screen pages. Examples in the UK include the BBC's pioneering service Ceefax and ITV's Oracle; similar services exist in other countries.

Viewdata. Another British first was the system invented by Sam Fedida for the British Post Office—Prestel—which is now being widely adopted and copied throughout the world. Such systems go under the generic name Viewdata (Videotex is the term more widely used internationally).

The brilliance of this concept is that it exploits the two most commonly used and accepted communications terminals, namely the telephone and television. Connect them together via a special interface decoder, and dial-up telephone line to a central processor: a powerful, simple-to-operate, low-cost colour terminal is available for use.

While, regrettably, public use of Prestel has fallen well short of expectations, business interest in Viewdata has been dramatic. This has encouraged a number of suppliers to market systems aimed at the business user.

Two typical examples illustrate the potential of this approach:

(a) *Motor vehicle manufacture.* A major car manufacturer has arranged to use a Viewdata system. All of its major dealer/distributors are to be equipped with Viewdata terminals able to dial the central Viewdata computer. If a potential customer enters a showroom and asks for a model/colour etc. not in stock, the dealer identifies the nearest available car, arranges an exchange of stock, and completes the sale.

Benefits

- The customer is satisfied quickly. The crucial issue is that he is not allowed to leave the showroom unsatisfied.
- Unusual items are sold more quickly.
- There is a better turnover of stock.
- A dealer carries less stock.

Problems

- The system requires an extra transportation infrastructure to be devised and operated as more cars move from dealer to dealer.
- A dealer is contractually bound to accept an exchange. This may be an inhibiting factor.

(b) *Holiday tour operators.* Many of the major UK tour operators have implemented systems which are available to the many thousands of travel agents. An increasing number of the latter now have Viewdata terminals installed which they use to access not only the tour operators' systems but also Prestel.

The holiday tour operators' systems not only provide up-to-date holiday information but also act as a 'gateway' into their seat reservation/booking systems.

Benefits

- Every marginal seat sold above break-even is highly profitable.
- Agents are not frustrated by telephone bottlenecks.
- Tour operators' administrative costs are reduced.
- The customer is satisfied quickly.

Phototypesetting

Phototypesetting is the modern process to produce 'professional' quality printing. The difference between word processors and photo-typesetters is narrowing. Both now have the QWERTY layout key-board. The majority have a screen of some sort, a microprocessor and program logic to control their performance. Nearly all have diskettes for magnetic backing storage. Both have sophisticated abilities to record text off the keyboard, revise it, and compose it for final output. The difference is that the word processor usually hammers an ink-impreg-nated ribbon against ordinary paper whereas the phototypesetter uses light-sensitive photographic paper. This is very much more expensive than normal paper but the quality of the final product is quite suitable for a book, magazine, or newspaper. The advantages of photosetting are:

- Much improved quality.
- Text is more easily and quickly assimilated.
- Up to 50% more text per page.
- 'Professional' presentation on every page.

Phototypesetter technologies have gradually converged to the point where they are now appearing in typing locations. Machines to convert text recorded on word processors into a form compatible with the photosetter are also now becoming available,

9.3.2 Voice processing

Voice communication is the dominant medium for information transfer between people. Man has a natural preference for face-to-face dialogue and it is widely believed that other sensory factors are important contributors to effective communication, for example, facial and hand expression—both components of body language.

Although face-to-face communication is preferred, the use of the voice is so important that the telephone constitutes a very useful and necessary alternative. However, according to a widely quoted statistic only 28% of telephone calls are successful. This is to say that in 72% of cases failure occurred because:

- the call was misdirected;
- the number was engaged;
- the relevant person was not available.

Most organizations are responding by trying to provide a more effective telephone system.

Private Digital Exchange (PDX)
The facilities available to a telephone user are constrained by what is available on the public service and by the features of the exchange to which he is connected. The electromechanical telephone exchanges in use for almost 100 years are now being superseded by electronic exchanges. An electronic exchange which is part computer is termed a Stored Program Control (SPC) exchange and offers users certain advantages through its ability to be reprogrammed instead of rewired.

The latest development is the emergence of the digital exchange in which the switching as well as the control is a computer operation. Public exchanges being introduced in the UK of the pure digital variety are of the System X design, while organizations can now obtain Private Digital Exchanges (PDX), carrying British Telecom approval, from a variety of suppliers. For the moment the telephone exchange plays its traditional role of voice telephone and data communications switch. However, increasingly, PDX suppliers are advancing the claims of their systems to be the 'nerve centre' of the automated office, encompassing text handling, data storage and image processing.

Examples of the facilities available on electromechanical, SPC and PDX exchanges are given in Table 9.3.

Table 9.3 Typical features of telephone exchange systems

Enquiry and transfer	An extension engaged on an external call can make an enquiry call to another internal extension and return to the outside caller when the enquiry is completed. The extension can also transfer an outside caller to another extension if required. These two actions are carried out automatically by the user without recourse to the operator.

Night service	Allows incoming exchange line calls to be answered from extension telephones when the switchboard is closed down.
Trunk barring	Controls the types of public network call that extensions can make. Access can be controlled to suit the business needs of the user, e.g. long-distance calls cannot be made at peak price times.
Group hunting	Extensions may be put into hunting groups for incoming calls, the call being offered to the first free extension in the group.
Absent extension transfer	If an incoming call to an extension is not answered in a set time it is automatically transferred to another extension.
Dictation access	Automatic telephone access to centralized dictation equipment.
Paging access	Connects to a paging system and enables extensions to call paging receivers by automatic dialling.
Direct dialling in	Incoming calls from the public exchange can be routed automatically to the required extension by direct dialling by the exchange line caller.
Operator controlled conference	The operator can set up a conference between an exchange line caller and a number of extensions.
Abbreviated dialling	Enables any commonly dialled number to be replaced by a two- or three-digit code.
Call booking—automatic call-back	When a call is made to an engaged extension the handset can be replaced; when the extension becomes free the caller is automatically rung back and the call is connected.
Refer back (brokers call)—repeated enquiry	During an enquiry call the originating extension can alternate between both parties without having to redial the number of the enquiry extension.
Extension controlled conference	An extension can set up a conference with a number of other extensions. One exchange line caller can be included in the conference.

Executive intrusion	Allows an executive to break into an existing internal call on a busy extension.
Follow-me transfer	Allows incoming calls to be diverted temporarily to another extension, diverted again from the second to a third extension and so on.
Call information logging	Enables details regarding exchange line calls to be recorded for later analysis. Note that the conversation is not recorded, the information being confined to: originating extension number digits dialled duration of call date/time.
External number repetition	When an outgoing exchange line call fails, e.g. number engaged, the number is stored and automatically redialled on command.
Data protection	Prevents either operator or executive intrusion on a busy data line.
Call pick-up	Enables an extension to pick up and answer a call that is ringing unanswered at another telephone.
Do not disturb	Incoming calls to an extension can be temporarily barred.

Voice messaging

It was noted earlier that 72% of telephone calls are unsuccessful. If this is aggregated across management and staff in large organizations, the cost implications are staggering. A further argument in favour of improved voice messaging facilities is that the successful 28% also have a negative effect because:

- they interrupt the person being called and break his thought processes, disrupt conversations or meetings etc;
- call time is wasted on pleasantries etc.

The contention is that a powerful voice-messaging system would increase the proportion of 'successful' calls and reduce the number of 'interruption' calls—and hence improve overall effectiveness. The favoured approach is to provide a store and forward voice-messaging facility on an office automation system. In its concept and mode of operation this is very similar to the electronic mailing of text messages.

Current examples of systems that provide voice messaging are the Information Management Processor (IMP) from OTL, the Alliance from Wang and Xibus from Xionics.

The IMP principal workstation supports voice input/output by handset or loudspeaker. Easy-to-use tape-recorderlike controls and volume control permit instant replay of voice messages which have been stored digitally on disk. Alternative uses are:

- send voice messages to other users;
- dictate and send for audio-typing;
- add voice annotations and commentaries to drafts and other stored documents.

In the last use a loudspeaker symbol alerts the reader to the existence of a voice note at a defined place in the text.

Voice recognition

It is surprising to discover that over 1000 voice recognition systems have already been installed worldwide. All but a few of these might be termed simple systems, capable only of accepting a limited size vocabulary. Nonetheless market forecasts expect explosive growth for this type of product as follows:

1983 sales forecast	\$155 million to \$340 million
1988 sales forecast	\$1 billion to \$1.5 billion

Accompanying this is considerable R & D expenditure on the development of advanced systems capable of recognizing any word from any speaker.

A typical simple voice recognition system consists of a number of operator terminals each equipped with a lightweight noise-cancelling (to eliminate background noise) head-mounted microphone with cable connection to a local recognition processor. This typically drives a local strip or screen display and also interfaces to a host data processing computer. For even greater flexibility it is possible to substitute telephone, tape-recorders, or wireless microphones for the normal cable-connected microphone.

The voice recognition terminal consists of:

- An audio spectrum analyzer which converts the analogue speech to a digital representation.
- A processing algorithm in ROM which transforms the digital input to a compact characteristic template.
- A series of stored vocabulary templates in RAM. These would

originally be generated by the designated operator(s) during a training session.
- RS232C ASCII interfaces to the terminal display and host computer.

Such terminals are capable of accepting data at up to 180 words per minute and achieve 99+% recognition rate, with a vocabulary of 40 to 370 words depending on the model. Prices for single terminals start at around £1500 (1982).

Voice recognition terminals are typically installed in situations where the hands are needed for principal tasks which would be interrupted if the alternative were keyboard data entry. Examples of application include:

- Quality control inspection.
- Vehicle assembly lines.
- Cash and carry checkouts.
- Cartography digitization.
- Credit control verification.
- Use by handicapped persons.

9.3.3 Image processing

Image-handling equipment, such as microfilm readers, facsimile (FAX) transceivers, photocopiers, has been the Cinderella of office technology and illustrates the gulf which has existed between the data processing professional and the office analyst. To the former the equipment is crude, of low technical content and generally beneath his dignity—yet at times he is aware of a feeling of guilt and he sporadically introduces systems which make use of imaging techniques, for example, using microfilm as an output medium. The office analyst has no such inhibitions; image equipment is generally of low cost, easy to understand, easy to operate and has a high significance in his scheme of things.

Microprocessor technology promises to change all that. It makes image processing respectable for the DP professional and gives the office analyst more opportunities to improve office efficiency. The latter recognizes the importance of an image as an information form, not only in the pure picture sense (diagrams, illustrations etc.) but as the means of capturing information which could not economically be handled as data (e.g. documents originating outside the organization).

However, the present situation of imaging is one of discrete technologies existing independently of each other. It is therefore sensible to review each of these in turn.

Micrographics

Most analysts are familiar with microfilm and microfiche and are aware of examples of their use. This will certainly include the realization that micrographics not only provides archive storage but is an acceptable alternative to on-line retrieval for many applications. A visit to the bank or a motor car accessory firm will quickly demonstrate that ease of access to reliable up-to-date information is a practical possibility.

Computer Output Microfilm (COM) is an output technique which can be considered as an alternative to line printers or image printers. Most companies with a COM application start by using a service bureau that converts magnetic tape output to microfilm or microfiche; the crossover point at which it becomes economic to install an in-house COM recorder lies between 200 000 and 500 000 pages per month.

One of the main shortcomings of micrographics, however, has been the inability to update the output records, although some newer systems do now offer an updating facility.

Facsimile (FAX)

Traditionally FAX has the reputation of slow speed and poor quality and transceivers from different manufacturers have not necessarily been compatible. Slowly the image of FAX is changing, helped by the emergence of international CCITT standards to which all manufacturers (with any sense) conform. The highest speeds and image qualities are achieved by machines that use digital representation of image data allied to data compression techniques. The current speed record is 35 s for an A4 page, with every manufacturer striving to better the speed and quality of his rivals.

The standard set by CCITT recognizes three primary groups of equipment:

Group 1 Facsimile devices which operate at 6 min with FM (frequency modulation) analogue modulation. A 4-min speed is also included in this class as a manufacturer's option.

Group 2 Facsimile devices which operate at 3 min with amplitude modulation (AM). A 2-min speed is also included as a manufacturer's option.

Group 3 Facsimile devices which operate at 1 min employing digital techniques and which may utilize redundancy reduction and bandwidth compression to enhance speed (e.g. to 35 s).

FAX is unique for the international transmission of picture images of documents and the UK Post Office now also offers a public service from certain public post offices.

Optical character recognition (OCR)

OCR has been around long enough for most analysts to appreciate its potential for data capture. Whether used on turnround documents or for capturing handprint numerics and special control characters from input forms, it forms the cornerstone of many implemented systems.

What is new is the emergence of reliable low-cost handheld scanning wands and low-cost document readers. Historically, document readers started at £100K whereas today for £10K one can obtain a very reliable hand-fed page reader. This is particularly useful as an adjunct to a word processing centre for capturing documents produced on electric typewriters, or existing documents/manuals typed before the word processor was implemented.

Handheld OCR wands are widely used in point-of-sale and inventory recording applications.

Image digitization

This inelegant expression refers to the use of an (electronic) pen and writing tablet to generate drawings or data. The result is normally shown on a graphics display screen and can be amended at will. In this way drawings, handwritten messages or notes, signatures etc. can be entered into a computer system as digitized images.

Laser printers

Non-impact laser printers score over conventional printers not only in increased speeds of output (e.g. 18 000 lines per min = 2 pages per s) but, especially, in the variety of print fonts and images that can be produced. The quality of the printed output thus exceeds that of a conventional computer printer by orders of magnitude. Laser printers are still expensive and justification usually depends upon:

- high average volume, i.e. over one million pages per month;
- peak workloads with critical deadlines;
- special graphical applications which traditional printers are unable to handle.

9.3.4 Office communications systems

Although Chapter 8 has dealt with data communications in detail, in this section we highlight some of the particular features of data communication in office systems.

Telex and Teletex

International telex networks have been in existence for many years and

analysts are familiar with their capabilities in providing electronic mail
links between locations and to suppliers and customers and of some of
the inefficiencies of telex preparation and distribution.

A multiplicity of devices now exist which aim to increase telex
efficiency. Many are similar to word processors in that they permit
efficient off-line preparation and editing of telexes and provide facilities
for automatic dialling and reception. Large users may implement a
telex 'switch' capable of supporting a number of satellite terminals in
unattended mode. An alternative approach is to use existing typewriters
or word processors by installing special attachments which produce
punched telex tape. Thus a number of secretaries may prepare their
own telexes and the tape can then be transmitted in the normal telex
terminals.

Teletex is a recently approved CCITT standard which aims to
supplant telex with better facilities and service. These include much
higher transmission speeds and support for a wide repertoire of
characters to allow the free use of various European character sets,
upper and lower case, etc.

Specifically, Teletex will provide:

- network-independent procedure and protocol;
- worldwide character set which includes graphic characters;
- choice of underlying network by the national PTT;
- terminal specifications for hardcopy and video terminals;
- addressing, directories and international numbering;
- interworking with other services, such as telex, Facsimile and
  Videotex.

West Germany is the first country to implement Teletex and most
European countries are committed to its introduction over the next few
years.

Packet switched networks
PSN was covered in detail in Chapter 8; of importance to the office
automation analyst, however, are the value-added services which grow
up around PSNs. In the USA two large networks, TYMNET and
TELENET, include in their value-added services access to proprietary
databanks. With various European PTTs now rapidly implementing
national packet networks—e.g. PSS in the UK, TRANSPAC in
France, Datex-P in Germany—these services are likely to grow and can
already interconnect under a service called EURONET which provides
access to a number of European databanks.

Local Area Networks (LAN)

Teletex and PSS provide dramatically improved facilities for improved communications between locations, but LANs represent new ways of communication within locations.

A typical LAN supplier defined his development objectives as follows:

- Open networking—freedom to choose the best equipment from different suppliers.
- High speed—to cater for a large number of users including the high data rates associated with voice and image.
- Resilience—avoidance of system failure, typically by duplicating key facilities; hardware is cheap!
- Comprehensiveness—covering all types of information.
- Security and privacy.

LANs are now in pilot operation in a number of organizations; two examples are given below.

(1) *Cambridge ring derivatives.* A cable loop is laid around the building using coaxial cable or twisted pairs (as appropriate), to which are attached the various user devices. Each is attached via an 'intelligent socket' which is capable of transmitting and receiving packets of data from the ring. Packets circulate round the ring and are sensed by each intelligent socket in turn. If the destination address corresponds to the device attached to the socket it is output onto that device, and the packet is sent back to the originating address with an acknowledgement flag set.

An empty socket can be filled by any data waiting in an intelligent socket's buffer.

A minimum configuration will include a central communications controller, which is associated with detecting incipient malfunctioning on the network, and also a file server to provide central filing and store and forward functions.

(2) *Ethernet.* Ethernet is a coaxial cable to which are attached connectors, transceivers and hence devices. The term 'Ethernet' implies that transmissions are out in the 'ether', which is being continuously sampled by all the transceivers to see if any signal (i.e. data) exists for a particular device. If so, it is received and output to the attached device.

LANs represent an area of dramatic development, with almost daily announcements of new systems and additional facilities.

Viewdata
The general arrangement is as for Integrated Office Systems, with central minicomputers handling file storage and communications. The most obvious difference is that the workstation is typically based upon a Viewdata television set, either in colour or black/white.

Private Digital Exchange (PDX)
PDX suppliers have announced their intention of supporting the full range of office activities with direct connection of workstations, file storage, etc. to the PDX.

9.4 Summary

At the beginning of the chapter we said that no one knows quite where the office of the future lies. There are, however, some clear indications of the components of this office and of the problems which analysts will be called upon to resolve.

Firstly, there will be dramatic social and organizational change. It is fashionable to believe that this will occur only in the long run, but we believe that it would be prudent to expect this long run to be a good deal shorter than is commonly supposed. We can equally expect this change to be painful. Chapter 10 discusses the role users are demanding for themselves in the design of their systems. Sadly, the evidence of practical implementations shows that these ideas are not generally understood. Without this understanding, the implementation of automated office systems will be revolutionary in more ways than one!

One can clearly see, however, the application in a step by step process of a variety of facilities implemented to improve efficiency in specific areas. Word processors, telex switches, electronic telephone exchanges, microfilm retrieval terminals etc. will all have specific application in most organizations. However, those organizations that have already achieved the most progress in this respect all seem to have arrived at a similar conclusion. This is that to increase office services efficiency, though valuable and desirable in itself, is only to target 20% of the cost. The name of the game should be to improve the effectiveness of managers and professionals, who not only constitute 80% of the cost but, more important, are responsible for the value of the output of the organization. The end objectives are better quality products and services made available on time, cost and customer satisfaction.

This conclusion seems to lead towards an integrated management system which will enable routine work to be handled more efficiently, while providing easy access to information and the ability to exchange it freely with one's colleagues. Such systems apparently now exist and are being implemented by many organizations.

A day in the life of tomorrow's office
On arrival at your desk, having disposed of your coat, exchanged pleasantries and obtained coffee etc. you switch on your desktop screen terminal. This is a high-resolution screen, flicker-free and with clear representation of text and graphics. You use black and white or colour according to preference and need.

You check your diary and list of reminders—including forward dated ones automatically brought forward—by pressing an appropriately labelled key, and you then probably also look to see if there are any new messages waiting for you. These have been entered by colleagues elsewhere in the building, at branch locations or even from home—stored and forwarded on the system. Messages can be replied to at once and are automatically forwarded to the originators or redirected to colleagues, or left on the DESKTOP (an electronic pending file) or else discarded.

If you next want to deal with other routine work you action some of the reminders to yourself and also work through your electronic in-tray. Having scanned each document in turn you discard some (to WASTE-BIN), aside others (to DESKTOP), mail some to colleagues—with perhaps a voice comment attached ('Bill, will you please deal with this, more in your line . . .'), and reply to others. Replies can be spoken, using the handset or microphone attached to the workstation, keyed or else dictated for a secretary or typist to key into the system.

Your in-tray also contains letters, memos and reports which have been typed for you by your secretary or typist and are now waiting to be checked. If you want to correct any mistakes yourself—it hardly seems sensible to print off and annotate the original and then wait for it to come round again—you can do it directly. Other documents are draft reports from colleagues for your comment. You voice annotate or key comments according to personal preference.

You regard your system not only as an essential communications tool but useful also to facilitate improved information retrieval. Therefore you file away useful and important documents and messages from the in-tray, sometimes using traditional hierarchical filing structures by assigning a document to an (electronic) file, within drawer, within cabinet. In other cases you see a need also to be able to access by content and you request the system to index by content, perhaps including some extra keywords added by yourself.

Progressing beyond the in-tray, you now attend to work outstanding on your action list: budgets to be revised and updated using spread-sheet calculation facilities on the system; progress reports to be updated with comments on the latest month's events. Requests for information cause you to examine stored files of information. Mostly these are text supplemented by graphical representations and digitized image/picture copies.

It should be apparent that most of the activity described so far is able, in tomorrow's office, to take place at home. Indeed, as a place from which to deal with routine work, review, analyze and draft, the home has much to commend it.

Typically, the reason for being at the office is to attend meetings, appointments and discussions and there will be no excuse that the minutes or papers failed to arrive or were late—these things are produced and circulated promptly to all via the system. The discussion does not get bogged down for want of the correct information or document—a terminal in the meeting room services that need. Audio conferencing enables you to involve a distant colleague in answering a specific question, and if he needs to 'see' the item you are discussing you telemail him a copy so that he can make his contribution effectively. At main branch offices the conferencing facilities can go beyond audio conferencing and telemail to provide also full video conferencing, so that participants can see each other.

Satellite transmission, national and international packet switched networks etc., mean that the sending of messages, documents, pictures and conferencing are all possible cheaply on an international scale.

In a snapshot—much routine work will be performed at home (or in the village community bureau if you prefer). Telecommunicating and teleconferencing will change 9–5 work patterns and the incidence of journeys between company locations. However, the organization will need to stimulate interpersonal synergy of ideas if an electronic bureaucracy is to be avoided. Hence, though routine meetings may diminish, conferences or seminars and brain-storming sessions will expand. The emphasis will be on stimulating and exchanging ideas, assisting personal development and satisfying our natural desires for social interaction.

10 Social aspects of information systems

10.1 Introduction

All organizations need information systems in order to function effectively. Every information system, whether for a one-man business, a parish council, a multi-national corporation, or the government offices of a large industrial nation, is made up of a number of components. Some of the components are artefacts—pencils and paper, word processors, computers and communication networks, operating systems and procedure manuals—but all information systems require people to construct, work with and operate the artefacts. Even a completely automated information system still requires people. In practice, then, information systems rely on people using and interacting with the artefacts.

Information systems vary enormously in the extent to which they rely on formal and structured information-handling techniques as against informal, often *ad hoc* and subjective techniques. All information systems use some elements of both. In Figure 10.1 we show a model of an information system illustrating the relationship between the different components and showing the formal and informal aspects. The information system exists in a real world which consists of objects, some concrete, such as machines and stock and buildings, and some abstract, such as budgets, accounts and sales forecasts. The system uses people (customers, managers, suppliers, clerks etc.), rules (embodied in legislation, in company procedures, in rule books and in codes of practice), norms (often deeply engrained ways of doing things and modes of thinking and practice) and commands (such as standing orders, checklists, etc.).

The information user in Figure 10.1 has to perform some task in relation to the real world. He may be a manager taking a decision or a clerk carrying out a task, but whichever he is, he needs information about the real world. Sometimes this can be obtained directly by, for example, walking into the store to check how much stock of a particular component is left; or the information can be obtained by the use of a

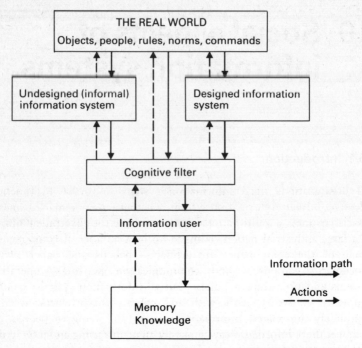

Fig. 10.1 Relationship of the information system with the real world

formal designed information system. This might consist of a stock ledger card on which receipts and issues had been entered, or alternatively it might consist of a computer stock system which the manager could interrogate to discover the level of stock by using the terminal. He also has a third option open to him, in that he can call up the stock-room supervisor and ask him how much material there is in stock. In this case he would be using the informal information system. Most information systems have these three major information sources: the real world itself, which can be inspected; the designed information system, which is intended to provide an exact image of the real world; the informal information system which sometimes substitutes for the designed system and which is often used to provide qualitative or evaluative information about the real world.

10.2 Types of information

A useful starting-point for the analysis of our model of an information system is to classify information according to three basic types—

descriptive information, probabilistic information and qualitative information.

To operate an enterprise it is necessary to make use of a great deal of data which describes the real world. This data attempts to provide a picture or map of the real world with sufficient accuracy so that a planner or a decision-maker can take appropriate actions, even if he is in fact at some distance from the world in question. This descriptive information describes the rules that govern or constrain the activities of an enterprise and these rules are often part of the designed system. A good example of this is the rule book of an industrial enterprise, which sets out in considerable detail the operating procedures to be followed by the workforce. Another example is the standing orders used in banking systems, which are instructions for the bank to make specific payments at a specified time to a specified payee. In many administrative systems the legal statutes which the system exists to apply—for example, the payment of social security benefits—are translated into instructions by means of a code of practice set out in a manual. The computer program, too, is the embodiment of a set of rules in the form of instructions and forms a part of the designed system. Commands also, however, exist in the undesigned informal system. They arise out of situations which are often unplanned or unforeseen and where immediate decisions are needed.

In practice the picture of the real world provided by the information system, its files and databases, may not correspond to the actual situation in the real world at all because the system may be incapable of providing a totally accurate view of the real world. There may be many reasons for this. In general, a formal system is based on the recognition of 'legitimate' transactions. Many systems, however, are subject to interference from unrecognized or non-legitimate sources. An inventory control system, for example, may be subject to petty pilfering of which the formal system has no knowledge. Informal practices may exist which go unreported, such as the storekeeper's habit in one company of issuing 36 inch stockings as 34 inch when he ran out of stock of the latter.

Information users therefore have to be aware of the extent to which the description of the real world that they are using is valid. One of the most common problems with computer-based information systems is that if the picture of the real world provided by the computer system ceases to be trusted, those expected to use it develop alternative sources of information—informal unofficial systems—or even attempt to sample the real world itself and to circumvent the designed information system.

Although descriptive information attempts to replace the real world of events by symbols which map the real world, it is not always possible to do this. Sometimes the real world has to be inferred from a description of a sample or by making guesses based on assumptions about the statistical behaviour of the real world. Information systems include large amounts of information which is inferred on the basis of assumptions of statistical distributions and behaviour and this kind of information is called probabilistic information.

Probabilistic information attempts, on the basis of statistical regularities and knowledge or guesses about the future, to provide a model of the real world in the future. All planning systems, for example, rely on predictive information and, to the extent that real world activity behaves in a regular way, it is possible to predict future activity by the use of these techniques. In more complex cases it is not possible to observe and measure all the relevant variables or even to know which of the many variables are relevant. In such cases it becomes necessary to construct a model of the real world and to simulate its behaviour. This is done, for example, in the construction of an economic model used by government forecasters to plan for the effect of tax changes and so on. Because these kinds of model are based on simplifying assumptions about the real world they can often provide only an approximate guide to the behaviour of the real world and are often dependent not on facts, but on assumptions derived from the designer's own preconceptions and personality.

Both descriptive and probabilistic information represent the objective real world as it is or as we expect it to be. However, if we have to plan future action or take decisions we need to know not only the facts about the real world but also some of the explanations and reasons that have given rise to these facts. In other words, we need to know about a variety of qualitative elements relating to the real world. To an extent this can be provided by the formal information system, but in this case the range of possible explanations has to be foreseen and some mechanism devised which enables these explanations to be encoded into the system. It is impossible, therefore, for formal information systems to provide the richness of explanation that a less formal system can provide. The tone of voice and the phrases used in a spoken reply can give the questioner a much better insight into the real cause of the variance that may be being explained than any number of formal written reports. Formal systems therefore are often supplemented by informal systems so that qualitative information can be provided.

While most designed information systems deal in objective verifiable data which supports the operational, planning and decision-making function of the enterprise, we do need to recognize that sometimes the information system is used for the purpose of shaping attitudes, beliefs and behaviour. In all organizations political processes are at work and the raw material for these processes is information. The information is selected, manipulated, presented, or concealed in such a way as to gain the maximum impact. To individual managers the availability of information thus represents power in the bargaining process and they may hoard information for use in their day-to-day negotiations with employees, customers, suppliers and so on. As a result, it may prove very difficult for the systems analyst to persuade information hoarders to release certain kinds of information for incorporation into the organization's database.

One of the most common complaints from systems analysts is that users cannot make up their minds what information they need and that, when the system is implemented, users demand different information. Studies have also indicated that what managers say they do in order to make a decision varies considerably from what they actually do when faced with a decision-making situation. One reason for this discrepancy, and for the difficulties faced by systems analysts trying to assess the information needs of managers, is the frequency with which the cue to take a particular action comes from an unexpected source which was not anticipated as being relevant when the system was first discussed. Because the source is unexpected, or the information was not thought to be relevant at the time the formal system was designed, this information cannot form part of the formal designed system. Although comprehensive databases with powerful query languages can help to overcome this difficulty, it is important to realize that information users will always make use of informal undesigned systems to supplement the formal designed system provided by the systems analyst.

10.3 How information is used

Different people use information in different ways and how a person uses information depends on a number of factors. Some of these are generic and some are related to the particular environment or situation in which the information is received. In understanding the social apsects of information systems, it is worth while to bear in mind the following factors which have a substantial influence on how people use information:

(1) Cognitive style and preference of the user. Some people prefer

and better understand information presented to them in the form of pictures or graphs. Others prefer narrative text, some preferring information presented formally whereas others prefer a more informal freer style. What determines a person's preference for the way information is presented to him is not well understood, but it is clear that it differs considerably between different individuals. As a consequence, even quite simple messages may be interpreted differently by different individuals. Complex messages, such as those involving the description of a complicated sequence of events or the rules embodied in a contract or, perhaps, set out in a systems specification will almost certainly receive many interpretations.

(2) Remembered knowledge. The working of memory is not well understood either, as there is no way of measuring what is in a person's memory or how that information is accessed, nor of discovering what knowledge the person possesses. Nevertheless it is the association of information received through the senses with the knowledge stored in a person's memory that determines the response to the received message and consequently the resulting action. Two people may thus respond quite differently to the same message and interpret the same structure in different ways.

(3) Language. All information is conveyed to us in the form of signals or messages and to be meaningful these need to be embodied in a code or language. Natural languages are very rich in the variety of information they can accommodate, but they are inherently ambiguous. Conversely, formal languages such as mathematical notation and programming languages can be very precise, but may lack the capacity to cope with a wide range of concepts. Consequently we have a situation where language, memory and cognitive style operate interdependently and their operation is often rooted in the individual's culture, education and experience. An understanding of the importance of these factors suggests that some approaches to the design of systems are to be preferred to others and we shall explore this later.

(4) Environmental factors. In addition to the generic factors already described, a number of environmental factors influence the way in which a person responds to information and which type of information source he may prefer to use. These environmental factors include his understanding of and his trust in the designed system, the trust placed in the judgement of his peers and subordinates, the time available to respond and take action, the pressure of work and the convenience or inconvenience of looking at the real world.

An information system is thus a *social system* that uses information technology. The extent to which information technology plays a part is increasing rapidly and it is impossible to design a robust and effective information system which incorporates significant amounts of the technology without treating it as a social system. It is not enough to design a technical system and then to make it 'user friendly', or to tell the designer to remember to take account of human factors.

10.4 Social policy issues

Social policy issues have a considerable effect on how people react to information technology and they therefore exert a material influence upon the work performed by the systems analyst. At the macro level—the level of public policy and the nation—a number of issues have received a great deal of attention in recent years and will no doubt be the subject of debate in the future. While these issues are of concern to the practising analyst, and may indeed have direct relevance to the system he is working on, we can only deal with them here in summary.

One of the major motivating forces in redesigning information systems has been to displace labour or to enable an increase in activity to take place without an increase in labour. Critics of technology argue that the primary effect of the implementation of new systems is to destroy jobs and there is considerable evidence that such job destruction can take place. On the other hand, it is argued that technology releases resources for more productive work elsewhere and enables new industries and new employment to be created. Evidence is cited of previous technological revolutions which resulted ultimately in more jobs and greater prosperity. In addition to the problem of labour displacement, it is also argued that new information systems can degrade and deskill work and reduce the quality of working life. It is argued that individuals should have the right to defend themselves against such uses of technology and to reject schemes which have an adverse affect on job satisfaction.

It is also argued that people should be involved in the design of the systems in which they work. In Norway, for example, a law was passed in 1976 which gave workers represented by their union the right to be consulted about changes in technology leading to changes in working practices. That law established a new position in Norwegian industry— that of the data steward—whose role is to lead the negotiations on behalf of the workforce on issues arising out of the proposed implementation of new systems. In other countries, unions and management are required by law to come to some co-determination agreement with regard to the introduction of a new system. In the UK, some trades unions have been able to insist on formal technology agreements with management before new systems can be introduced. These agreements aim to prevent redundancy, to ensure that management shares information about future plans with the union, that benefits are shared, that the workers have the right to be consulted about the design of new system and that strict environmental and health conditions laid down by the union are met.

This will seem strange territory to many analysts but it is certain that these kinds of agreement will increase rather than decrease and systems analysts will therefore inevitably find themselves working in situations where the systems they design will be subjected to scrutiny and even rejection by the people who will be expected to work with and use them.

10.5 Preconditions for information systems implementation

At the level of practical systems design it is possible to take into account social as well as technical factors in the implementation of information systems. For a designed information system to be truly effective and to provide the organization with cost-effective benefits, the system must normally fulfil a number of important preconditions. These are:

- It must obtain the approval and the esteem of those who work with it and those who use it. If a system fails to obtain approval before it is implemented the implementation will be resisted, probably resulting in delays and in the subsequent misuse of the system. If it fails to satisfy the users once it becomes operational it may be misused, supplanted by unofficial procedures or even sabotaged. The fact that a new system succeeds in obtaining approval before it is implemented does not necessarily imply that it will also be approved once it is brought into operational use.
- It must be capable of adapting or being adapted to meet changing conditions and changing requirements. A designed information system which cannot be adapted quickly may affect the ability of the organization to continue in business or may cause its decline and eventual failure. However, since information systems are social systems and most social systems are robust, the informal human component often finds a way of overcoming the failure of the designed system, but usually at the cost of some efficiency. Consequently, the failure of the designed system to adapt to change

may result in its losing the approval of its users, who will devise alternative unofficial procedures to cope with the new conditions. The designed system becomes bypassed and falls into disuse.

- The various components of the information system, the designed and the undesigned, the official and the unofficial, the formal and the informal, need to operate in harmony and provide mutual support to the users.

Analysis, design and implementation methods are therefore needed, which recognize these preconditions and which attempt to ensure that they are met. It is necessary to think about the way the new system is developed and how the tasks in its development are organized. This brings into question the respective roles of the professional systems analyst and the user. We need also to think about the process of implementing change and the tools and techniques which will be available to us to carry out the process efficiently and effectively.

10.6 Organizing for good social design

We have already mentioned our belief that the systems analyst will in the future be required to subject his systems designs to greater scrutiny from a wider variety of people than has been the case in the past, and we take this further now by discussing the role of the user as participant in the systems design process. Participation by users in the design process is a powerful technique which aims to prevent the isolation of the DP specialist and the loss of certainty and control by the user. It aims also to help strike a balance between the specialist's need to innovate and the line manager's requirement for stability. The model in Figure 10.2 shows this situation where users join in the design team so that they share in the control of the planning and design process. As a result, conflicts related to differing objectives are brought out into the open and an opportunity is provided for negotiation and resolution of the differences. Users gain in confidence as they learn to cope with the problems of design themselves and come to have more confidence in the DP specialist because he is perceived as a helper rather than an opponent. The DP specialist loses his isolation and becomes more identified with the organization than with his technique.

Because users do not lose control and because they have a clearer vision of what the new system will do for them, the extent of uncertainty is limited. It will still exist, because an innovative system cannot have a precisely predicted outcome, but the group of users and systems analysts have an improved capability for communication and

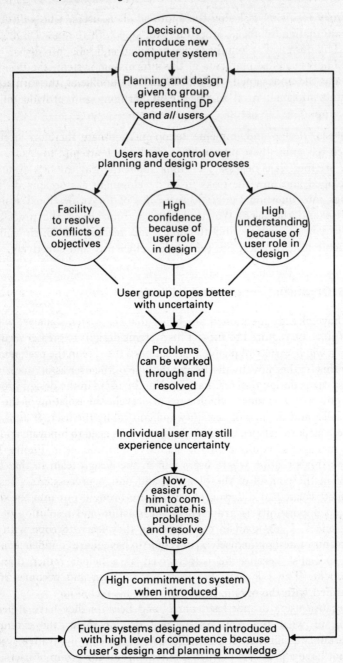

Fig. 10.2   The shared approach

for resolving problems. Users are more likely to regard future changes as a worthwhile challenge because they themselves played a part in setting objectives for the system and in evaluating its design.

We should expect, therefore, that their response to uncertainty will be positive, rather than an attempt to retain the *status quo* by means of counter-implementation strategies. Above all, users will share a high commitment to make the system work, they will learn from the experience of designing systems and achieve a higher level of confidence which will in turn lead to improved design of future systems.

The essential ingredient for this process is participation by users. This participation is effected at many levels and takes many forms: there is no simple prescription for the way participation should be introduced or practised. Introducing systems change into a large unit of public administration, such as the Inland Revenue, with 50 000 employees scattered throughout the British Isles, must be quite different from the introduction of new office technology into a company employing 150 people. Introducing change to a medium-sized family-owned company with a history of paternalistic concern for its workers must be quite different from introducing the same type of change into a company of equal size, but having a strong trade union and a history of management and union conflict. It is possible, however, to suggest some organizational framework within which the participative process can be considered. A distinction must still be drawn between participation in decision-making, where the participative process is concentrated on taking part in decision-making about a project (such as choosing between alternative designs) and participation in the analysis and design process, which does not involve the making of judgmental decisions.

Perhaps the most common form of participation is that known as consultative participation. Here participants are invited to give evidence to the decision-makers so that it can be taken into account when decisions are made. Much rarer is the democratic form of decision-making in which all participants have an equal voice in the decision-making process and where decisions are taken on the basis of the votes of the participants, but where the implementation of the decision is in the hands of some authority or some agency. A third kind of participation in decision-making is called the responsible form. In this case participants are given full authority to make decisions as they see fit and to involve other interest groups or specialists as advisers to help them. This is seen most frequently, for example, in organizations which give departmental managers and their subordinates authority to buy their own data-processing facilities based on microcomputers.

Participation in the analysis and design process occurs firstly at the top, where it is concerned with strategic planning; in the middle, where it covers systems definition for a number of divisions, functions or departments; and finally at the bottom, where it relates to the detailed design of an organizational subsystem for, perhaps, a department or function. The consultative approach is seen as being most appropriate for securing agreement on strategic planning objectives where the major planning decisions are taken by senior managers, perhaps at board level, whose hierarchical position enables them to take a broad view of the enterprise's future needs. However, they will only take these decisions after extensive consultations with interested groups lower down the organizational hierarchy and a consultative structure must exist or be created so that this sounding-out of opinion can be thorough and accurate. Representative participation is seen as appropriate for the system-definition stage when the powerful interest groups at middle management level wish to express an opinion as to where systems boundaries are to be drawn and on the broad form any future system should take. Consensus participation attempts to enable all the staff in a department to participate in the design of a new work system. They are involved when efficiency and job satisfaction needs are being diagnosed through feedback and discussion in smaller groups. As the design team formulates alternative design strategies, these are discussed at staff meetings and the subsequent choice of work organization and task structure to be associated with the technical part of the system is greatly influenced by the views of the staff. Experience shows, however, that a consensus on a new systems solution does not always emerge easily; the conflicts that result from different interests within a department may have to be resolved first.

10.7 Summary

Systems design is not merely a technical process that involves the choice of hardware and development of appropriate software. It requires that the set of new or changed computer-based procedures be inserted into an existing organizational framework that includes a network of people carrying out a variety of tasks, engaged in different roles and having individual relationships and job satisfaction needs. In most cases, the introduction of the computer systems requires the redesign of the functions that people at all levels of the organization are expected to perform. It requires of the members of the design team the ability to identify and specify both organizational and social needs and to create a system that facilitates the satisfying of these needs. For the designed system to be truly effective it must, on the one hand, be regarded as efficient in the sense of productivity and quality, coordination and control, and its ability to allow the organization to develop and adapt to changing requirements: it must deliver the anticipated, usually economic, benefits to its sponsors. On the other hand, the system cannot deliver these benefits unless it provides an environment for work in which people can achieve personal development and satisfaction. The design of the computer application therefore requires the ability to create a system which uses information technology to help in the attainment of efficient operating and decision-making procedures, together with human effectiveness and satisfaction throughout the organization as a whole.

Suggestions for further reading

Our list of suggestions for further reading is deliberately small. It is intended not as a researcher's bibliography but as a list of useful books or articles for students and practitioners alike.

Parkin, A., The scope of systems analysis, in *Computer Bulletin*, March 1978.

Lucas, H. C., *The Analysis, Design and Implementation of Information Systems* – McGraw-Hill, 1981.

Keen, P. G. W. and Morton, M. S. S., *Decision Support Systems: An Organizational Perspective* – Addison-Wesley, 1978.

Collins, G. and Blay, G., *Structured Systems Development Techniques* – Pitman, 1982.

Martin, J., *Computer Database Organization* – Prentice-Hall, 1977.

Davis, B., *Database in Perspective* – NCC, 1980.

Mayne, A., *Database Management Systems – A Technical Review* – NCC, 1981.

Doll, D. R., *Data Communication; Facilities, Networks and Systems Design* – Wiley, 1978.

Jarrett, D., *The Electronic Office* – Gower, 1982.

Lucas, H., Land, F., Lincoln, T. and Supper, K. (Eds), *The Computer Systems Environment*, North Holland, 1980.

Land, F., Adapting to changing user requirements, *Information and Management*, May, 1982.

Damodaran, L., Simpson, A. and Wilson, P., *Designing Systems for People*, National Computer Council, 1980.

Index